And all that jazz

Improvised sounds of 1930s Chicago noisy hall – loud American conversatio (cut off)
including 'Whoopee!', 'Skidoo', 'Hot', plus much laughter

Deliberate and gin-soaked ♩ = 130

PIANO

mf

mp

9 S. *p*

Come on, babe, why don't we paint the town,_ And

p

12

all that jazz, I'm gon-na rouge my knees and roll my stock-ings down,

15

S. A. *mp*

And all that jazz!_ Start the car,_ I know a whoo-pee spot where the

mp

4

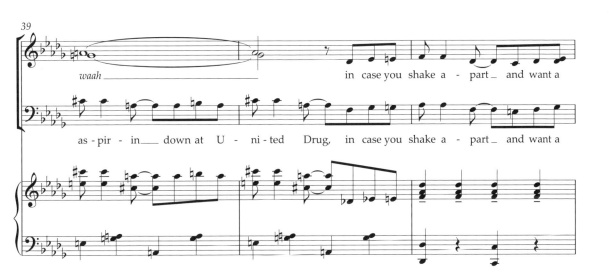

Roxie

Words by Fred Ebb
Music by John Kander
arr. Beale

16

When you're good to Mama

Words by Fred Ebb
Music by John Kander
arr. Beale

BATTLE OF BRITAIN
AIRFIELDS

BATTLE OF BRITAIN
AIRFIELDS

Philip Birtles

MIDLAND
An imprint of
Ian Allan Publishing

Opposite: By August 1942, when RAF Fighter Command was on the offensive, it was safe for 43 Squadron to line up the Hurricane IIcs at Tangmere and prepare them for the next ground attack in occupied Europe. *(RAF Museum)*

First published 2010

ISBN 978 1 85780 328 0

Published by Midland Publishing

an imprint of Ian Allan Publishing Ltd, Hersham, Surrey KT12 4RG.
Printed in England by Ian Allan Printing Ltd, Hersham, Surrey KT12 4RG.

Visit the Ian Allan Publishing website at www.ianallanpublishing.com
Distributed in the United States of America and Canada by BookMasters Distribution Services.

CONTENTS

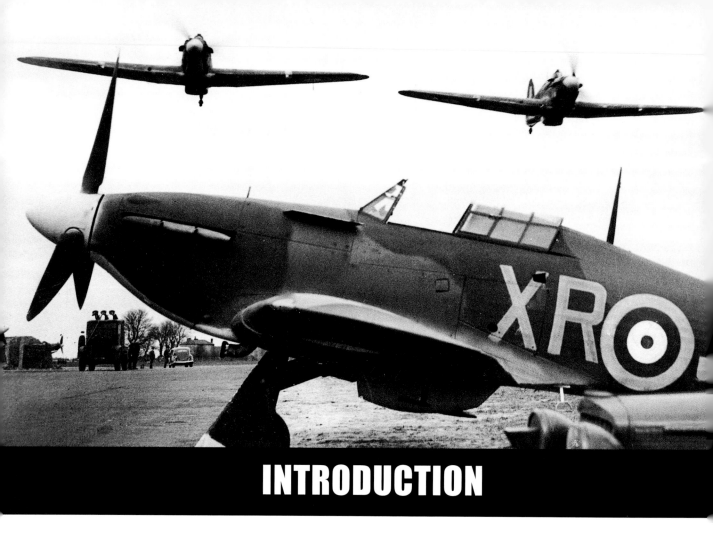

INTRODUCTION

The Battle of Britain took place from 10 July until 31 October 1940, and 2010 will be the 70th anniversary of what was probably the most decisive air battle of all time. Hitler's plan was to progressively annex or invade the middle European countries including Poland and Czechoslovakia, followed by Belgium, Denmark, The Netherlands and France in preparation for the invasion of Britain.

Once France had been taken the stage was set for the Battle of Britain which was to destroy the RAF in the air and on the ground, gaining air superiority to allow the invasion armada to head for the English southeast coast where the Channel is at its narrowest point. Following defeat during the Battle of France, RAF Fighter Command was weakened due to losses of aircraft and experienced pilots. Whereas the losses of fighters could be made up from the expanding production lines, the training of new pilots could not keep pace.

The Luftwaffe had four times as many pilots and they were on the offensive with He 111, Ju 88 and Do 17 medium to light bombers, and Ju 87 Stuka dive bombers which were terrifying to ground forces, but were vulnerable without air superiority. The bombers were escorted by Bf 109 fighters which outperformed the more numerous Hurricanes, but were matched by the Spitfires which were in smaller numbers.

The belief of senior RAF officers in the 1920s and 1930s was that the bomber would always get through, resulting in less investment in fighter aircraft. Fighter Command pilots therefore had to divert or shoot down the German bombers during the summer of 1940 until the winter weather made an invasion across the Channel too hazardous. The winter period would then allow time to rebuild RAF Fighter Command both in effectiveness of aircraft and the training of pilots. In 1940, both the Hurricane and Spitfire were armed with eight .303-inch machine guns mounted in the wings, which were not effective against armoured targets, to be replaced in 1941 by the more effective 20mm cannons firing explosive shells.

The Battle of Britain commenced with air attacks on coastal shipping, followed by the bombing of airfields and aircraft factories. The Luftwaffe would aim to attract the RAF into the air against the bombers to allow the Bf 109s the opportunity to destroy the British fighters while the bombers destroyed the RAF on the ground. It was therefore vital to destroy the enemy bombers before they dropped their bombs and avoid wherever possible fighter-to-fighter combat. The RAF had the advantage that in general the air battles were over home territory whereas any surviving German aircrew would be taken prisoner.

'Adler Tag', or 'Eagle Day', on 13 August was the day designated by Goering for a major air attack, but fortunately for Britain, much of the impact was lost due to poor co-ordination as well as to bad weather. When it appeared that the RAF Fighter Command would not be beaten, the enemy strategy turned to the bombing blitz of London and other cities, taking the pressure off Fighter Command to allow regrouping in preparation for the spring of 1941 offensive. The day bombing of London was a hazard as the fighter escorts were at the limit of their endurance and only had enough fuel for ten minutes over the target. When the Luftwaffe switched to bombing at night, although less accurate, airborne interception (AI) radar had not been developed and Hurricanes and Defiants were sent up in the darkness to attempt to locate and destroy the raiders with little success.

The 'Hardest Day' was 15 September when the Luftwaffe threw all their might against the RAF while the defenders were stretched to the limits with all the reserves committed. However, due to the early warning from the radar network and the Observer Corps, AVM Keith Park, the officer commanding the 11 Group frontline, was able to predict the Luftwaffe intentions and turn the tide of the battle. Although the battle continued to the end of October, the invasion was shelved and Hitler's attention focused on attacking his former ally, Russia.

Winning the battle allowed Britain to return to the offensive, and although it would not be until D-Day, 6 June 1944, when the Allies could again set foot on the European mainland, the day bombing offensive by the USAAF and night bombing by the RAF reduced the industrial and offensive might of Germany. Although the bomber will always get through, the losses were crippling with some 55,500 young RAF aircrew from Britain and the Commonwealth lost in the night bombing campaign over the Third Reich.

Battle of Britain Airfields attempts to outline what it was like for the people involved in the battle, from the top commanders to the local population who were living in the proximity of the airfields. The combat pressure for the pilots was high, requiring rest and recuperation, with the training of new crews to replace those lost in the fighting. When the RAF went on the offensive from 1941, they operated over hostile territory and when shot down were either killed or taken prisoner, being a total loss to the RAF. More pilots were lost on air and ground attack operations in the offensive over Europe than the total of the Battle of Britain.

Philip Birtles
Stevenage, UK,
June 2010

CHAPTER 1

THE GATHERING STORM: BEFORE THE BATTLE

The prototype Hurricane K5083 was first flown from Brooklands by George Bulman, the chief test pilot on 6 November 1935. Bulman was to remain chief test pilot with Hawker Aircraft for the duration of World War 2. *(British Aerospace Aircraft Group)*

Following the signing of the armistice at the end of World War 1 in 1918, the RAF's strength was reduced from 188 squadrons down to a mere 25. With the signing of the Treaty of Versailles, the German nation was forbidden to operate combat aircraft, but instead developed transport aircraft and kept the younger generation air-minded by encouraging the flying of gliders. Even in 1936, the RAF possessed 42 home-based squadrons, the majority being bomber units while only 13 were fighter units, still equipped with obsolete biplane fighters.

While many of the senior officers within the RAF were World War 1 veterans, new personnel had to be attracted to what was seen as the finest flying club in the world. The career RAF officers were 18-year-old school leavers who underwent their training at the RAF College at Cranwell. In the 1930s, with the acceleration of rearmament to counter the growing German threat under Hitler, extra officers, many from the Commonwealth, and with the right qualifications, were granted short service commissions without having to graduate from Cranwell.

The gentlemen's air force was the Auxiliary Air Force, formed in 1924 as a reserve where young men were recruited to form locally based squadrons, such as 600 (City of London) flying initially obsolescent aircraft. However, by 1939, due to the urgent need of Fighter Command, the 14 squadrons of weekend flyers were equipped with Hurricanes and Spitfires. With a continued shortage of pilots to match the build-up of fighter aircraft being produced in the rearmament programme, the RAF Volunteer Reserve was created in July 1936. In this case young men were paid to take a part-time flying course to provide a pool of pilots at the anticipated outbreak of World War 2. By the summer of 1939, some 200 pilots had completed their basic flying training, but lacked skills in operational flying.

Meanwhile, the aircraft needed maintaining and Sir Hugh Trenchard, the father of the RAF from its founding on 1 April 1918, created the Halton Apprentice School to provide a foundation of highly skilled ground and maintenance engineers. The Halton recruits were taken from secondary schools at the age of 14 or 15 and given three years of intensive tough discipline training. The Trenchard 'brats' created a high level of discipline at many of the pre-war RAF stations, the later 'Direct Entry' NCOs finding the standards somewhat demanding.

When Air Chief Marshal Sir Edward Ellington was appointed Chief of the Air Staff in April 1933, and Air Marshal Sir Hugh Dowding was Air Member for Supply and Research, there were at last senior officers in the RAF who believed the bombers must be stopped, although the major part of the air budget was still allocated to the bomber squadrons. Sponsored by Sir Thomas Inskip, Minister for the Co-ordination of Defence, the Cabinet accepted Scheme L in April 1938, allowing the RAF strength to reach 1,352 bombers and 608 fighters by April 1940. This insistence on an improved priority for fighters gave the RAF a small margin of strength which was so critical in 1940. Between 1935 and 1937, the combined strength of the RAF and Fleet Air Arm (FAA) increased from 91 to 169 squadrons, in effect doubling the numbers of aircraft to 2,031. Unfortunately some 80 per cent of the aircraft were obsolescent and required urgent replacement with Hurricanes and Spitfires to match the new generation of combat aircraft in operation with the Luftwaffe.

In addition to more modern aircraft, there was an urgent need for pilots to fly them in combat. The Commonwealth volunteers for the RAF were increased and 1,700 Short Service Commissions were granted with an additional 800 NCO pilots accepted. To cope with the increased training needs, the number of Flying Training Schools was increased from six to 11, but it took a year to teach a pilot to fly a fighter, let alone use one in combat. With the refusal of the Canadian Prime Minister, Mackenzie King, to permit RAF flying training in Canada, it was evident that the early burden of fighter pilots would fall upon the part-time Auxiliary Air Force and Volunteer Reserve. By August 1939, there were over 42 Reserve Flying Training Schools, all but two equipped with de Havilland Tiger Moths. Meanwhile, in 1938, to supplement the RAFVR schools, the Government-sponsored Civil Air Guard was formed to allow flying schools to train men and women between the ages of 16 and 60 to provide a pool of pilots for non-combat tasks. With the declaration of war in September 1939, all civil flying ceased and the Civil Air Guard was disbanded. Flying training schools were then not only set up in Canada, but worldwide under the Empire Air Training Scheme where new pilots were given basic training uninterrupted by weather or combat.

HM King George VI was invited to inspect the prototype Spitfire K5054 at Eastleigh. He is standing on the wing to view the cockpit; Reginald Mitchell is by the wing leading edge close to the nose. *(Unknown copyright via BAE Systems)*

In 1936, the old Air Defence of Great Britain was replaced by four functional commands: Fighter, Bomber, Coastal and Training. Air Marshal Sir Hugh Dowding was appointed Commander in Chief of Fighter Command and took up residence at Bentley Priory to the north of London in July 1936. From the new Fighter Command Headquarters, Dowding set up four Group areas for defence purposes, and with his staff began to create new direction systems for the control of the fighters when enemy aircraft were on the attack. One of the key defence systems was the secret early radar chain being set up under the approaches to Britain to detect the early advance of hostile aircraft. This would be supplemented by the Observer Corps, a civilian volunteer force whose organisation had been strengthened during the 1930s, who would visually track enemy aircraft flying over Britain.

The Hurricane

In mid-December 1937 the first Hurricanes were delivered to 111 Squadron at Northolt, a few months before the Luftwaffe accepted the new Bf 109 fighter. The Hurricane was the first RAF monoplane fighter, designed by Sydney Camm, the Hawker Chief Designer, as a company-funded private venture to be powered by the Rolls-Royce PV-12 engine, later to become the Merlin. Using traditional aircraft construction of a metal tubular structure with a wood and fabric covering, the Hurricane was a rugged aircraft that was resistant to battle damage and could generally be easily repaired. With the issue of Spec. F.36/34 calling for eight .303-inch machine guns to be located in stressed metal skin wings, the prototype made its first flight from Brooklands in November 1935.

Despite being a combination of old and new technology, and being outclassed by the Bf 109, the Hurricanes could give a good account of themselves in the hands of experienced pilots, especially as they could out-turn the Bf 109. It was also the primary type available as deliveries of the more complex Spitfire were in smaller numbers. During the duration of the Battle of Britain between July and October 1940, there were 1,715 Hurricanes in operation accounting for some 80 per cent of all victories against enemy raiders. By 1941, the Hurricane had been transferred to the fighter-bomber role in which it excelled for the remainder of the war.

Two flights of 73 Squadron Hurricane Is over France in early 1940. (*Imperial War Museum*)

Above: Sir Sidney Camm was the designer of the Hawker Hurricane. Camm was at the forefront of combat aircraft design from biplane fighters to the jet age Hunter and P.1127, the early development that led to the Harrier. *(Flight)*

Right: As part of the BEF in France, 85 Squadron operated Hurricanes, one example being L1648 from the first production batch. (*Flight*)

Below: Hurricane I L1582 of the first production batch fitted with a fixed-pitch wooden Watts propeller, which was delivered to 3 Squadron at Kenley in July 1938. However, the airfield at Kenley was unsuitable for operational Hurricanes and 3 Squadron reverted to Gladiators.

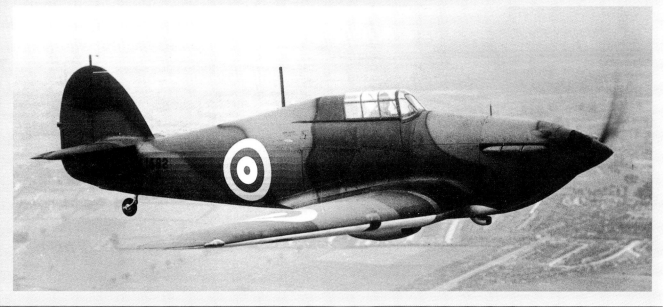

The Spitfire

The Supermarine Spitfire was designed by Reginald Mitchell, the company having become part of Vickers in 1928. Mitchell had created the Schneider Trophy racing seaplanes, achieving speeds of over 400 mph and winning the trophy for Britain. Towards the end of 1934, Mitchell worked on the design of a revolutionary new fighter to be powered by the Rolls-Royce PV-12 engine, later to become the Merlin as was powering the Hurricane. Work commenced on the new prototype in January 1935, the construction being an all-metal stressed-skin airframe, which with the elegant elliptical-shape wing caused some early production problems. The fuselage was in three sections, with the engine fairings mounted on a monocoque centre section housing the cockpit, and a removable aft section including an integral tail fin. The main wing spar was like a tapered leaf spring with a heavy gauge wing skin leading edge and light wing skin covering aft giving great strength and lightness. In the spring of 1935, Mitchell had to adapt the wing design to accommodate the Air Ministry's specified eight machine guns in the thin wing profile.

The modular structure of the Spitfire allowed dispersed production as Supermarine resources were limited, even for the initial order for 310 aircraft.

A large shadow factory was constructed at Castle Bromwich near Birmingham, which was the major production facility for the Spitfire. The first prototype made its maiden flight from Eastleigh on 5 March 1936. It proved a match for the Bf 109 below 20,000 feet, and with experienced pilots could hold its own above that altitude.

The first Spitfires were delivered to 19 Squadron at Duxford in May 1939 and mostly operated from the nearby satellite of Fowlmere. By September 1939, nine Fighter Command squadrons were equipped with Spitfires and at the start of the Battle of Britain in July 1940, there were 19 Spitfire squadrons. Sadly, Reginald Mitchell died at the age of 42 in 1937 from cancer and never saw the success of his creation. The Spitfire was at the start of its potential, being upgraded throughout the war with improved versions of the Merlin engine, until the advent of the more powerful Rolls-Royce Griffon engine, which prompted the design of a longer nose to accommodate the new power plant.

Right: A classic front view of an early Spitfire I, showing the elliptical wing shape. *(Vickers)*

Far right: Geoffrey Quill, the chief test pilot of Supermarine, was responsible for the overall flight development of the Spitfire. *(Flight)*

Left: Following the initial flight trials, the Spitfire prototype was painted overall light blue. *(Unknown copyright via BAE Systems)*

Middle left: Spitfire prototype K5054 rear view at Eastleigh with the classic Warren Truss girder hangars in the background. *(Unknown copyright via BAE Systems)*

Bottom left: Early production Spitfire I K9787 at Eastleigh fitted with a tail-wheel, unlike the prototype which had a tail-skid. *(Vickers)*

Below: Early Spitfire Mk.Is of 19 Squadron formate close to their Cambridgeshire bases of Fowlmere and Duxford in 1938.

Radar

In 1935, Britain conducted secret experiments on a system known as radio direction finding (RDF), but unknown to the British scientists, similar experiments were being undertaken in Germany, albeit with less success. Under the chairmanship of Sir Henry Tizard, a committee was set up in 1934 to consider possible means of defence against airborne attack. Robert Watson-Watt, a scientist at the National Physical Laboratory (NPL) identified three areas of research covering the complementary requirements of reflection of radio waves, radio communications between the ground and defending fighters to direct them to the located targets, and a coded signal transmitted from allied aircraft to differentiate from friend and foe (IFF).

Tizard established a reputation for having a practical knowledge of the needs of the military and could identify ideas which would find practical military applications and amongst other projects backed by him were the Barnes Wallis bouncing bomb and Frank Whittle's jet engine. Having become the superintendent of the NPL radio department at Teddington in 1933, Watson-Watt prepared with his assistant, Arnold Wilkins, a paper entitled 'The Detection of Aircraft by Radio Methods', the basis of his proposal to the Tizard Committee.

Tests were begun with 70-foot masts mounting the equipment in May 1935, and in 1936, the team of researchers moved into Bawdsey Manor on the Suffolk coast where scientists were able to mingle with the visiting civil servants and RAF officers to fully understand the requirements and problems to overcome. In 1936, Biggin Hill was used for a series of tests to explore the practical problems of linking the radar warning, as RDF had become to be known, of a hostile attack to the defending fighters, using teams of ground controllers and plotting tables to produce a rapid indication of the converging courses which would achieve interception.

Following the success of the experiments, a network of what was known as Chain Home radar stations was set up along the east coast from Scotland and round the south coast to the Isle of Wight. These were supplemented by Chain Home Low radar stations which could track low-flying aircraft. Once past the coastline, the formations were tracked by the volunteers of the Observer Corps, later to become the Royal Observer Corps (ROC).

A network of Chain Home Radar stations was set up around the east and south coast of Britain to give warning of the approaching enemy formations, allowing Fighter Command to react in good time to incoming raids. The one shown here was located at Rye. *(Imperial War Museum)*

Left: Sir Robert Watson-Watt led the development of radio detection, later to become radar, which reflected radio waves off aircraft and returned them to the base station, where they were detected on a cathode ray tube. *(Imperial War Museum)*

Above: A WAAF operator sits in front of a cathode ray tube at the Chain Home Radar station at Bawdsey, tracking approaching enemy raiders. *(Imperial War Museum)*

Left: Once past the radar coverage on the coast, enemy formations were tracked by members of the Observer Corps, later to become the Royal Observer Corps. Using specially developed instruments, they would judge the height, direction and numbers of the hostile formations allowing Fighter Command to deploy defending fighters to gain an advantage. *(Imperial War Museum)*

Above: The Hurricane prototype K5083 was a low-wing monoplane of rugged construction that adapted the early biplane fighter technology to the needs of World War 2 combat. Power came from a Rolls-Royce Merlin engine and armament comprised eight wing-mounted fixed 0.303-inch machine guns. *(British Aerospace Aircraft Group)*

Right: The rugged metal tubular structure of the Hurricane made it resistant to battle damage and easy to repair. The rear fuselage was faired over with fabric-covered wooden stringers and the outer wings were attached to the centre section. *(Flight)*

Left: Designed by Reginald Mitchell, the Spitfire was of all-metal stressed skin construction which created some challenges in the new techniques of production. The maiden flight was from Eastleigh Airport near Southampton on 5 March 1936 by Captain Mutt Summers, the chief test pilot of Vickers, and owners of Supermarine since 1928. *(Unknown copyright via BAE Systems)*

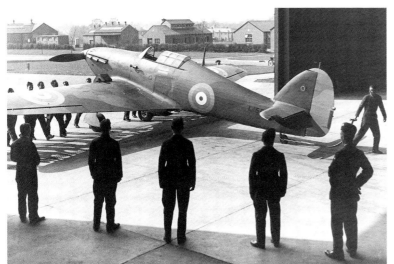

Left: Squadron Leader John Gillan, the Commanding Officer of 111 Squadron, flew I lurricane I L1553 the 327 miles from Edinburgh to Northolt in a record time of 48 minutes on 10 February 1938, taking advantage of a tail wind at an average speed of 408.75 mph. *(Flight)*

Below left: Early Hurricanes required the ground crew to hand crank the Merlin engine to get it started, with a member of the team in the cockpit and the sergeant ensuring the safety of the men. This Hurricane, P2617, was delivered in January 1940 initially to 111 Squadron. *(Photographic News Agencies)*

Below: Sergeant Brown of 111 Squadron at Northolt in full kit with parachute, ready to board a Hurricane I for another training flight. The Hurricane did not feature cockpit heating.

Top and middle: The Fairey Battles of the AASF were two-seat light bombers powered by an early Rolls-Royce Merlin engine. Although fairly advanced when designed, the Battle was outdated by the time World War 2 was declared. The Battle had an all-metal airframe and a total of around 2,200 aircraft were ordered. The first prototype made its maiden flight on 10 March 1936 from Fairey's Great West Aerodrome, now absorbed by London Heathrow. The aircraft carried a crew of three in a long tandem cockpit: pilot, bomb aimer/observer and radio operator/gunner. Normal bomb load was four 250lbs and armament was a fixed forward-firing 0.303 machine gun in the starboard wing outboard of the propeller arc and a Vickers K gun in the rear cockpit. Battles of 88 and 218 Squadrons saw action during the Battle of France. (*Imperial War Museum*)

Bottom: On 6 December 1939, HM King George VI visited Lille-Seclin airfield and inspected the Hurricanes of 85 and 86 Squadrons with Gladiators and a Blenheim IV in the background. (*Imperial War Museum*)

Left: An early Hurricane I of 87 Squadron after a mishap on landing. The wooden propeller is snapped and the guns have been fired.

Middle left: Poor ground conditions were often the cause of damage to aircraft. Hurricane I L2047 of 87 Squadron force-landed in France.

Below: An early Hurricane I LK-N of 87 Squadron with the fixed-pitch Watts wooden propeller in France in early 1940.

Bottom: Hurricanes of 87 Squadron at Lille-Seclin in March 1940 during a practice gas attack. (*Imperial War Museum*)

Right: Pilots of 87 Squadron scramble for their Hurricane Is in France in March 1940.

Below: An 85 Squadron Hurricane during exercises in France in 1939. (*Imperial War Museum*)

Below right: Winston Churchill, then First Lord of the Admiralty, inspects an RAF guard of honour in France before he became Prime Minister. (*Imperial War Museum*)

Bottom: 85 Squadron pilots climb aboard Hurricane Is as part of the BEF in France in 1940. (*RAF Museum*)

Top left: Nos. 1 and 73 Squadrons were part of the AASF with Hurricane Is, their duty being to protect Battle and Blenheim bombers on the ground and in the air. Hurricane I L1681 of 1 Squadron was lost in France in May 1940.

Top right: During the 'Phoney War', Hurricanes of 79 Squadron were on standby for the defence of France. This Hurricane I is being prepared for take-off with the ground crew attaching the 'trolley ack' mobile battery starter. (*RAF Museum*)

Above: Sergeant P V Ayerst of 73 Squadron AASF landing his Hurricane I in France in May 1940. (*Imperial War Museum*)

Left: HM King George VI with Queen Elizabeth escorted by ACM Sir Hugh Dowding on a visit to the HQ Fighter Command, Bentley Priory, on 6 September 1940. (*Imperial War Museum*)

CHAPTER 2
THE BATTLE OF BRITAIN

Spitfires of 610 (County of Chester) Royal Auxiliary Airforce on patrol from Biggin Hill during the Battle of Britain. *(Imperial War Museum)*

Upon the withdrawal of the BEF from France on 5 June 1940 – the famous Dunkirk evacuation – Winston Churchill, the British Prime Minister, made the following speech in Parliament.

"What General Weygand called the Battle of France is over. I expect the Battle of Britain is about to begin. Upon this battle depends the survival of Christian civilisation. Upon it depends our own British life and the long continuity of our institutions and our Empire. The whole fury and might of the enemy must very soon be turned on us. Hitler knows that he will have to break us in this island or lose the war. If we can stand up to him, all Europe may be freed and the life of the world may move forward into broad, sunlit uplands.

But if we fail, then the whole world, including the United States, including all that we have known and cared for, will sink into the abyss of a new Dark Age, made more sinister and perhaps more protracted, by the lights of perverted science. Let us therefore brace ourselves to our duties, and so bear ourselves that, if the British Empire and its Commonwealth last for a thousand years, men will still say: This was their finest hour."

With the Fighter Command Headquarters at Bentley Priory north of London, where the overall strategy was controlled, Great Britain was divided into four groups. 11 Group, headed by AVM Keith Park, was in the frontline in the South East and covered the defences of London, Kent, Surrey, Essex and parts of Hampshire and Suffolk. 11 Group was supported by AVM Sir Quintin Brand who commanded 10 Group defending Wales and the South West, and 12 Group to the north of

ROYAL AIR FORCE
CONTROL AND REPORTING SYSTEM
during the Battle of Britain 1940

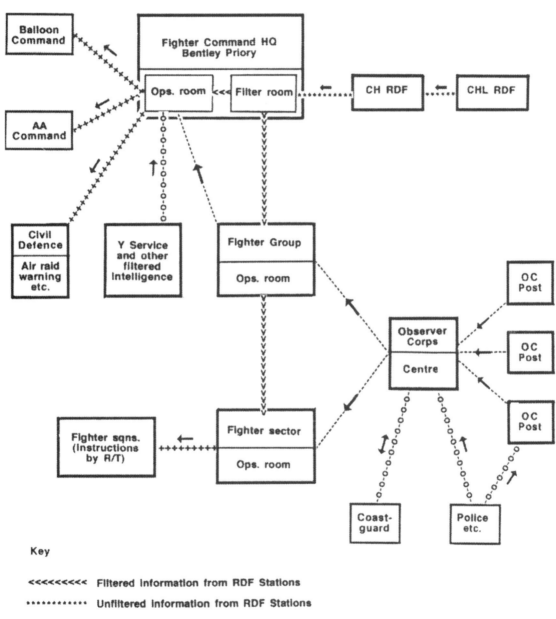

Key

<<<<<<<< Filtered information from RDF Stations

••••••••••• Unfiltered information from RDF Stations

----------- Observer Corps information

-o-o-o-o-o Information from other sources

++++++++++ Combined information

Right: The Operations Room at HQ Fighter Command at Bentley Priory was the overall control centre for the Battle of Britain. The WAAF 'Chorus Girls' plotted the positions of the enemy attacks, allowing the overall deployment of RAF fighters to defend against the Luftwaffe bombers and the escorting fighters. *(Imperial War Museum)*

Below: New Zealander Air Vice Marshal Keith Park was the AOC 11 Group tasked with defending the front line of the south-east of England and approaches to London. He was the only senior commander with modern fighter aircraft experience and flew a Hurricane based at Northolt to visit his front line squadrons. *(RAF Museum)*

Above: AVM Keith Park in the cockpit of his personal Hurricane. *(Imperial War Museum)*

Top left: South African-born AVM Sir Christopher Quintin Brand was AOC 10 Group with responsibility for the air defence of the west of England and South Wales. In this picture, he is seen presenting a parachute to 'Ginger' Lacey. *(RAF Museum)*

Top right: AVM Saul was AOC 13 Group responsible for the air defence of the north of England and Scotland, usually with battle-weary squadrons from the south who moved north to reorganise and train new pilots before returning to the battle. *(RAF Museum)*

Bottom left: Air Vice Marshal Trafford Leigh-Mallory was the AOC 12 Group with the task of defending the industrial Midlands and providing support to 11 Group. He was an exponent of the 'Big Wing' method of defence which often proved ineffective during the Battle of Britain due to the time taken to form up and fight the Luftwaffe. *(RAF Museum)*

Bottom right: Air Chief Marshal Sir Hugh Dowding was the Air Officer Commanding Fighter Command in the build-up to and during the Battle of Britain. *(RAF Museum)*

London to defend the Midlands and north up to Yorkshire and commanded by AVM Trafford Leigh-Mallory. The defence of the north of England, Scotland and Northern Ireland was the responsibility of 13 Group commanded by AVM Richard Saul. Each group was divided into sectors, controlled by sector stations supported by other airfields and satellites. The sector stations were responsible for the tactical control of the fighter defence within their area and to provide additional reinforcements to 11 Group when required. Each sector station had its own control room and comprehensive maintenance facilities.

Air Chief Marshal Sir Hugh Dowding was the architect of Fighter Command, having been working on its reorganisation since 1936. 'Stuffy' Dowding, as he was sometimes known, was a difficult man to work with, and as well as having the Luftwaffe as his enemy, he also had a number of enemies within the Air Council. He was given the task of leading Fighter Command, as it was seen as the 'Cinderella' service, the main perception being that the bomber would always get through to its target. It was Dowding's job to disprove this theory. His bosses were Chief of the Air Staff, Air Chief Marshal Sir Cyril Newall, and the Air Council, together with the political masters headed by Winston Churchill and the War Cabinet. There were times, particularly during the Battle of France, that Dowding rejected the political wish to send reinforcements to France, which would have resulted in a fatal loss of Britain's defence capability. As it was, irreplaceable experienced aircrew were lost, while it was not difficult to build more Hurricanes and Spitfires.

Dowding was a man of formidable personality with a sharp tongue and could be more direct in correspondence. However, with subordinates, and with men and women who clearly worked as hard as he did, Dowding was polite, and if someone had a promising case he would provide full backing. When necessary, he would stand up for his principles with other authorities, however high. Dowding was very demanding of his staff, but had a great sense of justice that earned him the respect of his colleagues. He did not accept ideas because they were orthodox, often being in conflict with generally accepted views. He did not see the need to persuade opponents that they were wrong, or even to compromise with them. He gained the nickname 'Stuffy' in his thirties, but maverick would have been more appropriate. Although not of a jovial disposition, he could be very entertaining away from work with a keen sense of humour and good stories.

With Dowding's tenure as chief of Fighter Command due to end in July 1939, he was to be replaced by AM Sir Christopher Courtney. This did not happen due to Courtney being injured in an air accident from which he required time to recover. Dowding was advised that he could stay in service until he reached 60, but not necessarily in his current role, although Newall confirmed that Dowding should continue in his existing appointment until at least the end of March 1940. On 30 March 1940, the day before he was due to retire, Newall asked Dowding to stay on until 14 July, but there was no word of whom his successor might be. There was then a further extension until the end of October, but Winston Churchill finally came to the rescue and confirmed Dowding as Fighter Command chief, approved reluctantly by Newall and Sir Archibald Sinclair.

On the morning of 7 September, Goering and his senior officers view the white cliffs of Dover across the Channel, ready to start the bombing of London. *(Imperial War Museum)*

The speed of the German advance across the Benelux countries and northern France had been so rapid that the logistical support required for an invasion of Britain would be considerable. Hitler therefore spent time in the pleasant summer weather touring the battle sites from World War 1. Dowding was aware that it was his strategic task to defend Britain until the bad weather across the Channel made an invasion impossible. When the good weather returned in the spring, Fighter Command would be stronger and the army would be re-equipped and reorganised.

It was not until 21 July that Goering called together his senior commanders to prepare plans for air superiority in advance of the invasion. Hitler decreed that a major air assault be launched from 5 August codenamed 'Eagle Day' with 15 September the target date for 'Operation Sealion', the invasion of Britain. Of the 2,800 Luftwaffe aircraft facing the RAF in July 1940, 760 were Bf 109 fighters against 700

HERMANN GOERING

Dowding's main adversary was Hermann Goering, commander of the Luftwaffe, a leading member of the Nazi Party and Hitler's designated successor. Goering was a World War 1 fighter ace with 22 kills and was the final Commanding Officer of Jagdgeschwader 1, the squadron of Manfred von Richthofen, the Red Baron. From his early service in the military, Goering was arrogant and unpopular, weak in character and violent when challenged. He joined the Nazi Party in 1922 and was Luftwaffe General on its founding in 1935.

In 1939, Goering had boasted that not a single bomb would be dropped on Germany, and he declared that if ever an Allied bomber reached the Ruhr he was to be called 'Meier', which had the meaning that something was impossible. As early as 1940, the RAF had hit targets in Germany, reportedly landing bombs on Berlin during a Hitler-led Nazi rally, interrupting the proceedings. This was in retaliation for a mistaken Luftwaffe raid on London, when the bombers were off course, jettisoning their war load on London. As a result of the bombs on Berlin, Hitler declared London as a potential target, which was supported by Goering. From 1942, the Allied bombing campaign was established against Germany in retaliation for the blitz on London and other cities, but by then Goering had withdrawn from the military scene to enjoy the pleasures of wealth and power.

Goering surrendered to the Allies on 9 May 1945 in Bavaria, and during the subsequent trial for war crimes at Nuremberg, he claimed not to be anti-Semitic. However, he was the leading force in German aggression, second only to Hitler, and directed the slave labour programme as well as leading the oppression of Jews and other races. He finally admitted to all the crimes, unique in their enormity, and in his appeal agreed to accept the death penalty, but requested to be shot as a soldier rather than hung like a common criminal. This request was refused and the night before he was to be executed, Goering committed suicide by taking a cyanide pill. He was 53 years old.

Above: The initial eight Hurricane Mk.Is at Kenley preparing for Empire Air Day in 1938 with the grass surface airfield beyond. These aircraft are fitted with the fixed pitch wooden Watts propeller which was later replaced by three blade variable pitch propeller for improved performance.

Below: Hurricane Is and Gladiators in the Warren Truss girder hangars at Kenley in 1939 during the transition between the two types. (*RAF Museum*)

Above: Luftwaffe bombers were protected mainly by Bf 109 fighters during the Battles of France and Britain. The Bf 109 was designed by Messerschmitt as a single-seat all-metal monoplane fighter, powered initially by a Jumo and later by a Daimler Benz engine. It was armed with four 7.9mm machine guns, two mounted above the engine firing through the propeller arc, and two 20mm cannons in the wings. The Bf 109 had a top speed of 310 mph (with the Jumo engine) and a range of up to 420 miles. In the latter part of the Battle of Britain, some Bf 109s were adapted as fighter-bombers and carried a single 50kg (110lb) bomb. (*Imperial War Museum*)

Below: Also used on bomber escort duties were the twin Daimler Benz-powered Bf 110s with four 7.9mm machine guns and two 20mm cannons in the nose and one 7.9mm gun in a dorsal turret. There was a crew of three, consisting of pilot, radio operator/navigator and a rear gunner, although in combat the radio operator/navigator was not always carried. The Bf 110 was vulnerable in combat against fighters and often flew in a defensive circle for mutual protection. During the Battle of Britain, the Luftwaffe lost 223 Bf 110s, having started the battle with only 237. (*Imperial War Museum*)

Right: A fine formation of later Spitfire Mk.Is with three-blade variable-pitch propellers operated by 65 Squadron. *(Unknown copyright via BAE Systems)*

Hurricanes and Spitfires. The weak link was that the German pilots were better trained and experienced than the allied pilots. Weather further delayed Eagle Day to 13 August, although the official dates of the Battle of Britain were from 10 July to 31 October.

The Luftwaffe's combat-ready air fleet in July included 1,300 bombers, of which over 300 were dive bombers, and 1,050 fighters, of which 250 were the vulnerable twin-engine Bf 110s. Dowding had 450 Hurricanes and 300 Spitfires, of which 600 were combat ready, supplemented by a number of inferior Blenheims and Defiants. To combat the massed Luftwaffe attacks, Dowding practised an air reserve policy, making use of tactical reserves and using the individual squadrons as the largest practical unit, ensuring there was always a challenge offered to enemy forces. This allowed preservation of resources and denied the Luftwaffe the opportunity to destroy large numbers of RAF fighters in any particular engagement.

When it was realised that the main attack would be against the south-east of Britain, nearly half the fighter force of 21 squadrons were allocated to Park in 11 Group, distributed around seven sectors. 10 Group, commanded by Brand, had ten squadrons in four sectors and Leigh-Mallory in 12 Group had 14 squadrons in six sectors. Saul had 14 squadrons in six sectors in 13 Group, although a number of these northerly units were in training or resting from combat. The group commanders were delegated conduct of operations in their areas, the most demanding being Keith Park, who had been Dowding's deputy at Bentley Priory from July 1938 until April 1940 when he was posted to the 11 Group HQ at Uxbridge.

The priority was to destroy enemy bombers before they hit their targets, but as the German frontline had moved to the coast of the English Channel, fighters were able to provide cover. When raids were detected by

Below: A pilot of 64 Squadron scrambles to his Spitfire I at Kenley. The Merlin is running and his parachute is on the tailplane ready to be strapped on in the cockpit. *(Imperial War Museum)*

radar, it was important to concentrate on the bombers, while trying to evade the escorting fighters. The Luftwaffe often sent fighters in raids to lure and destroy RAF fighters, but these were avoided as much as possible.

Park divided the battle into three phases, the first spanning 8 August to 10 September. In this first phase the Luftwaffe had flown over in massed formations of bombers escorted by high-flying fighters which proved ineffective as the Hurricanes were able to attack the bombers before the escorts could swoop down to protect them. Their targets were ports, advanced airfields, coastal installations and radars.

Park's second phase of the battle was from 19 August until 5 September, the Luftwaffe switching their attacks to inland aerodromes, aircraft factories, industrial targets and residential areas. There was a five-day lull after 18 August and the new raids consisted of smaller formations of bombers closely escorted by fighters, making it difficult for the RAF to concentrate on the destruction of enemy bombers. It was also limiting for Luftwaffe fighters to be tied to close escort of the bombers. The smaller, but more numerous formations made predicting targets more challenging, and while Park's 11 Group concentrated on the enemy over the south-east, he called upon 10 and 12 Groups to protect the sector stations and aircraft factories. In addition to Observer Corps information, the pilots were asked to report approximate numbers of fighters and bombers, with their height, position and heading to allow the appropriate use of reinforcements. Enemy bombing attacks by day did extensive damage to five of the forward airfields and six of the seven sector stations. Manston and Lympne, close to the frontline, were unfit for operations for a number of days and Biggin Hill was so severely damaged that it could operate only a single squadron for over a week. While other airfields were available, they lacked the vital communications links with Uxbridge and the sector stations. Also, there were inadequate resources available to make the most basic repairs, including the filling in of bomb craters to make the operating area serviceable. During this second phase, the Luftwaffe lost more than three aircraft for every RAF fighter, and nearly five times as many German aircrew were killed as RAF pilots. Although fighter production and repairs were keeping pace with losses, the pilot situation was critical, as the Luftwaffe had plentiful trained aircrew. Of the RAF fighter strength of around 1,000 pilots, 106 had been killed with nearly as many seriously injured, and the training system was unable to match the casualties suffered.

Park's third phase of the battle, from 6 September to 31 October, commenced with the first major raid on London. At a meeting in Berlin on 3 September, a decision was made to change Luftwaffe tactics to make London its target, the reasoning not being rational but due to Goering's impatience, as there appeared to be no significant progress in destroying Fighter Command. The primary aim had been for the Luftwaffe to gain air superiority, but their formations were still being faced by significant numbers of RAF fighters despite the great damage done to airfields and infrastructure. Park was concerned that the damage to the 11 Group airfields was so bad that the defensive power of the fighter squadrons was greatly reduced. With the destruction of numerous telephone lines, the dispersal of operations rooms and the complete disorganisation of the defence systems made the control of fighter squadrons difficult. Had the attacks on the 11 Group Sector airfields, such as Biggin Hill and Kenley continued, the fighter defences of London would have been overwhelmed.

The change of German strategy to bomb cities gave great relief to 11 Group, allowing it to recover rapidly. If the relentless attacks on the airfields continued, it is likely that Fighter Command would have had to withdraw out of the range of Luftwaffe bombers and fighters.

For the third phase, Park instructed that the fighter squadrons should be employed in pairs, and he was concerned that some units flew in close 'Vic' formation of three aircraft, which limited their capability in combat. He ordered that the pilots should fly in a loose line abreast formation of four aircraft which was more flexible with a broader field of view, and would be able to offer rapid mutual support. When engaged in combat it was important that the fighters operated in pairs for better chances of survival. To maintain effective control while the sector stations were being repaired, temporary operations rooms were commissioned clear of the sector stations.

15 September 1940 has been referred to as the 'Hardest Day' and is now commemorated as Battle of Britain Day. By this time, Fighter Command had regained its strength, with the first Polish squadron in action and the novice pilots with a few weeks' service becoming combat veterans. A tremendous effort had brought all but the hardest hit of Fighter Command stations close to full operational capability. Over the previous week Dowding replaced his most battered squadrons with fresh units from the north, and added new pilots to those most depleted by losses, while giving the new arrivals an opportunity to train in preparation for action.

Luftwaffe crews were discouraged by the continuous attacks and losses as the defenders appeared undiminished. Morale suffered with the failure to achieve any major success and constantly changing orders demonstrated a lack of focus and misjudgement of the situation of the battle. Unjustified accusations of the inefficiency of Luftwaffe pilots were demoralising and they were exhausted by the continuous physical and mental strain.

The clear dawn of 15 September turned into a glorious late-summer day with conditions perfect for the Luftwaffe massed attacks, but they were late in coming. Park had

time to bring to readiness a full squadron at each sector station, while individual patrols were flown along the east and south coast from Harwich to Land's End to maintain an awareness of approaching formations and confirm information as processed by the Observer Corps and radar. The occasional Luftwaffe reconnaissance flight was forced to return home or destroyed, a lone He 111 being shot down near Exeter by Hurricanes of 87 Squadron.

On the morning of 15 September, Park received an unscheduled visit from Winston Churchill who happened to be passing Uxbridge. This was an auspicious day to have chosen. Soon after the visitors were seated a radar report was received of forty-plus bandits forming up over Dieppe, followed by a report of another forty-plus in the same area, but no height information. Several squadrons were scrambled to climb south east of London, and more ordered to 'standby' with pilots in the cockpits ready for take-off. The remaining squadrons were brought to 'Readiness' – take-off within five minutes. Although the targets were unknown to Park, he had to make a calculated guess and encouraged his squadrons to attack the bombers, causing them to jettison their bombs over the sea or open country. Soon

The He 111 was an all-metal monoplane powered by a pair of Jumo 211A engines giving a cruising speed of 233 mph and could carry between 300kg of bombs over a distance of 1,745 miles, or 2,000kg over 552 miles, the normal range being 1,366 miles with 1,000kg of bombs. It carried six 7.7mm machine guns, one in the nose, two below the fuselage firing fore and aft, one on top of the fuselage firing aft and one on either side mounted to fire through the side windows. The crew consisted of six. (*Imperial War Museum*)

Led by Squadron Leader Douglas Bader, 242 Squadron Hurricanes heads up the 12 Group Wing from Duxford and Fowlmere in October 1940. *(Imperial War Museum)*

all squadrons in 11 Group were engaged with no reserves and Park called Dowding to request reserves from three squadrons in 12 Group.

The target turned out to be a major attack on London in two stages. The Luftwaffe had been led to believe that Fighter Command was virtually destroyed. However, they found a determined opposition with some 170 defending fighters ready to meet them and around 50 bombers turned for home before reaching Chatham. The enemy fighter escorts were fighting hard and held off many RAF fighters. In reaching the outskirts of London, the German aircraft flew into a heavy barrage of newly installed anti-aircraft batteries, and as they emerged from this hazard, they were faced by the largest concentration of defending fighters they had ever encountered. There were 15 squadrons facing the enemy, ten from 11 Group and five from the 12 Group Wing – the weight of the force being sufficient to put the Luftwaffe on the defensive as they were outnumbered. The combination of the RAF fighter assault and thickening cloud spared the main German target of the Royal Victoria and Surrey Commercial Docks from serious damage. Instead, bombs were scattered across west, north and south London as well as one on the Strand. Attacks on the retreating bombers continued all the way to the south coast when a force of Bf 109s arrived to escort the remainder home. Before the end of the day, it was clear that a decisive battle had been won. And although the Air Ministry announced the destruction of 183 enemy aircraft shot down, the real figure was 56, the heaviest daily loss by the Luftwaffe so far, and a severe blow to morale and strength. In the space of 90 minutes 250 RAF fighters from 28 squadrons had been in action, belying Goering's boast that Fighter Command was down to its last 50 fighters.

RAF pilots felt a strong sense of victory at the end of the day. A total of 26 fighters had been shot down with the loss of 13 pilots. The organisation of Fighter Command had worked well with detection, interception followed by destruction of significant hostile aircraft as well as turning away many of the bombers. The entire communications infrastructure had worked, from the Observer Corps, radar and group and sector stations, to the pilot with his finger on the trigger. Park's careful and skilful management of the situation had worked well and the Luftwaffe's poor performance had contributed to the RAF success, the main clash being at the point of Park's choosing where the escorting fighters were at the extreme of their endurance. The Luftwaffe's attempt to win air superiority had failed to achieve the conditions for an invasion, but the attacks did not finish there and then. The greatest danger had passed on 15 September, and although it was not obvious at the time, the Battle of Britain had been won.

CHAPTER 3
LIFE ON A BATTLE OF BRITAIN AIRFIELD

The 19 and 616 Squadron rest room at Duxford in September 1940.
(Imperial War Museum)

In 1935-36, the whole structure of the Royal Air Force was reshaped. What had been a Directorate of Supply and Research was divided into Research and Development and Supply Organisation. In May 1936, a Training Command was established, followed on 14 July by a Bomber Command, Coastal Command and Fighter Command. All these officers were directly responsible to the Air Council through the CAS. It was a big advance upon the clumsy existing organisation: a Commander-in-Chief of Air Defence with both fighters and bombers under him, standing in an indeterminate relationship to the Chief of the Air Staff. Air Marshal Sir Hugh Caswall Tremenheere Dowding had on 14 July 1936 become the first Air Officer Commander in Chief of Fighter Command. Three days later civil war broke out in Spain. While the German *Legion Kondor* exploited the war for its own ends, sending 370 handpicked pilots and aircrew, devising tactics

and honing its skills, Dowding set about correcting "some lamentable deficiencies" at Fighter Command. Dowding was of the opinion that the next war would be won "by science thoughtfully applied to operational requirements". In 1931, he had been appointed Air Member for Research and Development and in the mid-1930s he had grasped the importance of Radio Direction Finding (RDF, later radar) and integrated it into the defence system.

In 1934, A P Rowe of the Directorate of Scientific Research in the Air Ministry informed his director, H E Wimperis, that unless science could come effectively to the rescue, any war in the next ten years was bound to be lost. A scientific committee was formed within the Air Ministry at the end of 1934 to survey air defence and its first meeting was on 28 January 1935. One of the first matters to come before the committee was Radio Direction Finding of aircraft proposed by

Robert A Watson-Watt, Superintendent of the Radio Department of the National Physical Laboratory. A Post Office Report of June 1932 mentioned that aircraft interfered with radio signals and re-radiated them and Watt considered the possibility of transmitting a radio pulse which would be reflected back by aircraft as a signal to the ground. Further calculations by one of his staff, A F Wilkins, enabled Watson-Watt to submit to the Air Ministry on 12 February 1935 a document entitled *Detection and Location of Aircraft by Radio Methods*. Using as a basis his experiments in calculating the height of the ionosphere by the reflection of radio pulses, Watson-Watt explained how pulses would be similarly reflected from the metal components of an aircraft, and how this reflection could be recorded. Air Vice-Marshal Dowding insisted on a demonstration of the proposed system. On 26 February, a Handley Page Heyford aircraft from the Royal Aircraft Establishment at Farnborough flew a straight course up and down a beam transmitted from the nearby BBC short-wave station at Daventry and in a caravan in a field near Weedon, a wireless receiving set to which was attached a cathode-ray oscillograph showed a green spot elongated as the aircraft came nearer, contracting as it went away. The range of this early locating equipment was only eight miles but it had been demonstrated beyond doubt that electro-magnetic energy was reflected from an aircraft and that these reflections could be depicted visually by the cathode-ray apparatus.

By the end of March, sites for laboratories and towers had been selected at Orfordness and work had begun on the design of suitable transmitting and receiving apparatus. The developments that followed, first at Orfordness and then at Bawdsey Manor, made it clear that RDF – or radar as it came to be called – had many uses, not only for detecting aircraft but also for use in aircraft. By September 1935, the Air Council was sufficiently impressed with progress to recommend the construction of a chain of ground stations from Southampton to the Tyne. As an intermediate step the Treasury agreed to the erection of five stations between Dover and Bawdsey. The building of these was beset with all kinds of difficulty and delay, and approval for the main chain of twenty stations did not follow until August 1937. In 1938, the decision was made to erect a chain of 18 Chain Home (CH) stations between the Isle of Wight and St Abbs Head, the first operational masts (apart from research masts at Orfordness) being erected at Bawdsey and handed over to the RAF in May 1937. These were followed by masts at Dover and Canewdon.

During the air exercises in the summer of 1937, Britain's embryonic air defence system only just passed its first serious examination but RAF Fighter Command's biplane fighters were often too slow to catch the new Blenheim bombers. By 1938, three fighter squadrons had been re-equipped with Hurricanes and the radar chain had been increased from three to five stations. The air exercises of 5-7 August 1938 proved promising and provided the

Although 61 Squadron did not operate Blenheims in France, this line-up at a Royal Aeronautical Society garden party at Fairey's Great West Aerodrome in May 1938 illustrates the type used for bombing by the AASF in an attempt to stop the German advance. The Blenheim was an all-metal aircraft powered by two 840hp Bristol Mercury engines. It had a maximum speed of 285 mph, a range of 1,125 miles, a service ceiling of 32,000ft and carried a crew of three. The prototype made its first flight from Filton, Bristol, on 25 June 1936 and was armed with a dorsal turret with single Lewis gun. First deliveries to the RAF were in March 1937.

reward for Dowding's "forceful, cogent and entirely outspoken protests" to the Air Ministry. On the assumption that the Luftwaffe would likely mount daily raids of 200 aircraft it was estimated that 10 per cent would be destroyed. Dowding knew differently. Early in 1939, faced with taking early retirement, he wrote to the Air Ministry: "I can say without fear of contradiction that since I have held my present post I have dealt with and am in the process of dealing with a number of vital matters which generations of Air Staff have neglected for the last fifteen years: putting the Observer Corps on a war footing, manning of Operations Rooms, identification of friendly aircraft, unserviceability of aerodromes and adequate Air-Raid Warning System. This work had to be carried out against the inertia of the Air Staff, a statement which I can abundantly prove if necessary. [...] In spite of my intense interest in the Fighter problems of the immediate future ... there is little in my past or present treatment at the hands of the Air Ministry to encourage me to undertake a further period of service." Dowding's retirement was deferred, but only until the end of March 1940.

The battle for survival that lay ahead could not be fought by the pilots of RAF Fighter Command alone. An incident in late May 1939 was a portent of things to come. RDF stations on the east coast picked up a strong radar response from a large slow-moving object over the North Sea. The echo turned out to be the German airship LZ130 *Graf Zeppelin*, which was carrying General Wolfgang Martini, the Luftwaffe's Chief of Signals, on a mission to investigate the British radar defence system. Flying in cloud, the airship radioed its position off the Yorkshire coast to its home base. The Zeppelin was actually several miles inland over Hull, but the temptation for British radar operators to issue a correction was resisted because any contact would have confirmed that the airship was indeed being tracked by radar and revealed the extent of the system's efficiency to the Germans. By July 1940, there were 51 operational radar stations situated around the approaches to Britain. Twenty-one of these were Chain Home (CH) fixed mast stations, located around the east and south coast from the north of Scotland to Cornwall and South Wales. They could determine the range, bearing, height and strength of a hostile raid. Each CH station was capable of providing a long-range picture of the air situation at medium and high altitudes within a fixed 120 degrees arc at a range of about 150 miles at 18,000ft from shore, but for technical reasons the CH radars could not track aircraft flying over land. When, in the early months of the war, German aircraft commenced to lay mines in the estuaries of the East Coast, it was found that the CH stations failed to detect these aircraft when flying low. Thirty smaller stations known as Chain Home Low (CHL) were constructed to provide low coverage to the estuaries of the Thames, Humber, Tyne and other rivers. CHL stations could detect aircraft flying at 500ft out to 18 miles and aircraft flying at 2,000ft out to 35 miles. The first CHL station, at Fifeness in Scotland, was commissioned on 1 November 1939. In 11 Group's operational area there were 16 coastal radar sites, eight of which were CH sites and eight of which were low-level CHL, stretching from Suffolk to Ventnor on the Isle of Wight.

But while radar was fundamental, a great deal more was involved in the air defence system. Between the radar 'plots' of approaching hostile aircraft and the fighters which climbed to intercept them, and the guns, searchlights, balloons and air-raid sirens (all of which had their vital functions) there existed a highly intricate system of communications manned by hundreds of men and women. Once the raiders crossed the coast, tracking them was the responsibility of the Observer Corps, which was made up of 32 centres whose 30,000 volunteers manned over 1,000 posts around the clock monitoring the height, speed and strength of the enemy formations overhead. The Observer Corps plotted the 'hostiles' by sight or sound, depending on the visibility, and passed their plots by landline to their own Group HQ, which relayed them to the Fighter Command filter room for onward transmission throughout the system. The filter room concept was developed by Squadron Leader Hart at Bawdsey, where the first one was built, but parts were later removed and taken to Bentley Priory in October 1938. The first filter training school opened in March 1940 at Bawdsey. The filter room collated, sorted and filtered all incoming reports before the information was used operationally. This was intended to eliminate duplication and to display identified tracks on the group Operations Room plotting table. The results were broadcast to all operational users within the designated area of responsibility of a fighter group, such as sector Operations Rooms and Observer Corps centres. The filter room was originally part of the group Operations Room but later became a protected building in its own right known as a filter block, built using the cut-and-cover technique in two levels. The roof consisted of a 1ft thick rcinforccd concrete subroof and a thinner upper roof with a 4ft 6inch void filled with sand and gravel, the complete area then being covered with earth.

Dowding recognised the potential afforded by new fighters and radar and to this he soon introduced Operations Rooms at all Commands. He also saw the need for all-weather runways at his airfields, many of which dated back to the very early days of aviation. In 1939, only nine airfields in the United Kingdom had runways and these were of maximum dimensions of 1,000 yards by 50 yards. The rest were grass fields for all types of aircraft and for all purposes – training or operational.

In 1939, the first runway programme was initiated at 12 stations, two runways 800 yards by 50 yards being put in and connected with a perimeter or taxi track 50ft wide. By the autumn of 1938, paved runways were recognised as essential. At each of eight fighter stations – Biggin Hill, Church Fenton, Debden, Hendon, Kenley, Northolt, Tangmere and Turnhouse – the construction of two 800-yards-by-50-yards runways was begun.

One other airfield requirement causing considerable planning and constructional problems was the provision of aircraft dispersal and parking standings round the airfield perimeter. Immediately before the war it was realised that some provision must be made for aircraft dispersal around the airfield boundary so that in war concentrations of aircraft in hangars and on aprons could be avoided. Accordingly, on operational airfields, reservation of outlying fields and flat areas suitably located adjacent to woods and farms was made and temporary hardcore access tracks constructed. Two main types of fighter dispersal pens, both with earthwork traverses, were intended for the protection of two aircraft. Type B differed from the Type E in that its outer arms were cranked whereas the arms of the E were straight. Cranking offered better protection to the aircraft but as space was limited with this arrangement it was necessary to have two different sizes of pen. One had a maximum width of 54ft for an aircraft the size of a Hurricane and the other at 76ft was large enough to accommodate a Blenheim. It was the normal practice to provide six Type B fighter pens per squadron of 12 aircraft while satellite airfields were provided with just six pens. Other stations had two separate groups of six pens. The floor of the pen was either concrete or tarmac. Type E pens could be found at Biggin Hill, Hornchurch, Kenley and North Weald.

As Hurricanes of 32 Squadron return from combat on 15 August 1940, personnel with red flags indicate bomb craters on the airfield. A typical dispersal is in the background.

The hangar arrangement has always been the dominant feature of all airfields and fighter stations under Air Defence of Great Britain were thought to be liable to attack in the event of war. Up until 1939, most hangars were A, B or C Type but then hangar design was changed and stations laid down pre-war were completed with J and K Type hangars with curved ¼-inch steel plate covering roofs. Some stations, like Duxford and Martlesham, retained hangars of 1917 vintage. At Duxford, Belfast Trusses in the roof have given the name 'Belfast Type' to the sheds.

Another structure thought to be one of the most vulnerable to air attack was the Operations Rooms and so these were protected by 6ft high earthworks. The standard Operations Room for stations under the ADGB Scheme of 1925 was a brick-built bungalow-like building which accommodated up to three squadrons and which was invariably built immediately behind the station headquarters, connected to it by a corridor. It was often a detached building which required a basement to house a heating chamber. The building was 97ft 9in long and 27ft 9in wide, built with solid walls 13.5in wide and faced with red facing bricks. King-post timber trusses with hipped gable ends and large-size purlins supported by vertical struts carried rafters supporting rough boarding and slates. A protected central entrance through the earth bank gave access to a corridor connecting a store and workshop on the far left, while the Operations Room was at the opposite end. The PBX, battery room, wireless and signals office were all in the centre of the building. A protected roof version was very well defended against the effects of incendiaries and bomb blast from near misses. Surrounding the whole building was a 9ft high reinforced-concrete traverse wall with an angled earth bank having a maximum thickness of 17ft. The building was further protected with a thick-section concrete subroof slab supported by twenty large section RSJs.

There was a plan in place for squadrons to use airfields of other commands if ever it became necessary to evacuate Fighter Command's main bases. The plan would never be put into practice but in 1940, 11 Group alone used 27 airfields spread across Kent, West Sussex, Surrey, Greater London, Essex and as far east as Suffolk. All Groups had several satellite fields where fighters could be dispersed. In 12 Group, on 3 July 1940, Spitfire pilots of 19 Squadron moved to Fowlmere, which was complete with sleeping

Spitfire Ib R6923 QJ-S of 92 Squadron was one of the first to go into action with the eight .303-inch machines guns replaced by a pair of the more destructive 20mm cannons. The cannons fired high explosive rounds, whereas the 0.303 machine guns fired solid rounds. To accommodate this bulky armament in the wing, additional fairings had to be fitted on the upper surface close to the trailing edge. *(Unknown copyright via BAE Systems)*

huts for the pilots and tents for the ground staff, cooking tender, PBX telephone exchange and the Welsh regiment to guard them, for what amounted to a 21-day sojourn. The village had no shop and only two pubs. The officers frequented the 'Chequers' but the landlord did not want the ground staff. Their abode was the 'Black Horse' where they had beer and played a lot of cards including gambling games, which were illegal, though everyone turned a blind eye. If pilots wanted a bath, they had to go to Duxford once a week. On 23 July, 19 Squadron returned to Duxford and on 2 August the squadron flew its first combat patrol.

Permanent stations had an armoury, guardhouse, stores, M/T sections, workshops and modern messes, a NAAFI and modern barracks, but if they were lucky some pilots who were billeted off base were able to better enjoy the comforts of home. In August 1940, Nigel Rose, a Spitfire I pilot in 602 City of Glasgow Squadron, arrived at Tangmere with the rest of his squadron from Scotland. He wrote to his parents telling them that "we live for the moment in a typical Sussex rectory (perhaps I'm not really qualified to call it that!) but there's that delightful smell of soap and flowers and new mown grass and wasps in abundance. The squadron bagged two 'certains' and three unconfirmed at tea just after we arrived yesterday."

No-one understood the true nature of Fighter Command and its battle system better than Dowding, who created an air defence system without parallel based on what he would call "science thoughtfully applied to operational requirements". His assessment of his own, and the Command's, task in 1940 was clear: "Mine was the purely defensive role of trying to stop the possibility of an invasion, and thus give this country a breathing spell ... it was Germany's objective to win the war by invasion and it was my job to prevent an invasion from taking place." When the battle was joined, German listeners were amazed to find "the air full of voices, calmly and systematically placing fighters here and there and guiding others back to base. It dawned on the listeners that this was part of a complex and smooth-running organization of great size."

In December 1939, serious investigation of German signals had started – not a moment too soon – and in February 1940, Flight Lieutenant (later Group Captain) Scott Farnie established the first listening post at Hawkinge. Thus began the invaluable 'Y Service', which kept the Luftwaffe under permanent radio surveillance, one of the war's well-kept secrets. The ever-increasing requirement for fluent German linguists soon made it obvious that women would have to be recruited for this work as well as men. The Women's Royal Air Force had previously briefly existed at the end of World War 1. The Women's Auxiliary Air Force was formed on 28 June 1939 by Royal Warrant. At the outbreak of war on 3 September, there were fewer than 2,000 women on strength. Its object was to replace men in the RAF where possible to free them for other active service. When war was declared, an appeal for recruits to the WAAF was broadcast over the radio by the BBC and hundreds of women immediately volunteered.

In early 1940, a public campaign was launched to recruit WAAF personnel from the Norfolk area to work in the Operations Room at Coltishall. This campaign was held at the Odeon Cinema in Norwich with Squadron Leader Bader on the stage to promote recruitment. Those who volunteered were summoned to Coltishall, uniformed and taken straight to the Operations Room with no training for the task or for RAF life in general. The original Operations Room at Coltishall was soon closed as it was deemed inadequate for the increase in work generated within the sector, especially with the additional sorties being flown from the satellite airfield at Matlaske. Within weeks a new Operations Room near Norwich was in full swing with the Duty Watch being transported from Coltishall on a daily basis. These facilities soon became were unsuitable and vulnerable to enemy raids and the Operations Room moved again, to Stratton Strawless Hall on the Norwich to Aylsham road, where a purpose-designed Operations Room was built adjacent to the original buildings with Nissen huts being constructed in the grounds to house the RAF and WAAF personnel.

Corporal Bunty Walmsley, a locally recruited WAAF, recalled that not long after joining up, she with other members of her watch were suddenly roused from their beds and told to immediately assemble outside to be addressed by the WAAF Commanding Officer. Garbed in various forms of night attire, they all staggered outside looking the worse for wear. The next moment their Commanding Officer appeared, dressed in full uniform and, to their amazement, proceeded to inform them that the Germans had invaded the south coast and that further landings were likely. She went on to say that if Coltishall should be involved, she expected each one of them to defend the station by any means possible. Bunty's only weapon was a poker allocated to her billet! In the morning, they were all due to report for their watch at 0800 hours. On meeting up with some of the RAF section of her watch, the WAAFs discovered that none of them had been disturbed and were equally unaware of an invasion.

Bunty and her colleagues worked a six on–twelve off shift pattern in three watches – A, B and C. This shift pattern continued throughout the war years, even over the Christmas periods. There were numerous visits by Wing Commander Max Aitken who would travel to the hall from Coltishall to observe his squadron from the decks when they were involved in major operations. With the plots being moved around the tables and the R/T messages coming over the radio, he often felt he was in the aircraft with the crews. This is why he chose to be at the Operations Room rather than at the airfield when things were 'hot'.

It often got hot at Duxford, in 12 Group, as Jean Mills, who went to RAF Leighton Buzzard in early August 1940 to train as a plotter and tracer with Fighter Command, recalls.

"I was in a contingent of about a dozen WAAFs that had just arrived at the little railway station at Whittlesford. We were quite excited because we were all pretty young, 18 or 19, I suppose, and most of us hadn't been away from home before and life was a great big adventure and we were feeling very hyper I should imagine. And the truck bumped over the country roads and suddenly we reached the brow of a hill and we could see Duxford stretched out before us and it was a very sunny day. And there was the aerodrome, mostly grassed and the big hangars there and you could see the main gate. To the right was what looked like a little housing estate, which were the previous married quarters for the airmen and their families. And suddenly as we looked

there had obviously been something going on because planes seemed to be landing from all directions. And as we looked one of them appeared to hover for a moment and then it nose-dived straight down into the ground. And there were smoke trails rising. The noise just stopped absolutely instantaneously and we looked at each other a bit shocked. And the mood changed and we were all very much sobered up. And I think we then realised that it wasn't a great lark and it was quite serious business that we were in for. Actually, we were reminded of this because the pilot was killed, of course, and he'd owned a large Alsatian dog, which for the next few days just seemed to roam the camp looking for him all the time until somebody else took him over. It was quite sad. There were moments like that, but most of the time you were so busy that you just didn't let it get at you."

Section Officer Aileen ('Mike') Morris MBE, recalls: "By the end of the summer of 1940, the Air Ministry Intelligence had an almost complete picture of the Luftwaffe Order of Battle, particularly in Western Europe. With all this knowledge added to the information that we were amassing at Kingsdown [Bentley Priory] about the call signs and frequencies used by the various German squadrons to which we were listening, we were able, for instance, to advise 11 Group that the enemy raid that was approaching Beachy Head was probably made up of Me 109s of III JG 51 at St-Omer. This would be most helpful for the controllers, who would then be able to anticipate the probable return route of the enemy aircraft. Later, when we had direction-finding [D/F] facilities, we could pinpoint the transmissions and thus knew the exact position of the enemy formation whose messages we were hearing. But even in those early days of the summer of 1940, we could almost certainly confirm the height at which the formations were approaching, and we might also be able to give some indication, from what we were hearing, of their intended action."

Section Officer Morris believed that the German equivalent of the Y Service – *Horchdienst* – "may at that time have been rather more efficient than ours. There were occasions when we would intercept a message from a German formation approaching RAF fighters ... having spotted our aircraft before they themselves were observed. We were then likely to hear: '*Indianer unten fuenf Uhr, Kirchturm 4, Aufpassen!*' ['Bandits below at 5 o'clock, height 4000 metres, look out!] In those days we were unable to get this information through in time for it to be of tactical use, and would get hopping mad that we had no means of warning our fighters that they were about to be jumped. Then '*Angreifen!*' [Attack!] the formation leader would yell, and we would know that the German fighters were diving on their target. I would often hear one of the WAAF operators murmuring: 'Oh God ... oh God ... please ... *please* look up ...' and I knew how helpless she felt. Eventually, we were able to bring the time-lag down to one minute."

Everything began with the intercept. The monitoring of all German signals, whether in low-grade or high-grade cipher, radio-telephony, or non-Morse transmissions, was the responsibility of the Y Service. Station X, Bletchley Park, the Government Code and Cipher School, was entirely dependent upon Y. It was here that brilliant academics broke the German *Enigma* codes and produced the *Ultra* decoding system. During the period of the invasion threat, *Ultra* played a significant part in permitting the British leadership to build up a complete picture of German intentions in the Battle of Britain. Apart from Dowding, Air Vice-Marshal Keith Park, commanding 11 Group, alone of the fighter commanders was in on the *Ultra* secret. The early and authentic information that came from Bletchley about forthcoming raids was also available to Dowding from the beginning, at first via the Air Ministry, then direct from Bletchley by teleprinter through a Special Liaison Unit lodged in a sound-proof cubicle next to the Operations Room in Bentley Priory.

At the heart of the whole Dowding System was the 166-year-old Bentley Priory, atop a hill at Stanmore just north of London, his headquarters, and at the heart of that the Operations Room, which had only been securely lodged underground and under concrete in March 1940. Here sat Dowding with his duty controller, the Commandant of the Observer Corps, liaison officers from Bomber and Coastal Commands, the Admiralty, the War Office, the Ministry of

Home Security (air-raid warnings) and Lieutenant-General Frederick Pile of Anti-Aircraft Command. AA Command controlled guns positioned within a 25-mile-wide belt stretching from Newcastle down the East Coast, around London and south-west to Portsmouth. Included in the belt were 960 searchlights. The whole system was manned by 23,000 personnel. Even before the war, the Chiefs of Staff had recommended the provision of just over 4,000 guns; a fresh survey of requirements now placed the figure at something over 8,000, but the total number actually possessed by Anti-Aircraft Command at the beginning of August was less than 2,000. Responsibility for the protection of London belonged to the 1st Anti-Aircraft Division, with more than 120 heavy guns. The rest of the south-east was the responsibility of the 6th Anti-Aircraft Division with almost 200 heavy guns, mainly old 3-inch guns plus the newer 3.7 inch and 4.5 inch ones. In addition there were a few hundred more light guns (mainly two-pounders and Bofors 40mm) and 700 light machine guns protecting the airfields and other key targets. Air Vice-Marshal O T

Airfield ground defence was sometimes basic with twin Lewis guns of World War 1 vintage. *(Imperial War Museum)*

Boyd's Balloon Command was also under the operational control of Fighter Command No 30 (Balloon Barrage) Group that was responsible for the protection of London and the south-east of England with more than 500 balloons, which were able to reach heights of up to 5,000ft.

A neighbouring filter centre shared the same concrete bunker where filter officers – one for each radar station – identified all the plots received from the two radar chains and the Observer Corps. Each raid was allocated a number and the filter offices checked them against 'friendly', 'hostile' or 'unknown' ('X-

One of the many barrage balloons, this one close to the Houses of Parliament, which were raised on steel cables designed to bring down enemy aircraft as they approached their targets. *(Imperial War Museum)*

raids') before they appeared on the map in the Operations Room where Dowding could view the battle situation anywhere in the British Isles. This was the only place where the complete picture was available to the Commander-in-Chief 24 hours a day. Sadie Younger, a filterer at Bentley Priory during the battle, recalls:

"I can remember working flat out on the Estuary/Channel area of the filter room table. The heavy enemy attacks, meant for London, were continuous, apart from a lull at midday. Radar stations passed mass plots to plotters, working at high speed, and tellers were doubled up, as there was so much information to be passed to Operations Rooms. I needed both hands to filter tracks. I even remember telling the controller on the dais that the heights on enemy raids could be anything between 15,000 and 25,000 [feet], but the weather was fine and the visibility good."

The track of the raid would be given simultaneously to the Fighter Group controllers, who as well as the filtered radar plots from Fighter Command, received plots direct from the Observer Centres. This was the only independent source of information in the Groups, which it was their duty to pass to Fighter Command and other Groups. Balloon barrages, too, were in direct touch with Group Operations Room, which was modelled on the 'master' at Bentley Priory, but displaying on its key map only the Group area and immediately adjacent sectors. The Group Commander and his Controller could see simultaneously at any moment the exact situation on the table map of the Group area. Around the map sat WAAF girls with headphones and croupiers' rakes, moving coloured discs, which represented aircraft according to the plots received.

Fighter Command did not make any tactical decisions about the air fighting. Operational

One of the many Luftwaffe He 111 bombers over the Thames and London Docks at Rotherhithe on the first daylight attack of the London Blitz. *(Imperial War Museum)*

command rested with the Group Commanders who would bring squadrons to varying states of readiness according to the scale and direction of a threatening raid and it was they who then decided when to send up which aircraft. No 11 Group, commanded by Air Vice-Marshal Keith Park, a New Zealander, with headquarters at Uxbridge, covered the whole of Southern England from Portsmouth round to the Thames Estuary. At the beginning of July 1940, there were eight sector airfields in 11 Group: North Weald, Hornchurch, Biggin Hill, Kenley, Tangmere, Middle Wallop, Northolt and Filton (Bristol). Within days of the battle opening the number of sectors was reduced to seven, lettered A, B, C, D, E, F and Z, controlled from Tangmere, Kenley, Biggin Hill, Hornchurch, North Weald, Debden (transferred from 12 Group) and Northolt respectively. No 12 Group, under Air Vice-Marshal Trafford Leigh-Mallory, extended

across the Midlands to the East Coast, north from the Thames Estuary to Yorkshire, with six sectors (Coltishall, Duxford, Wittering, Digby, Kirton-in-Lindsey and Church Fenton). The North and Scotland were the defence responsibility of 13 Group under Air Vice-Marshal Richard Saul DFC with sectors at Catterick, Usworth, Acklington, Turnhouse, Dyce and Wick. It had for some time been realised that 11 Group, with London and the South-East, as well as important ports and industries (particularly aircraft factories), was too large for one command. By 8 July 1940, it had been divided again and a new group, No 10, was operational under Air Vice-Marshal Sir Christopher Quintin Brand KBE DSO MC DFC, with sectors at Middle Wallop and Filton (Sectors W and Y respectively) both of which were transferred from No 11 Group.

The Sector Operations Rooms were the final link in the control system; it was they

The Hurricane had a rugged structure consisting of metal, wood and fabric covering which could absorb combat damage and bring its pilot back home.

who scrambled the squadrons into the air, positioned and fed them with essential information and brought them back again, advising the best available airfield if bomb damage meant that they could not return to their home airfields. Sectors were given letters but were usually known by the name of their Sector Station, which was the airfield controlling them. This airfield had its own Operations Block which was a temporary building. It was unusual in that it consisted of a standard Laing hut (60ft by 18ft 6in) on top of a brick ground-floor structure to form a two-storey building with a D/F plotting room, four R/T rooms, a controller's office and WCs. The first floor contained the upper part of the D/F room, the Operations Room proper, the plant room, VHF room and a large spare room at the rear. The D/F room followed its own fighters by means of radio fixes, which it obtained from the IFF [Identification Friend or Foe] or 'Pip Squeak' – a small automatic transmitter fitted in every aircraft. The D/F room passed the fighters' position on to the Operations Room. There, arranged around a balcony like a theatre, two deputy-controllers (one listening in to other sectors and the other dealing with air-sea rescue) and two navigators rapidly calculated the fighters' interception courses and passed them to the Sector Controller who directed all the aircraft at the sector stations under his control. On either side of the deputy-controllers were 'Ops A', who was in permanent contact with group, and 'Ops B', who got through to dispersal and scrambled the pilots from the airfields. On the wings of the balcony, which Churchill called the 'dress-circle', sat liaison officers who were in direct contact with Observer Corps Headquarters and Anti-Aircraft command respectively.

The ground floor of the Operations Room contained a 10ft square grid-lined map table showing the group and sector boundaries and the airfields within the sector. From his raised dais, the controller had a perfect view of the large table map, swiftly and silently manipulated by WAAFs who worked in three shifts of about ten hours each and were usually known as the 'beauty chorus'. At sector stations each of them was assigned to a radar station and Observer Corps centre within the sector. They wore headsets and, using magnetised croupier rakes,

dutifully moved wooden blocks representing each raid around the grids like a board game as the enemy raids developed. The blocks had numbers slotted into them to show the raid designation; for example, H06 for Hostile 6. Underneath would be the hostile strength – e.g. 30+ – to show the minimum size positively identified by the Observer Corps posts or by radar return. Arrows were placed behind the blocks to show the direction of the raid. There was a clock on the wall with each five-minute segment colour-coded red, blue or yellow and the arrows coloured to show during which of the segments they had been updated. During July and August 1940, all information was shown on the main table but by September this was becoming so congested that a slotted blackboard known as the 'totalisator', or 'tote', showing squadrons and their states of readiness recorded all details of enemy raids and fighters sent to intercept. Observers and controllers could therefore see how up-to-date the information on the table was. Friendly aircraft were plotted in a separate room and other WAAFs put their blocks on the board showing the units concerned, their strength and height.

The sectors were able to control up to six squadrons but most usually controlled two or three. The respective sector Operations Room controller, generally of Squadron Leader or at most Wing Commander Rank, would possess exact, up-to-date information of pilot and aircraft availability. Squadrons which might be on the ground, either at the sector station or one of the forward airfields, would be at one of the prescribed states – that is ten minutes on 'available', five minutes on 'readiness', or two minutes on 'standby'; the latter with pilots in their fighters with engines running. Take-off orders were passed to the pilots by the sector controller by telephone or loudspeaker. Flight Lieutenant Denis Robinson of 152 Squadron at Warmwell recalled:

"The worst time was just waiting. When the phone rang the orderly would shout 'Squadron Scramble – Angels 15 [15,000ft].' In an instant we were running to our aircraft, grabbing the parachute off the wing, buckling it on as you scrambled into the cockpit. Then pull on the helmet already attached to radio and oxygen supply, whilst somehow starting the engine. It was a grass field without runways, so it's a matter of getting into the

Pilots of 601 Squadron scramble to their Hurricanes for another sortie from Exeter while the ground crews start the Merlin engines. *(Imperial War Museum)*

wind, keeping a sharp look-out for other aircraft, full throttle and away we go."

Further instructions followed over the aircraft radio after take-off.

The sector controllers therefore were the key men; each one "retained executive authority over the aircraft he dispatched until the fighters saw the enemy. When combat was broken off the controller resumed command." Heavy responsibilities lay upon these officers. The duties of a sector controller meant those fulfilling the role "needed a sense of judgement amounting to an Intuition". And they were unique to the RAF. A Luftwaffe intelligence report dated 16 July 1940 derided the superb RAF fighter direction system, claiming that "the command at high level is inflexible in its organisation and strategy. As formations are rigidly attached to their home bases, command at medium level suffers mainly from operations being controlled in most cases by officers no longer accustomed to flying [station commanders]. Command at low level is generally energetic but lacks tactical skill."

In fact the sector control rooms were presided over by experienced career officers like Wing Commander Lord Willoughby de Broke "who impressed with his calm and clear messages" and Wing Commander Alfred Basil Woodhall, at Duxford. 'Woody' Woodhall was

a South African who in 1914 had been a lance corporal in the Witwatersrand Rifles before joining the Royal Marines. During the early 1920s, he had flown biplane torpedo bombers before transferring to the RAF in 1929. When war came, Woodhall had a desk job at the Air Ministry and he was posted to Duxford on 12 March 1940 as senior controller.

When the sector controller directed his fighters to intercept a hostile raid a simple code was used between them: 'Scramble', take-off; 'Angels (ten)', height (10,000ft); 'Orbit', circle (a given point); 'Vector' (one-eight-zero), steer (course of 180 degrees); 'Buster', full throttle; 'Tally-ho!', enemy sighted; 'Pancake', land.

Each sector station and each fighter squadron had a codename – curious two-syllable inventions like Jaunty, Tennis, Waggon, Lumba, etc. A tactical unit of 12 fighters, each squadron was divided into four sections of three aircraft: Red and Yellow in A Flight; Blue and Green in B Flight, with the pilots in each numbered 1, 2 and 3. Blue 1 led Blue Section, followed by Blue 2 and Blue 3. The whole was an intricate and highly organised system of communications – from the hostile target to the radar station by radio-magnetic waves then on by telephone line to Fighter Command, to Group and to Sector then by radio-telephone from Sector Ops to the fighter pilot in the sky. A serious break at any stage in this elaborate system would more or less render it impotent.

A low-level attack on 18 August by nine Dornier Do 17s of KG76 restricted the use of Kenley. In the Operations Room, the station commander, Wing Commander Thomas Prickman, had watched his station's fighter squadrons being vectored to intercept high-altitude raiding forces coming in from the south-east. Then another marker appeared on the plotting table, showing the low-flyers heading across Sussex. The only fighters in his sector that were not yet committed were 111 Squadron's 12 Hurricanes, waiting at readiness at Croydon. Prickman ordered the unit to scramble and patrol over Kenley at 3,000ft. Thanks to efficient plotting by the Observer Corps, Kenley's ground defences were at full alert. Whilst the number and type of defences varied from airfield to airfield, those at Kenley consisted of two obsolete 3-inch anti-aircraft guns, four smaller 40mm Bofors guns and about 20 .303-inch Lewis machine guns. There was also a parachute and cable installation, known as PAC which fired salvoes of rockets at any raiders at about 500-700ft. Two Dorniers were shot down and the survivors came under repeated attack by 111 Squadron's Hurricanes. Two of the Dorniers ditched in the English Channel and two more crash-landed in France. A follow-up raid by 27 Dorniers delivered a high-altitude attack on Kenley. Altogether, three out of four hangars and several other buildings were destroyed and four Hurricanes and a Blenheim fighter were destroyed also.

A neglected area of the Battle of Britain is the courage and heroism shown on the ground by RAF and WAAF personnel, and also the casualties suffered during attacks. In May 1940, Corporal Daphne Pearson at the Coastal Command station at Detling, Kent, dragged the badly injured pilot of a crashed Anson clear of the burning wreckage and shielded him as bombs exploded. She was awarded the EGM, later converted to the George Cross. Squadron Leader Tony Pickering, a Hurricane pilot in the battle, said that his major memory of 1940 was of the young WAAFs who endured the bombing of the aerodromes such as Biggin Hill and Kenley and carried on at their posts with great bravery.

Wing Commander Carnegie had already been given some inkling of how the WAAF would behave under fire. In the early months of the war Carnegie, having received a draft of WAAF at Wittering, only because the Commanding Officer at a nearby bomber station refused to take them, ordered them away from the airfield when an approaching raider was plotted. The next day the WAAF officer in charge demanded an interview and informed him that if he ever gave a similar order she could not be responsible for the discipline of the girls or for their obedience to his instructions. During the Battle of Britain, military medals were awarded to six WAAFs. During the big attack on Biggin Hill on 18 August, Sergeant Elizabeth Mortimer, a telephone operator who was also in charge of the despatch of ammunition to the gun positions, remained at her very dangerous post throughout the raid, then, as soon as the bombs stopped falling – and long before the

Below: The Dornier Do 17 was a twin Bramo 323-powered all-metal monoplane with a crew of four consisting of pilot, bomb aimer/navigator and two rearward-facing gunners. Normal bomb load was 250kg (550lb) with a range of 745 miles (1,200 km) and a cruising speed of 275 mph (440 km/h). (*Imperial War Museum*)

Bottom: A pair of Luftwaffe Do 17 bombers over the Royal Victoria Docks and Silvertown in the East End of London on the first day of the London Blitz, 7 September 1940. (*Imperial War Museum*)

all clear – began planting red flags round the craters in which there were unexploded bombs. That same day at Poling, Sussex CH station, diminutive Corporal Avis Hearn ignored the order to take cover as a large Luftwaffe formation approached because she "had a lot of plots to send and I loved my country". Avis, who was only 4ft 10½in tall, was soon promoted to Flight Sergeant and sent to a top training establishment. Yet her mother had once chided "you'll never amount to anything". On 1 September, two telephone operators at Biggin Hill, Sergeant Helen Turner and Corporal Elspeth Henderson, continued to maintain communications even after the operations block in which they were working received a direct hit. Such calm behaviour, to which the superb example of the WAAF officer in charge, Assistant Section Officer Felicity Hanbury, greatly contributed was an inspiration not only to airwomen on other stations but also to their male comrades. Felicity was awarded a military OBE.

Two other military medal awards were made to Sergeant Jean Youle who was on duty in a station telephone exchange when the station was attacked and bombed by five enemy aircraft, and Corporal Josephine 'Josie' Robins, who was in a dug-out which received a direct hit during an intense enemy bombing raid. Josie recalled in a radio programme for the BBC:

"I really do not know why I have been given the Military Medal, as I only did what everyone else would have done. The actual raid was a lightning one; we saw the German planes coming and at first thought they were our own as they were so very low, then we made for the nearest shelter as the bombs rained down on us. Two of us were literally blown into the dug-out by the blast of a bomb which burst just behind us, and the next nearly blew us out again as it was a direct hit on the shelter, killing four men and injuring others. We helped some out of the dug-out which was full of awful dust and fumes from the explosion, and got a stretcher for a seriously injured man ... The morning after the raid we turned into carpenter and demolition squads, as each section had to make the building habitable. The roof of ours was decidedly impaired so we climbed up to investigate, and were forced into a perilous slide to the ground

every time the siren sounded or there were signs of air activity overhead."

Donald Elliott, a Norfolkman, had joined the RAF in 1938 and went to 1 School of Technical Training, Halton, as a boy-entrant. After training as an engine fitter and passing out in the rank of LAC he was posted to 66 Squadron at Coltishall. He wrote in his diary:

"We got to our new station last night. I am posted to 66(F) Squadron, Coltishall. It's on the main road between Norwich and Mundesley. It's eight miles from Norwich so I may be seeing you sometime. ... We lost one of our Spitfires over the sea on Wednesday afternoon. His engine seized up and he had to jump. ... Every little job you do, however small, is done perfectly. ... The other morning, when that German machine raided Norwich, it could be seen from this aerodrome by our pilots but, as usual, another muddle and they were not allowed to take off. ...We have managed to get one or two Jerries in the last day or two. ...Yes, of course, I have worked on some of the machines that have shot down the Nazis. I expect I have been on all of them; there's not many of us for the engines of the whole squadron. ...We start at eight in the morning now and every night it's either been eight or nine before we have packed up. Sunday is exactly the same as any other day up here, so we don't know one day from another now."

Donald Elliott was at the dispersal on the morning of 10 July 1940, the day that 66 Squadron recorded the first kill of the Battle of Britain. His diary went on to tell the story of the damage to Pilot Officer Cooke's aircraft on his return to Coltishall:

"The Germans' burst of gun-fire went straight through the revolving airscrew and into his bulletproof windscreen – it's a piece of glass about three times the size of this paper and is an inch thick. It was like looking at snow through it. It's been fitted since the war started. If it hadn't, the pilot would have got it in the head. As it was, he said that he said his prayers when the windscreen splintered. I have got a piece of it."

On 19 August, Donald reported: "Out of the blue about 3 o'clock this afternoon came one of those Nazi things. He let go six or eight over the next hangar. I am sorry to say there were about a hundred workmen working on and around it. A few were killed and a good many injured. It shook us up a good bit – some of the boys couldn't remember where they were and what they were doing before the bombs dropped. The air-raid siren went after all the bombs had been dropped."

His diary for 22 August went on to say: "Jerry came again yesterday dinner time, only our fighters were ready for him. It was like disturbing a hornet's nest when he came over. Both Squadrons, 66 and 242, shot up after him and then began a lovely game of hide-and-seek in and out of the clouds over the camp. Presently one of our Hurricanes came back full-out, dived down low over the drome and shot up again, doing a complete roll. That's the sign they all give if they have scored a victory." LAC Elliott left Coltishall with his squadron for Kenley on 3 September 1940.

Joe Crawshaw, an airframe rigger on 222 Squadron, recalled: "Relationships with pilots varied. Some would acknowledge their ground crews and have a bit of a chit chat, others remained remote figures but we always took a keen personal interest in our own pilot's welfare and would wait anxiously for his return from a sortie."

Sergeant [later Squadron Leader] Ian Hutchinson on 222 Squadron at Hornchurch adds: "The airfield was under attack and chunks of shrapnel were raining down. When I taxied towards dispersal no-one was to be seen; they were all in the airfield shelters taking cover. Before I rolled to a halt and cut the engine, B Flight ground crew, under their flight sergeant, were swarming around my Spitfire, the bowser racing out to refuel the aircraft, while the armament men, laden with ammunition, were re-loading the guns. The noise from the explosions going on around us was terrifying but not one of those magnificent men faltered in the tasks. I was frankly relieved to be taking off again."

Sergeant pilot [later Squadron Leader] Cyril 'Bam' Bamberger adds: "In September 1940, having been engaged in combat with Me 109s, during which my Spitfire was damaged I came in to land at Hornchurch airfield. As I touched down there was a twanging noise and both port and starboard ailerons drooped down. Whilst taxiing towards my squadron dispersal I had time to reflect on the fatal consequences if the control wire, obviously hit by enemy fire, had failed as I came into land.

As I parked my aircraft, still trying to relax, the senior Commanding Officer i/c ground crew greeted me with a curt comment, 'Now we have another unserviceable A/C.'"

Wing Commander Michael Nicholson Crossley, Commanding Officer of 32 Squadron for part of the battle said: "The ground crews were past all praise. If we had long hours they had longer ones by far. There were always laughing and ragging around the place, betting cigarettes or drinks as to whether A Flight would do better than B. A lot of publicity and glamour comes the way of the pilots but not all the praise in the world would do justice to these back-room boys."

A fighter squadron was normally led by a Squadron Leader, with Flight Lieutenants commanding A and B Flights. Commanding Officers who commanded squadrons in the battle included Squadron Leader George Denholm of 603 Squadron and Squadron Leader Harold Starr, who was machine-gunned and killed under his parachute by a Bf 109 on 31 August. Squadron Leader 'Jimmy' Fenton, a former Army Co-Operation pilot and instructor, took over 238 Squadron on 15 July and led it for the rest of the battle, although he was away wounded for over a month. Of Monday 12 August, Squadron Leader Crossley, Commanding Officer of 32 Squadron wrote: "Coo! What a blitz! Patrol base. All of a sudden we sight a cloud of Huns and move unwillingly towards them, but sight another cloud complete with mosquitoes a bit nearer; we move even more unwillingly towards them and attack.

A 19 Squadron Spitfire at Duxford on 21 September 1940 with armourer Fred Roberts and rigger Sgt Jennings in the cockpit. (Imperial War Museum)

Everyone takes a swing at the 50 Dornier 215s and the Messerschmitt 109s. Hell of a lot of zigging. Very hectic. Day's bag nine 109s, three 215s." They were a happy set in his squadron, each of whom was known to the others by a 'trade' name, among them being The Mandarin, Jackdaw, Grubby [Flight Lieutenant Douglas Hamilton Grice], Hector, Pete B [Pete Brothers], Polly [Sergeant R J Parrott], Humph [John Bernard William Humpherson], Jimmy, and David, while they dubbed Squadron Leader Crossley the Red Knight.

Squadron Leader Crossley afterwards referred to Thursday 15 August as "a remarkable blitz afternoon". His squadron started by chasing some Germans up to Harwich, where they had a mix-up with Bf 109s. Returning to their base to refuel, they were ordered down to Portsmouth to help beat off a very heavy attack by German bombers, after which they flew to base to refuel again. They were then sent away to patrol off Dover, and had climbed to 10,000ft in the neighbourhood of Maidstone when the control called them up and told them an attack on Croydon was pending. They needed no second invitation. Up to then they had destroyed six German aircraft that day and were keen to add to their score.

"We turned round and beat it for Croydon as hard as we could. Sure enough when we approached I saw a large party in progress. Masses of Me 110s were dive bombing the place. As they did not appear to notice our approach, I steered straight past them, with the object of getting between them and the sun. This was successful and we charged at them. I put a long burst into the first one I saw and he promptly caught fire and went down in flames. Then I saw another detach itself and make off, so I made after it and gave it a long burst, at which the starboard engine caught fire. I broke away and the Mandarin gave it a long burst and it altered course inland as if looking for somewhere to land. I nipped in and gave it another bang, and as I broke off I saw the starboard airscrew revolving slowly and then stop. Another burst from the Mandarin and one of the crew bailed out and the aircraft crashed in flames in a wood near Sevenoaks."

One of the most inspirational leaders was Douglas Bader, Commanding Officer of 242 Canadian Squadron. To see the Canadians lounging in their chairs at the dispersal point, with the yellow dope on their Mae Wests almost rubbed away by continual usage and to watch the way they were galvanised into life by the entrance of their squadron leader and his terse 'Come on!' was to witness a living example of leadership. He was the captain of their team and they would have followed him anywhere, as they did. They flew into the fury of the fight undismayed by any odds. It must have been a sad blow to them and to him when his promotion to the rank of Wing Commander in March 1941 compelled him to relinquish his command and go elsewhere. "Tactics," Bader said later, "were not for the Battle of Britain." All the fighter pilots could do was to get at the German bombers the quickest way possible, risking interference from Me 109s. These enemy fighters took a heavy toll particularly of 11 Group squadrons based in Kent and Surrey, which were too near the Channel to climb to the enemy height in time. As a result they were frequently clobbered on the way up. Duxford was 43 miles north of Tilbury, an ideal position for intercepting an enemy approaching London from 80 miles southeast of the capital. Quite naturally, the 11 Group controllers, who bore the heaviest burden of responsibility during the Battle of Britain, committed all their own squadrons before calling on Duxford in 12 Group.

It was Bader who said, "The Royal Air Force seemed to breed unusual characters." Generally, the brotherhood that made up the RAF fighter squadrons in the summer of 1940 were the happy few, a band of brothers unique in British military history who came from all walks of life and from all over Europe and the far flung reaches of the Empire. Canadians, Australians and New Zealanders, some of them fed up with their dead-end jobs, answered the call to arms with gusto. Of the 3,080 airmen awarded the Battle of Britain clasp, only 141 (6 per cent) were educated at the top 13 public schools. During the Battle of Britain, just 188 pilots achieved 'ace' status, shooting down at least five hostile aircraft. A further 233 of those claiming successes during the battle became 'aces' later in the war. But it was not all about becoming an 'ace'. Some station commanders could not resist the temptation to go into action themselves. Group Captain Stanley Vincent of Northolt became probably the only RAF pilot credited with destroying enemy aircraft in both world wars. On 15 September, he took off in his Hurricane and charged head-on at a *Staffel* of eight Dorniers. The veteran pilot watched in astonishment as they broke and wheeled away to the south. He was awarded a Bf 109 victory on 30 September. Wing Commander Victor Beamish of North Weald was another station commander who relished action. On 9 July, he listened with mounting impatience to the sector controller's commentary on the approaching plot over the airfield broadcast system and, on hearing his Hurricanes ordered off, dashed out of his office calling for his own aircraft to be started up. He was soon in the thick of action. Wing Commander Johnny Dewar, station commander at Exeter, who was killed on 12 September when it is believed that his Hurricane was shot down over Hampshire, was the highest ranking RAF officer to die in the air during the battle.

Leadership was needed at all levels. Bader was at the forefront again on 31 August, which before the war would have been a Bank Holiday weekend with time to laze, the day remaining mainly fair with haze in the Thames Estuary and the Strait of Dover, so there was still a chance of action. Finally, at around half past four, Wing Commander 'Woody' Woodhall, the Duxford controller ordered "242 Squadron scramble! Fly vector 190 degrees for North Weald. Angels 15." North Weald is 30 miles south of Duxford and the usual way to have covered the airfield would be to patrol over the airfield and wait for the enemy to appear. The Hurricanes took off and took 15 minutes to reach 15,000ft but Bader ignored the request to "Vector one-nine-zero. Buster [full throttle]." Instead he led the formation further west to get up-sun and climbed them to nearer 20,000ft to gain full advantage of the attackers, who he guessed correctly would approach from the west with the sun at their backs. The target for the Heinkel He 111H-2s of KG53 escorted by Bf 110s was not North Weald as was thought, but the Vauxhall Motor Works at Luton. Just north of North Weald Bader received directions to vector 340 degrees. At about the same time he saw three unidentified aircraft below and to the right of the squadron and ordered the three Hurricanes of Blue Section to investigate. At around 17.00 hours Bader spotted a tight enemy formation stepped up from about 12,000ft with their escort

fighters at 15,000 to 20,000ft, which he thought were 50 Dorniers escorted by a similar number of Bf 110s. Bader led his remaining Hurricanes down into the German formation west of the reservoirs at Enfield, heading for the Hatfield-North Weald area. He ordered Green Section to attack the top of the lower formation of 110s. Red Section (Bader, McKnight and Crowley-Milling) and Yellow Section (Eric Ball, Dickie Cork and Sergeant Robert Henry Lonsdale) formed into line abreast to dive down through the middle of the bomber formation. Heavily outnumbered, Bader's only aim was to try to break up the Heinkel formations and take the Bf 110s on individually in dogfights. It seemed to work because the tightly packed enemy formation immediately broke up fan-wise and were badly mauled by the Hurricanes. 242 claimed eight Bf 110s destroyed, one probably destroyed and one damaged. They also claimed five Heinkels shot down. On the way home to Duxford Bader picked up Green Leader and Blue Section, who were highly disgruntled to have missed the battle and not even fired a single round in anger. Six Heinkels were actually lost and two returned to base badly damaged while four Bf 110s were lost and three returned to base damaged. The Heinkels that did get through to their target hit the Vauxhall Works badly; 53 civilians were killed and 60 were injured. Bader felt that 242 had had a "successful" first engagement with the Luftwaffe "under favourable circumstances. Although, as was usual in 1940, heavily outnumbered, we had the height, the sun, and controlled the fight. We felt that with more aeroplanes we would have been even more successful."

Fighter Command lost 39 fighters on 31 August when the RAF flew 2,020 sorties and the Luftwaffe almost 2,800 sorties against London's sector airfields. These were the worst losses of the battle so far and they brought the number of RAF pilots killed and wounded that week to 115, with 65 of the fighters downed on the 30th and 31st. South of the Thames only two RAF Sector stations were still operational. At Coltishall, 242 Squadron had been scrambled three times to patrol North London but they had found no sign of the Luftwaffe. More RAF fighters had to be brought to bear against the enemy raids. Air Vice-Marshal Trafford Leigh-Mallory landed at the Norfolk station and talked 'Wings' to Bader between

Top left: London's Dockland and East End ablaze during the first mass air attack on London on 7 September 1940. In the foreground is the Tower of London and Tower Bridge. *(Imperial War Museum)*

Top right: A direct hit by an enemy bomb on the first night raid on London on 22 August 1940 demolished this cinema. As a result the RAF bombed Berlin, starting the chain reaction of the bombing campaigns of British and German cities. *(Imperial War Museum)*

Middle left: Fighting fires in London caused by bombing were very challenging and hazardous. Streets were blocked with rubble and buildings could collapse at any time. *(Imperial War Museum)*

Middle right: Fighting fires in Queen Victoria Street after a daylight attack on London on 10 November 1941. *(Imperial War Museum)*

Bottom: When daylight bombing attacks by the Luftwaffe became too hazardous due to the RAF defending fighters, the Luftwaffe switched to night bombing, which was less accurate but proved harder for the RAF to catch the raiders. *(Imperial War Museum)*

two patrols. The commander told Bader that, starting on the morrow, 242 and 310 Squadrons' Hurricanes would use Duxford daily. Together with 19 Squadron operating out of the satellite at nearby Fowlmere, they would form the 'Big Wing'.

The Duxford Wing began to operate on the morning of Friday 6 September but no contact was made with the enemy. Six of 11 Group's seven sector stations and five of its advanced airfields were very badly damaged during three main attacks by the Luftwaffe, which were largely broken up. Even so, only seven out of 18 squadrons dispatched engaged the enemy formations. It was obvious that some controllers were ordering squadrons intended to engage the enemy bombers to patrol too high. When Group ordered a squadron to 16,000ft, sector controller added 1-2,000ft and the squadron added on another 2,000ft in the vain hope that they would not have any enemy fighters above them. As a result some of the enemy bombers slipped in under 15,000ft and bombed without interruption. The majority of the formations were only intercepted after they had dropped their bombs. Fighter Command lost 23 aircraft, the pilots of 12 fighters being saved. Luftwaffe losses were 35.

Air Vice-Marshal Park issued an instruction on Saturday 7 September drawing attention to the number of squadrons failing to intercept incoming raids because controllers were sending aircraft in too high and squadrons were adding height to the instructions they were given.

The sector stations had expected annihilation and a signal (Invasion Alert No 1) was sent that an invasion was imminent. The Luftwaffe, however, switched their daylight attacks, sending 348 bombers escorted by 617 single- and twin-engine fighters to hit London in the first of their 'reprisal' attacks on the capital following raids by RAF Bomber Command on Berlin. This vast aerial armada, the greatest yet seen, assembled 88 miles away over the Pas de Calais and headed towards the Thames Estuary on a 20-mile front stepped up from 14,000ft to 23,000ft. The more than a mile and a half high formation covered an astonishing 800 square miles, a sight which must have sent shock waves throughout Fighter Command when the radars first picked up the mass formation. The RAF pilots who were sent up to intercept became

embroiled in melees and attacks that might begin and be pressed home at any height from 25,000ft down to near the ground. One moment there could be as many as 140 separate fights going on at the same time, the next pilots were seemingly alone. It was a situation that must have frozen the blood of even the bravest of men, if they had time to dwell on it. The situation demanded the utmost alertness and once sighted, the RAF pilots opened fire at an average of 200 yards, closing sometimes to less than 50 yards.

At 1617 hours, Air Vice-Marshal Park ordered 11 squadrons into the air and six minutes later he brought all remaining Spitfires and Hurricanes to readiness. By 16.30 hours, all 21 squadrons stationed within 70 miles of the capital were in the air or under take-off orders. As the first four squadrons of RAF fighters attacked the southern flank of the huge formation it was soon apparent to Dowding and Park that the Luftwaffe was heading for London and not the precious Essex and Kentish fighter airfields. Despite the spirited and strong resistance put up by the fighter squadrons, not least the Poles of 303 Squadron, many of the bombers had a clear run over the capital, which was heavily bombed. Nineteen Fighter Command pilots were lost from the 28 fighters shot down and 41 German aircraft were destroyed.

At Coltishall, 242 Squadron had spent another frustrating day at readiness waiting for 11 Group's call. To them 7 September must have seemed like another opportunity missed as the squadron spent most of the day kicking its heels as reports filtered through of waves of German bombers attacking London. Finally, at 04.45 hours, Operations rang and Bader and his pilots, straining at the leash, at last got the order to scramble. Once airborne 'Woody' Woodhall at Duxford calmly told Bader that there was some 'trade' heading in over the coast. The South African asked Bader to "Orbit North Weald. Angels ten" and added, "If they come your way you can go for them." Bader climbed to 'Angels 15'. Nearing North Weald Woodhall called Bader again. "Hallo, Douglas. Seventy-plus crossing the Thames east of London, heading north." In the distance Bader saw black dots staining the sky. They were not aircraft. They were anti-aircraft bursts. This could mean only one thing. Over the radio Willie McKnight called out, "Bandits. 10 o'clock." Bader recalled, "We had been greatly looking forward to our first formation of 36 fighters going into action together, but we were unlucky. We were alerted late, and were underneath the bombers and their fighter escorts when we met 15 miles north of the Thames." All Bader could do was attack the formation of about 70 Dorniers of KG 76 and Bf 110s of ZG 2 heading for North Weald as best they could while eight Spitfires of 19 Squadron tried to hold off assaults from the Bf 109s flying high cover. When the claims were totted up they totalled 11 enemy aircraft and two probables; all for the loss of two Hurricanes and one pilot killed.

On landing Bader rang the Operations Room in a fury to be told that they had been sent off as soon as 11 Group had called for them from Duxford. This was one of the recurring problems during this heavy last period of the battle.

Next morning, 242 Squadron flew to Duxford where Bader and his pilots again spent a frustrating day waiting in vain to be summoned by 11 Group as the German bombers returned to bomb London. On Monday the 9th, Bader and his pilots again waited at readiness as the German raids reached a tempo during the late afternoon when their targets were aircraft factories in the South London suburban area. At 17.00 hours, radar had detected a build-up of over 100 German aircraft over the Pas de Calais. Nine squadrons engaged the enemy bombers but only when they headed in were 242 and 310 Squadrons' Hurricanes and 19 Squadron's Spitfires permitted to scramble. 'Woody' Woodhall asked Bader, "Will you patrol between North Weald and Hornchurch, Angels 20?" Anticipating that the enemy formation would swing west and come out of the sun Bader disregarded this and climbed southwest to 22,000ft over the reservoirs at Staines, still climbing. When he sighted the bombers at around quarter to six, he ordered 19 Squadron's Spitfires to climb higher and provide cover as the Hurricanes attacked a formation of Dornier 17s in line astern through the middle of the enemy bomber formation. The Duxford Wing routed the bombers and claimed 11 of the 28 officially destroyed this day. Two of 242 Squadron's

Hurricanes were shot down with one pilot lost and three of 310 Squadron's failed to return although two were safe. Despite the high claims for victories Bader was still not satisfied, feeling that with more fighters the Duxford Wing could have destroyed more enemy aircraft than it had. Bader was later given two more squadrons – 302 (City of Poznań) with Hurricane Is, and 611 (West Lancashire) AAF, with Spitfires. On paper this was the equivalent of 60 or more fighters.

Then came the day that is forever etched in RAF folklore and the glorious annals of world history. On Sunday 15 September, Goering intended that his bombers carry out two heavy attacks on London in an attempt to further sap and perhaps finally break the morale of its long-suffering inhabitants. Vera Shaw, a plotter at 11 Group Headquarters, Uxbridge, recalls:

"Early duty. Lovely day dawning, though trouble expected. Around 8am, warning from Command of a big raid. It came! 250-plus aircraft approaching Dover. Plots came thick and fast. Soon table covered with raids. Noise indescribable – why must everyone shout so? Squadron board shows all squadrons in combat. Final score 185 shot down, and 26 of ours. By midmorning the King and Mr Churchill appear in the Controller's room. At one stage, Mr Churchill asked if we had any more squadrons to call on. 'No,' said the Controller. As the raids die down everyone relaxes at last. Mr Churchill comes down to congratulate the WAAF and RAF on their efforts. Really feel we have earned it! Crawled up those 100 steps to Rest Room feeling 100."

Squadron Leader Walter Myers Churchill DSO DFC, Commanding Officer, 605 (County of Warwick) Squadron recalled:

"The 15th of September dawned bright and clear at Croydon. It never seemed to do anything else during those exciting weeks of August and September. But to us it was just another day. We weren't interested in Hitler's entry into London; most of us were wondering whether we should have time to finish breakfast before the first blitz started. We were lucky. It wasn't till 9.30 that the sirens started wailing and the order came through to rendezvous base at 20,000 feet. As we were climbing in a southerly direction at 15,000 feet we saw 30 Heinkels supported by 50 Me 109s

4,000 above them, and 20 110s to a flank, approaching us from above. We turned and climbed, flying in the same direction as the bombers with the whole squadron stringed out in echelon to port up sun, so that each man had a view of the enemy. 'A' flight timed their attack to perfection, coming down sun in a power dive on the enemy's left flank. As each was selecting his own man, the Me 110 escort roared in to intercept with cannons blazing at 1,000 yards range, but they were two seconds too late – too late to engage our fighters, but just in time to make them hesitate long enough to miss the bomber leader. Two Heinkels heeled out of the formation.

"Meanwhile the Me 110s had flashed out of sight, leaving the way clear for 'B' flight, as long as the Me 109s stayed above. 'B' flight leader [Bunny Currant] knew how to bide his time, but just as he was about to launch his attack the Heinkels did the unbelievable thing. They turned south; into the sun; and into him. With his first burst the leader destroyed the leading bomber which blew up with such force that it knocked a wing off the left-hand bomber. A little bank and a burst from his guns sent the right-hand Heinkel out of the formation with smoke pouring out of both engines. Before returning home he knocked down a Me 109. Four aircraft destroyed for an expenditure of 1,200 rounds was the best justification for our new tactics."

Claims by the Duxford Wing at the end of the day were high: 44 enemy aircraft shot down, with eight probables. Overall, Fighter Command claimed to have shot down 185 aircraft, but the true figure was 56 German aircraft shot down for the loss of 26 RAF fighters but 13 pilots were saved. On the 17th, there was gloom in Germany where Hitler postponed Operation *Sealion* indefinitely.

The 11 Group Operations Room, located at the Headquarters at Uxbridge, was mainly operated by WAAF personnel. *(Imperial War Museum)*

CHAPTER 4
11 GROUP AIRFIELDS

Three Hurricanes at Tangmere in 1940 being refuelled and rearmed for the next 'scramble'. The pilot standing on the left is Max Aitken, son of Lord Beaverbrook, the Minister of Aircraft Production.

Bearing the brunt of Luftwaffe aggression was 11 Group Fighter Command. With Uxbridge as its headquarters and led by Air Vice-Marshal Sir Keith Park – a gentleman who very much cared for his men, whatever their role – Park regularly visited his airfields to witness first-hand the battle's progress, using his personal Hurricane, making him unique amongst the commanders. The battle was defined by Dowding as having started on 10 July and finished on 31 October 1940 for which the pilots were awarded the 1939-1945 Star with a Battle of Britain clasp as their campaign medal, in addition to any other awards earned.

On 13 August 1940, which the Luftwaffe designated 'Eagle Day', Fighter Command bases were set up as follows: the sector stations in 11 Group were Debden in Essex (which was allocated from 12 Group at the last minute), North Weald and Hornchurch, also in Essex, Biggin Hill in Kent, Kenley in Surrey, Tangmere

in Sussex and Northolt in Middlesex. Debden was home to 17 and 85 Squadrons, both with Hurricanes and a satellite at Castle Camps. The Commanding Officer of 85 Squadron was Squadron Leader Peter Townsend.

North Weald had advanced airfields at Stapleford Tawney, Martlesham Heath, and also operated from Rochford near Southend. The North Weald station commander was Wing Commander Victor Beamish and the squadrons based there included 56 and 151 Squadrons, both operating Hurricanes. One of the Commanding Officers of 151 Squadron was Squadron Leader 'Teddy' Donaldson who joined the RAF High Speed Flight after the war flying Gloster Meteors, and later became the air correspondent at the *Daily Telegraph*.

The Hornchurch Sector was one of the largest with five squadrons, many operating from the Manston satellite, close to Dover. 54, 65, 74 and 266 Squadrons were all equipped with Spitfires, with 266 Squadron also

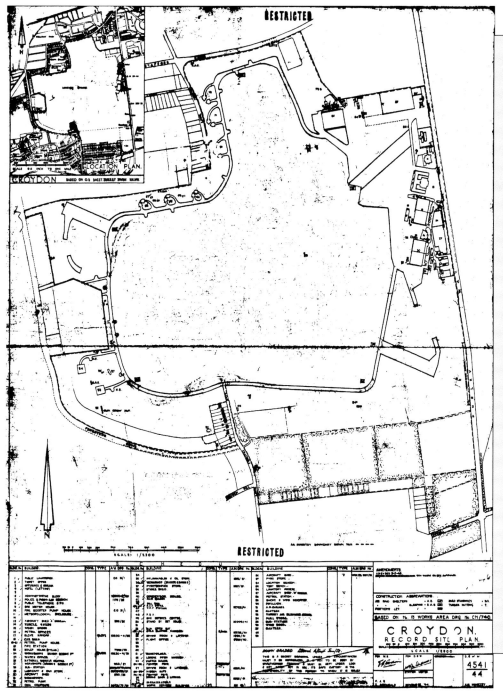

CROYDON

AP.2: TQ306635, three miles south-west of Croydon, Surrey, by the A23.

Croydon was first used for flying in January 1916 and became London's major civil aerodrome from 1920. All civil flying ceased on the declaration of World War 2, the first RAF unit being Gladiator-equipped 615 Squadron. Croydon was a satellite to Kenley with Hurricanes of 1 (RCAF) and 111 Squadrons amongst others during the Battle of Britain. Civil flying returned in mid-1946 with commercial airliners, general aviation and aircraft maintenance. The aerodrome was finally closed in 1959, and although the flying field has been developed commercially, many of the original buildings remain including the historic control tower which is preserved.

The grass landing area was surrounded by a concrete perimeter track with aircraft dispersed hardstandings around the boundary. There were hard surfaced take-off strips at both ends of the main runway, and on approach and take-off from close to the control tower. The main hangars and airfield buildings were along the eastern boundary, with more commercial hangars in the north-east corner.

operating from Eastchurch. 600 Squadron was equipped with the ineffective Blenheims, which was based at Manston for night readiness only, and later moving to Redhill, the forward airfield for Kenley.

The major critical sector airfield at Biggin Hill housed 32 Squadron with Hurricanes, 610 Squadron with Spitfires and 501 Squadron which operated from the Gravesend satellite, with Hawkinge as a forward satellite and Lympne as an emergency landing field. The other critical sector station was Kenley with 615 Squadron Hurricanes, 64 Squadron Spitfires which left for Leconfield in 13 Group on 19 August, 111 Squadron operating at the Croydon satellite with Hurricanes until 19

KENLEY

AP.1: TQ328580, four miles south-east of Croydon on the hill by Kenley, Surrey.

The airfield was first opened as an aircraft acceptance park in 1917 and remained a permanent RAF station until April 1944 when it became inactive. Flying commenced after World War 2 for training and communications aircraft until final closure in May 1959, the site being returned to common land where gliding operations continue. As illustrated in the plan, it was home to 23 and 32 Fighter Squadrons and was an all-grass surface, which was later extended and had two runways constructed which still exist.

The main runway was located approximately in the north-south direction with the airfield boundary extended to the north to provide room for the operation of RAF fighters, although it was too small to accommodate post-war jet fighters. When the runways were built, they were connected by a perimeter track with earth-bank protected aircraft dispersals, which also accommodated air-raid shelters for the airmen. The aircraft were accommodated in two sheds of the World War 1 Warren Truss girder Belfast type, and the modest technical area was entered by a standard guard room followed by 'H' airmen's barrack blocks, a parade ground, station headquarters and other accommodation and workshops.

August when it transferred to Debden, and 1 (RCAF) Squadron working up on Hurricanes from Croydon, to become operational at Northolt on 17 August.

Northolt, west of London, used Hendon as a satellite from time to time and housed 1 Squadron, the first of the Polish squadrons – 303 which became operational on 31 August – and 257 Squadron, all operating Hurricanes. Finally there was the Tangmere sector station based on the south coast in Hampshire which again was operational with Hurricanes. The units were 43, 145 (which operated from Westhampnett now Goodwood) and 601 Squadrons.

Kenley airfield was situated on a ridge of the North Downs on Kenley Common with approaches from the north over a chalk quarry and valley where the village of Kenley is located. Construction commenced in June 1917 with the first RFC personnel arriving on the site on 30 May, the initial role being an aircraft acceptance park. Initially accommodation for personnel and aircraft was under canvas, Bessonneaux canvas hangars being erected prior to the building of

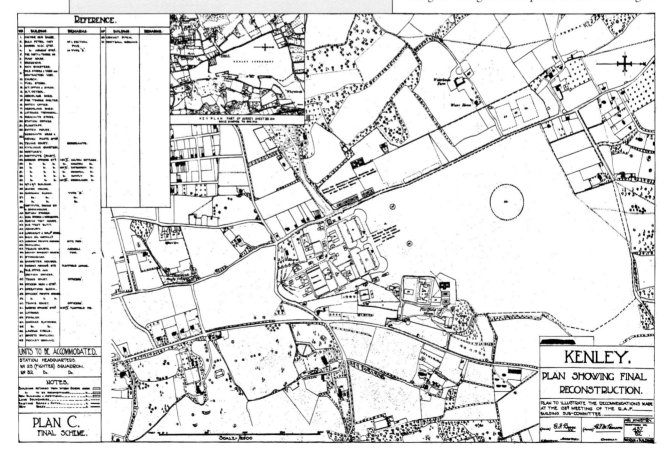

the more permanent Warren Truss girder hangars. Local empty large houses were taken over for accommodation and by 1918 the aerodrome was well established. It was one of the permanent RAF airfields functioning initially with a grass surface, but to ensure all weather operations two tarmac runways were constructed soon after the start of World War 2.

Accommodation for personnel was dispersed to ensure that not only did the pilots get the necessary rest, but were also clear of attacks on the airfield, although during the Battle of Britain most raids were conducted during the day. The sector operations building was surrounded by an earth bank for protection against bomb blasts, but the fighter control systems were relocated from the airfield on 3 September 1940. There was a station headquarters where administration of the airfield was controlled, an airmen's mess and officers' mess, sometimes located off base.

Following the defeats during the Battle of France, 615 Squadron flew their surviving Hurricanes to Kenley on the evening of 20 May with the ground crew returning the following day. 607 Squadron arrived the same day, to join 3 Squadron that had been withdrawn to Kenley giving station commander Tom Prickman problems finding accommodation for this unexpected influx of personnel and aircraft. Some of Squadron Leader Joe Kayll's men, the Commanding Officer of 615 Squadron, were billeted in a girls' school in Croydon, while other pilots were allocated places in the Surrey Hills Hotel in Caterham. With the runways completed, the first Spitfires arrived with 64 Squadron on 16 May. HM King George VI visited Kenley to award Squadron Leader Kayll with the DSO and DFC, and a fellow pilot with 615 Squadron, Flight Lieutenant Sanders, with the DFC.

With the start of the Battle of Britain, the Luftwaffe made tentative raids over southern England while also attacking supply convoys in the English Channel. The first raid on Kenley came on 3 July when a Dornier on reconnaissance dropped bombs in the area without causing significant damage. On 12 July, the Prime Minister, Winston Churchill, accompanied by Air Vice-Marshal Keith Park, included Kenley on his tour of Fighter Command airfields. The resident Hurricanes were mainly involved on convoy protection

patrols, a major attack being on 14 July when some 40 Stukas dive bombed a convoy, escorted by Bf 109s.

To provide a faster response to German raiders, one of the Kenley sector squadrons was sent to Hawkinge, high above the cliffs behind Folkestone, flying to the satellite at first light and remaining until relieved at midday or in the evening. The convoy attacks were at low level, so there was no need to climb to high altitude. In addition to protecting the convoys, a number of Hurricanes were used to escort RAF bombers hitting the build-up of invasion preparations in Calais. When returning home from the advanced landing ground, the pilots followed the railway line from Ashford to Redhill, joining the Kenley circuit.

August started quietly with convoy attacks and small-scale inland incursions, but on 12 August the Luftwaffe changed the emphasis when attacks were made on radar stations, including one at Pevensey, which was put out of action for a few hours. Fortunately the Germans did not know the significance of the early warning capability of radar, otherwise the stations would probably have been attacked more frequently.

Sunday 18 August was a typical warm, sunny summer's day with little cloud over Britain. At 12.45 hrs, as the Operations Room shifts were changing over at Kenley, a high degree of German activity was detected by the coastal radar stations. Senior controller Squadron Leader Norman remained on duty with the relief controller, Pilot Officer David Owen-Edmunds, to determine the enemy intentions. With the threat growing rapidly, 11 Group HQ instructed the scramble of 615 Squadron Hurricanes led by Joe Kayll, followed by eight Spitfires of 64 Squadron led by Squadron Leader Aeneas MacDonell.

Stephen Reid was a local air-raid warden who lived in a bungalow bordering the airfield close to the north gate, and heard the instruction over the loudspeaker system for the pilots to scramble. He was able to warn the local civilian population of a potential raid before the air-raid sirens were sounded, giving them ample time to take cover.

Soon after 13.00 hrs a force of nearly 60 enemy aircraft crossed the south coast in two waves split between medium and high altitude which was detected by the radar. While the

Observer Corps kept a watchful eye on the formations, a small force of nine Dornier Do 17s crossed the coast at low level by Beachy Head, avoiding radar detection. This was a special low-level attack unit flying at around 50 feet across country towards their target of Kenley. On arriving at the ridge of the North Downs, the aircraft climbed up the steep slope passing over Caterham.

Meanwhile a dozen 111 Squadron pilots were at readiness at Croydon, strapped into their Hurricanes awaiting instructions from the Kenley controller. When it became clear that Kenley was the target the first six pilots were scrambled at 13.05 hrs, soon followed by the remainder of the squadron. They were initially told to patrol at 20,000 feet, but progressively requested to fly at 5,000 feet, 3,000 feet and finally to intercept the enemy formation at 50 feet.

In Caterham High Street, Mrs Whittaker, the wife of the local greengrocer, was taking a break and playing darts in the back garden when her attention was diverted by the sound of approaching aero engines, the vibration causing the windows to rattle. Looking up she saw the German aircraft just above the rooftops, one of them opening fire with a machine gun and hitting a local resident in the legs as he stood at the entrance to an air-raid shelter. The German aircraft separated into three groups of three aircraft as the first of 111 Squadron Hurricanes made contact, before breaking away as they approached the airfield defences.

The greengrocer, Mr Whittaker, was on duty at the Westway fire station where he was an auxiliary fireman, throwing himself to the ground as the aircraft approached; the machine-gun bullets hit a row of five ambulances parked in the yard, putting them out of action. The aircraft were so low that Mr Whittaker could see the German aircrew. From the third floor of St Lawrence's Hospital, Reg Williams could see into the cockpit of the leading Dornier, as the steel-helmeted pilot flew up Coulsdon Road before turning with the other bombers lining up on the airfield, one group having come from behind the hospital and over Caterham Barracks.

Bombs damaged three cottages in Oak Road, killing one of the residents, Mrs Charlton. The local Registrar of Births, Mr Wright, was hit by shrapnel as he stood in Burntwood Lane, and a horse pulling Latham's Dairies' milk float was killed between the shafts.

The airfield defences had been forewarned thanks to the Observer Corps. As the leading German aircraft approached the airfield boundary, Pilot Officer Lofts was starting his take-off run in a Hurricane towards the

Viewed from the cockpit of a Dornier Do 17 bomber is a Spitfire in one of the blast pens on the boundary of Kenley airfield during a raid on 18 August 1940. A bomb is seen exploding just beyond the blast pens. (RAF Museum)

attackers, and to avoid a collision, he pulled the aircraft round in a tight right turn.

The 615 Squadron dispersals were on the Whyteleafe side of the airfield where Gene Roux was standing at the entrance of an air-raid shelter as the bombers came roaring in, the leading aircraft aiming its bombs at the hangars. When he became aware of shots close to him, he dived into the shelter for protection. The bombs dropped were fitted with short delayed fuses, to allow the low-flying aircraft to get clear before the explosion, but the hazard was for the following aircraft, one of which reared up alarmingly, yet managed to stay airborne. The hangars, station buildings, taxiways, runways and dispersals were all targeted, not only with bombs, but also machine gun and cannon fire. Three of the four wooden Warren Truss girder hangars were destroyed while a gunner on top of No.7 hangar continued to fire at the raiders with an ancient Lewis gun as the hangar crumbled around him. Bombs hit the hospital block and around the adjacent shelter where hospital staff had sought refuge. The raiders continued across the airfield at minimum height with the defenders firing back while the airfield resembled a battlefield.

Pilots of the three lead aircraft were approaching the northern boundary when they were confronted by a line of rockets dragging

steel cables fired in their path. The leader managed to scrape through, but one of the others caught a cable and began to descend towards Whyteleafe with the parachute trailing behind. Unfortunately the cable came off and the aircraft survived. In the house occupied by the Scots Guards, a gunner on the roof fired his Lewis gun at point-blank range at the bomb aimer of a Dornier as the bombs were released, reducing the house to a pile of rubble and killing the gallant gunner. One of the damaged Dorniers staggered over the airfield, hitting a rocket-fired cable before it crashed into a tree and a cottage. Two 111 Squadron pilots spotted the fleeing Germans and dived down to attack, and as the surviving Dorniers departed in disarray, 111 Squadron was in hot pursuit.

At the end of the raid the hangars were burning fiercely, marking the target for the approaching high-altitude bombers, the first wave being 12 Ju 88s which should have dive

Above: Wreckage of a Luftwaffe Do 17 bomber after being brought down by Kenley anti-aircraft defences during the air raid on 18 August 1940. *(A E Jessop via Imperial War Museum)*

Below left: Wrecked fuel bowsers at Kenley after the German air raid on 18 August 1940. *(A E Jessop via Imperial War Museum)*

Below: One of the wrecked Warren Truss girder hangars at Kenley following the air raid on 18 August 1940. Within the wreckage are the remains of Hurricanes and vehicles. *(A E Jessop via Imperial War Museum)*

The Junkers Ju 88 was an all-metal bomber/reconnaissance and dive bomber powered by two Junkers Jumo engines. Its normal bomb load with 2,900 litres of fuel was 1,800 kg (3,960lb) and armament was three to seven 7.9mm machine guns. Cruising speed was around 280 mph and the typical range was 1,500 miles. (*Imperial War Museum*)

bombed the airfield to prepare it for the low-flying Dorniers, but they were too late. The Ju 88 crews decided that their mission had already been achieved and turned for their alternate target at Manston, but the high-flying Dorniers began to drop their bombs on the damaged Kenley, while a few overflew to drop bombs on Croydon.

Air-raid warden Stephen Reid and his colleague Mr Robbins were caught out in the open as the bombs started to fall, detonating close by and hitting a pair of semi-detached bungalows, destroying one and slightly damaging its neighbour. The scattered Dorniers were chased by the 111 Squadron Hurricanes, one being shot down near Biggin Hill and two more suffering engine failure over the Channel and falling into the sea. Unfortunately there were losses to the RAF fighters with Flight Lieutenant Connors leading 111 Squadron hit by enemy fire and crashing in flames fatally. Peter Simpson had his Hurricane disabled by German fire and force-landed successfully on Woodcote Park Golf Club, his only injury being a piece of shrapnel in his right foot. Twenty-year-old Sergeant Harry Newton was still very inexperienced but spotted a Dornier trying to escape from Kenley. He gave chase and fire was exchanged; the German's bullets had greater effect and Newton was forced to climb to gain enough altitude to bail out, landing close to the wreck of his Hurricane with his hands and face badly burned.

615 Squadron had some success with the high-flying raiders, Flight Lieutenant Sanders claiming a He 111 from which four crewmen bailed out before it crashed close to Kenley.

He then claimed a Ju 88 which crashed near Sevenoaks, close to where a Bf 109 was seen to be diving with smoke pouring from it after being hit by Squadron Leader Joe Kayll. On the debit side, one pilot had to abandon his Hurricane and two had to make forced landings after battles with Bf 109s. Twenty-year-old Sergeant Walley attempted to make a forced landing in Morden Park after receiving serious damage to his Hurricane, but in trying to avoid some houses, he hit trees and died in the subsequent crash. Spitfires of 64 Squadron intercepted the high-altitude raiders as they turned for home with indecisive results.

Meanwhile, on the ground, the men and women in the rather vulnerable operations building had continued to control the fighters as best as they could. Fortunately the building was not hit as it had not been built to withstand an attack, the only protection being the earth banks with camouflage netting over the top, making it a difficult target for the enemy to spot. The only link remaining with the outside world was a land line to Bromley Observer Corps Centre, resulting in effective control of the sector being lost, but contact could be maintained with the other control centres. Controller Owen-Edmunds congratulated his staff on their performance.

With the sounding of the all clear, personnel emerged from the shelters to see the devastation caused by the attack. A column of thick black smoke rose from the burning hangars and there was the occasional explosion from bombs continuing to detonate. Scattered around the airfield were wrecks of aircraft and motor transport. Rescuers began to clear debris around

No 13 air-raid shelter close to the burning hospital where their colleagues were trapped. Bombs had fallen at both ends of the curved shelter, killing those near the entrance and trapping the survivors inside, many of whom were wounded. Amongst those who died was the 615 Squadron medical officer, Flight Lieutenant Crombie, who had also been a GP in the local area before joining up. Leading Aircraftman Holroyd was killed by shrapnel at one of the dispersals and Leading Aircraftman Turner was wounded in the cab of his lorry, later to die of his wounds in Purley Hospital. The returning fighters diverted to other less damaged airfields or found a clear path through the bomb craters at Kenley.

Even if the station fire appliances had not been damaged, the task of controlling the fires would have been daunting and local brigades were called in to assist in fighting the fires. The first arrivals from Caterham attempted to control the hospital block fire and were soon joined by appliances from Purley, which came up Old Lodge Lane and through the demolished north gate of the airfield. By this time any hope of salvaging anything from the burning hangars was gone, but one hazard was exploding oxygen cylinders, one of which hit a fire engine. Another hazard was a burning fuel bowser that was expected to explode at any time, but a soldier towed it away in a lorry. There was a shortage of hoses, and due to damage to the mains, water was in short supply so pumps were used to pipe water up from the valley and surrounding area.

Reports of parachutists landing near Kenley, amplified by church bells incorrectly warning of invasion troops, prompted a scare, resulting in police and home guard setting up roadblocks that restricted the movements of civilians and rescue services. Mobile emergency services began to arrive in large numbers, further contributing to the congestion. Dr Lewis, the district senior medical officer, found it quicker to park his car and walk to the airfield, where he was able to set up a temporary medical post in the surviving hangar.

By late afternoon a safe landing strip had been marked out in brightly coloured tape to identify the bomb craters and the Hurricanes were able to return from their satellites. Earlier in the afternoon, a Hurricane of 615 Squadron had been damaged when it ran into a bomb crater.

Of the 100 or so bombs dropped, 25 had failed to detonate; a Royal Engineers bomb disposal team made these safe. The three hangars were filled with the wreckage of aircraft and vehicles. The Station Headquarters and hospital were reduced to rubble, while barrack blocks and the Sergeants' Mess had also been damaged. The Officers' Mess was slightly damaged with gunfire damage around the airfield and local residential area.

Considering the severity of the attack, casualties were surprisingly light. One officer and eight RAF men were killed, with eight others, including a WAAF, injured. One soldier was fatally injured and two from the anti-aircraft regiment were slightly injured. Ten aircraft including six Hurricanes from 615 Squadron had been destroyed, and six more including a Spitfire and two Hurricanes were damaged. Of the nine Dorniers, four failed to return to France and two crash landed. The personnel from Kenley had stood up to the attack very well despite having faced the threat of death or injury.

The next day the airfield was fully operational, the runways repaired by men of the Royal Engineers, while Post Office engineers repaired the telephone lines, allowing the Operations Room to resume normal control of the sector. The battle-weary 64 Squadron was withdrawn to Leconfield to rest and train new pilots and was replaced by 616 Squadron. Squadron Leader John Thompson led 111 Squadron from Croydon to Debden on the same day as 64 left Kenley, which was hardly a rest tour, as it was one of the 11 Group sector stations. Squadron Leader Peter Townsend arrived at Croydon with 85 Squadron but after only two weeks, 14 of its original 18 pilots had been shot down and Peter Townsend was in Croydon Hospital with a bad injury to his foot.

Damage in the surrounding area, mainly from the high-flying raiders, was considerable where some 150 bombs had been dropped, some aimed at the railway lines. A large number failed to explode, causing disruption while they were made safe, and a number of houses in Caterham and Whyteleafe were destroyed, or severely damaged but repairable. Morale was helped by visits from the Duke of Kent and Winston Churchill.

Following the raid a few days of poor weather allowed time for repairs and preparation for further attacks on Kenley and

Croydon. To create further problems, the Luftwaffe began to bomb major towns and cities at night, including London. The Observer Corps were unable to track these raids effectively and fighters were not equipped to cope. On 26 August, 616 Squadron lost seven Spitfires in a few minutes to Luftwaffe Bf 109s during a clash over Dover resulting in the death of two pilots and three injured. 615 Squadron did little better when four of their Hurricanes were shot down with three pilots wounded. In return two Bf 109s were shot down. This was a waste of aircraft as fighter-to-fighter combat was not a way of stopping the bombers getting through. At the end of the month 615 Squadron took a well-earned rest and opportunity to train at Prestwick.

As a replacement for 615 Squadron, 253 arrived at Kenley from Prestwick under Squadron Leader Harold Starr, with the leadership shared with 32-year-old Squadron Leader Tom Gleave. On his first day, Tom Gleave with two of his colleagues attacked a large formation of Bf 109s, forcing three to leave the formation in difficulties before being obliged to break off the action. By the end of the day, two of his fellow squadron members were dead, one was missing and another wounded. The following day Gleave's luck changed when, while leading seven Hurricanes against a raid on the south east of Kenley, his aircraft was hit and blew up, throwing him free from the burning cockpit. Upon landing by parachute, Gleave was grounded for a considerable time. His friend Squadron Leader Starr was shot down and killed earlier the same day.

A further raid on Kenley was mounted on 1 September with eight enemy bombers escorted by around 50 Bf 109s, their aim to attract the fighters into the air and destroy the strength of Fighter Command. The bombs were inaccurate, falling outside the airfield boundary. Two days later an exhausted 616 Squadron was replaced by 13 Spitfires of 66 Squadron moving into Kenley from Coltishall.

The vulnerability of the Operations Room had been noted and the decision was made to move it off the airfield. There had been a successful butcher's shop owned by Spice and Wallace at 11 Godstone Road in the Caterham valley. It had closed just before the outbreak of war, making the premises vacant. It had been used for the training of staff in operations-room duties and it was decided to convert it to the station sector operations room, in the midst of the main Caterham shopping street. The

Spitfire I R6800 LZ-N of 66 Squadron at Gravesend in September 1940 with a Hurricane in the background and another Spitfire on finals to land. *(RAF Museum)*

complicated communications equipment was transferred by Post Office engineers and none of the local population had any idea what was going on behind the door of the old shop. Apart from a thick coat of whitewash over the windows the exterior of the building remained much the same, with the equipment adapted to the current internal layout of the building, and the front door was blocked off. The former cash desk became the telephone exchange and the signals and wireless operations were fitted into the former slaughterhouse and cold store at the rear. The Operations Room was on the first floor overlooking the street and on the top floor were two sleeping quarters, one each for men and women.

Changes to the shifts were achieved by using a coach to transport the staff from the airfield to the gates at the rear of the yard, and those being relieved boarded the coach for the return journey. Such was the interest in this improvised facility visitors included Lord Beaverbrook, the Minister for Munitions, and Winston Churchill. Staff had to be adaptable to the less than desirable conditions but coped well with the job in hand.

After six days 501 Squadron moved from Gravesend with Hurricanes, replacing the remnants of 66 Squadron, and were soon used

GRAVESEND

AP.7: TQ665720, two miles east of Gravesend in Kent, between the A2 and the A226.

The site was opened as a civil airport in October 1932 and combat operations commenced with 32 Squadron in January 1940 followed by many other Hurricane, Spitfire and later Typhoon squadrons of the 2nd Tactical Air Force. The site had been requisitioned by the Air Ministry as an advanced satellite for Biggin Hill. The original airfield was grass surrounded by a metalled perimeter track with access to a number of dispersal pens. In November 1940, Gravesend became an independent RAF station and more suitable accommodation was erected that winter. The station went on the offensive in 1941 and became increasingly busy in 1942 which required both runways to be extended. It remained an offensive fighter base until June 1944 when it supported the invasion of Europe, and in April 1944, 140 Wing 2nd Tactical Air Force (TAF) arrived from Hunsdon with Mosquito FB.VIs of 21, 464 (RAAF) and 487 (RNZAF) Squadrons which flew intruder missions over France in preparation for D-Day.

Flying at Gravesend ceased with the launching of V1s as it was in the direct line of their flight, the site being surrounded by barrage balloons. With the end of the war, the airfield was put on Care & Maintenance, and in March 1956, it closed to civil flying, the site developed as a housing estate. The plan of the site shows the station with the runway extensions from the original airfield to the north, south and east.

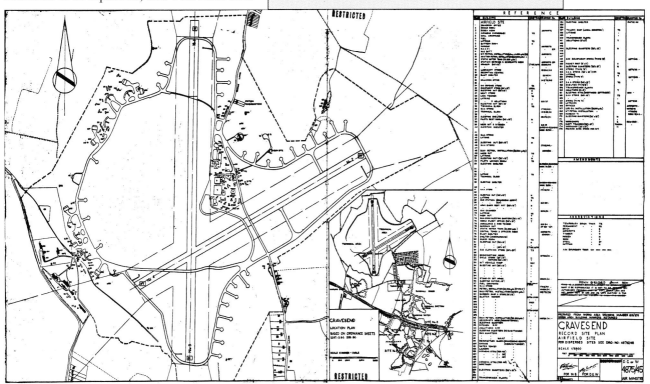

Right: Defiants of 264 Squadron were based at Gravesend until it was realised that they were vulnerable to attack from behind and below where the rear gun turret was ineffective. These aircraft are ready for take-off on 25 July 1940. *(Imperial War Museum)*

Below: 85 Squadron operated Hurricane Is as night fighters from Gravesend without the benefit of AI radar during the winter of 1940-41.

in a new experiment to better understand the details of approaching raids. Selected pilots were sent off on reconnaissance duties when the build-up of a raid was detected and maintained a direct link with Group HQ, giving information on the composition of the approaching formations. This was successful enough for 421 Spotting Flight to be formed in October. 501 Squadron was a veteran of the Battle of France, and although having been very busy at Gravesend for the previous six weeks, was still a potent force. They took over the northern dispersal at Kenley and some rooms in local hotels were allocated to the new aircrew with part of the old married quarters taken over as squadron offices. The personnel of the squadron not only came from all over Britain, but also Poland, Czechoslovakia, Belgium and South Africa.

One of the more famous members of the unit was 'Ginger' Lacey, who was to become a high-scoring pilot in the Battle of Britain.

Probably his most notable achievement was the destruction of a He 111 which had bombed Buckingham Palace. He took off from Kenley in very poor weather conditions with little chance of being able to return and after a long chase through cloud, both aircraft exchanged fire, Lacey's Hurricane being hit and set on fire. He continued to press home his attack using up all his ammunition, setting fire to both engines of the bomber and sending it down. He was able to abandon his fighter and came down near Leeds Castle in Kent, sustaining superficial burns to his face.

In fine weather conditions people on the ground could see the high-altitude battles above with the weaving fighters creating white contrails. On 30 August, a Hurricane was shot down over Waldingham, the spectators below relieved to see the pilot bailing out; however, to their horror a Bf 109 machine-gunned the 253 Squadron pilot as he descended. Two days later a Hurricane crashed in a cornfield, the pilot's body found in a Kenley garden wrapped within a parachute that had failed to open.

During the second week in September, the German strategy altered to raids penetrating further inland, giving 11 Group commander Keith Park greater warning to prepare his defences more appropriately. He took advantage of this change and was able to deploy his squadrons in pairs, but with a common aircraft type, making the Hurricane the dominant type in the sector. Kenley was home to 253 and 501 Squadrons with 605 based at nearby Croydon. By the middle of September the Luftwaffe began to spread their targets more widely with attacks round the clock on towns and cities including London, giving a respite to the frontline airfields.

No 253 Squadron was commanded by Squadron Leader Gerry Edge who had pioneered head-on attacks, and had taken over the squadron after it had suffered severe losses during its first week of operations. In one sortie on 15 September the squadron shot down 17 of a group of 28 Do 17s in the first attack. The large force of escorting fighters managed to inflict one bullet hole in a RAF fighter.

Most of the RAF personnel lived in requisitioned houses locally, but after the airfield was bombed, accommodation was more widely dispersed. The cramped accommodation for the operations room in the converted butcher's shop was replaced by the Grange in Old Coulsdon in December 1940. The full complement of operations room staff was just over 100 people working three shifts consisting of mornings, afternoons or nights, followed by a day off.

Small raids continued on Kenley airfield from mid-October 1940, but the heavy daylight raids ceased when Hitler abandoned the planned invasion of Britain and turned his attention to opening a second front against the Russians, his former allies.

Tuesday 13 August was designated 'Eagle Day' by Reichmarschall Goering, the Luftwaffe Commander-in-Chief, commencing the major effort to destroy Fighter Command in preparation for the invasion of Britain. Kenley was not the only airfield to be bombed by the Luftwaffe, the vital sector station of Biggin Hill nearby being a major target. Biggin Hill was officially opened on 14 February 1917 as an RFC Radio Signals Unit and later in the year 141 Squadron with Bristol Fighters arrived as part of the inner defence of London. The initial airfield development was on the South Camp; later followed expansion of a new technical site known as North Camp. With the site development completed, 23 and 32 Squadrons arrived in 1930, with more expansion taking place in 1938. After the Munich crisis the buildings were camouflaged, air-raid shelters built and many trees planted to help disguise the site. By this time the resident units were 32 and 79 Squadrons, who began to exchange their biplane fighters for Hurricanes.

On the eve of the declaration of war, 601 Squadron arrived at Biggin Hill from Hendon equipped with Blenheims fitted with four Browning 0.303-inch machine guns under the fuselage. Number 601 was the County of London Squadron, Royal Auxiliary Air Force (RAuxAF), and Churchill adopted it as his own, making an informal visit to the officers' mess at Biggin Hill on 2 September on his way to Chartwell. It was the next day that Neville Chamberlain announced over the radio that war was declared.

The RAuxAF was known for attracting wealthy young men who wished to spend their weekends flying as amateurs. They were keen to demonstrate that given the opportunity, they were equal in combat to the regular RAF pilots. The well-off auxiliary pilots, however, had little regard for the strict discipline of the regular service. One of the members of the 'Millionaire's Mob' was Max Aitken, born in Canada in February 1910, the son of Lord Beaverbrook, the Minister of Aircraft Production, and later to become a distinguished fighter pilot. He became the Commanding Officer of 601 Squadron in June 1940, which by which time was operating Hurricanes until 20 July. He took over as Commanding Officer of 68 Squadron from February 1941 specialising in night fighting, during which period he claimed four night victories. After service in the Middle East he was appointed Wing Leader of the Banff Strike Wing in 1944 with Mosquitos, reaching the rank of Group Captain with a total of 14 victories. Having flown on the first day of the war, Aitken achieved a unique record, as on the last day of the war he flew an anti-shipping patrol over Denmark, the only pilot to fly on both the first and last day of the war. After a postwar career as head of Beaverbrook Newspapers, he died on 30 April 1985 at the age of 75.

Among the other members were Whitney Straight, Loel Guinness, Willy Rhodes-Moorhouse, Roger Bushell and Sir Archibald Hope, most of the squadron members owning their own aircraft. They adapted their uniform to wearing blue instead of black ties and lined their tunics with bright red silk.

Whitney Straight was born in the USA and was an aviator, Grand Prix racing driver and by the time he was 16 years old, had flown over 60 hours solo, although he was still too young for a pilot's licence. He was educated in England and adopted British nationality in 1936. In the early 1920s, he headed up the Straight Corporation which operated airfields and flying clubs, and in

1936 he was involved in the development of the Miles Whitney Straight light touring aircraft. He had over four kills to his credit during the Battle of Britain and was badly injured in Norway in 1940 while laying out a runway on a frozen lake. After recovery, he rejoined his squadron near the end of the Battle of Britain. He was shot down over France in August 1941 and although he evaded capture on his way to Spain, he was eventually caught but subsequently escaped from a POW camp. Promoted to Air Commodore, Straight was in charge of RAF Transport Command operations in the Middle East and after the war he became CEO of BOAC, later also deputy Chairman of Rolls-Royce. He died in Fulham at the age of 66.

Loel Guinness was a member of the Guinness brewing family. He was raised in the USA and Britain and had inherited a considerable fortune. When flying with 601 Squadron from Biggin Hill in 1940, he was frustrated that due to rationing he was unable to obtain sufficient petrol to drive his car, and to overcome this problem, he bought a petrol station close to the airfield.

Willie Rhodes-Moorhouse flew Blenheims and Hurricanes with 601 Squadron, but was shot down over Kent and killed during the Battle of Britain. His father was the first airman to be awarded the VC when he died from his injuries sustained during combat in World War 1.

Squadron Leader Roger Bushell was born in South Africa of British parents, and was educated in Britain and read law at Cambridge, where he also excelled in sports. He joined 601 Squadron in 1932 as a weekend flyer and combined his flying and legal duties by being appointed as an RAF prosecutor against personnel charged with various offences. In October 1939, he was given command of 92 Squadron and promoted to squadron leader on 1 January 1940. During his first engagement with the enemy on 23 May 1940 when patrolling near Calais, he damaged two Bf 110s before being shot down. He crash-landed his Spitfire in German-held territory and was taken prisoner. Bushell dedicated himself to causing as much trouble to the Germans as possible by attempting to escape. After two unsuccessful escapes, he masterminded what has been termed the Great Escape, with plans to liberate 200 POWs and tie up a considerable amount of enemy resources. The escape was made from

Stalag Luft III at Sagan where he arrived in October 1942. He planned the Great Escape in the spring of 1943, and although not all of the planned 200 escaped, Roger Bushell and his partner Bernard Scheidhauer were among 76 officers to get clear. However, they were rounded up the next day and murdered by the Gestapo as a reprisal, two of 50 POWs who were recaptured and shot.

These weekend warriors more than justified their existence in the RAF, serving with distinction and courage, when in many cases they could have taken a much softer option. They proved they were equally as effective as regular RAF officers despite in many cases their considerable wealth and aristocratic heritage.

At the outbreak of war the station commander was Wing Commander R Grice. Tarmac runways were constructed and during the first year of the war Biggin Hill was threatened only by high-flying Luftwaffe reconnaissance aircraft. On 21 November 1939, two Hurricanes operating from the Satellite at Manston were ordered to patrol in the area of Hawkinge in bad weather during the morning. At 10.20 hrs, a potential target was detected by radar and the two 79 Squadron pilots alerted. American Flying Officer Jimmy Davies and Flight Sergeant Brown were directed towards the target over the Channel, which turned out to be a Do 17 on a weather reconnaissance flight. Both pilots attacked the enemy aircraft, which dived into the sea and exploded, opening the score for Biggin Hill.

On 29 November, 601 Squadron made their first combat operation, taking six Blenheims to Northolt where they were joined by six aircraft from 25 Squadron. Their target was the Luftwaffe seaplane base at Borkum in the Friesian Islands, a flight of 250 miles across the North Sea. One of the leaders was Flying Officer Max Aitken. Flying over the target at 100 feet firing their machine guns at the aircraft and installations, it was all over within five minutes, leaving five wrecked aircraft and sunk patrol boats; the aircraft returned without damage. This was the first RAF action against German territory and Michael Peacock was awarded the DFC in recognition of his action. The other four 601 Squadron pilots were Flt Lieutenants Sir Archibald Hope and Tom Hubbard, plus Flying Officers Carl Davies and Willy Rhodes-Moorhouse. Both Davies and

A Hurricane of 213 Squadron being rearmed at Biggin Hill on 3 June 1940. *(Imperial War Museum)*

Rhodes-Moorhouse were shot down and killed on the same day in September when flying Hurricanes.

The evacuation of Dunkirk, known as 'Operation Dynamo', was covered by the squadrons at Biggin Hill, but by then 32 and 79 Squadrons were on a rest tour, having been in action since early May, and were replaced by 213 and 242 Squadrons who went into immediate combat. On day one, the Hurricanes of both squadrons were patrolling over Gravelines when they encountered ten Bf 109s and claimed two without loss. On day two, 213 Squadron attacked a large formation of Ju 88s and He 111s escorted by Bf 109s which were bombing the troop concentrations on the crowded beaches. In combat which lasted about five minutes, seven enemy aircraft were claimed as shot down and a number damaged, for the loss of one Hurricane pilot.

As the evacuation continued, 610 Squadron claimed eight victories and four probables, but they lost six Spitfires, which was half the squadron, resulting in them being replaced by 229 Squadron Hurricanes from Digby on 25 May. By the end of the first week of June, the evacuation was over. Remarkably, over 338,000 members of the BEF had been evacuated successfully by the Royal Navy and a flotilla of civilian boats of all sizes while under constant attack. The squadrons from Biggin Hill had maintained regular defensive patrols over the beaches and in nine days of combat had claimed

36 Luftwaffe aircraft with 20 more as probable.

The cost had been high. 68,000 men were killed, missing or taken prisoner during the retreat, with 243 ships sunk and 474 aircraft lost in the air and on the ground during the overall Battle of France. Biggin Hill had lost eight Hurricanes and six Spitfires, with eight pilots either killed or taken prisoner.

By June 1940, Biggin Hill had a new runway, air-raid shelters had been constructed and the landscaping was in excellent condition with new trees and shrubs. Having done their duty during 'Operation Dynamo', 213 and 242 Squadrons had departed for a rest and 32 and 79 had returned after rebuilding their strength, ready for the upcoming battle. The Hurricanes were soon into action escorting Blenheims on bombing raids and fending off enemy Bf 109s. On 7 and 8 June, the two squadrons shared a total of 14 claims plus four probable, with no losses to 79 Squadron, but three pilots of 32 Squadron were missing, although one was able to return.

In July, Gocring targeted Allied shipping to not only reduce supplies by sea, but to attract Fighter Command into the air over the Channel where he hoped the Luftwaffe could destroy the remnants of the defending fighters. Although the RAF was short of pilots, additional Allied airmen were escaping from occupied Europe, and more were coming from the Commonwealth, while fighter production was rising steadily.

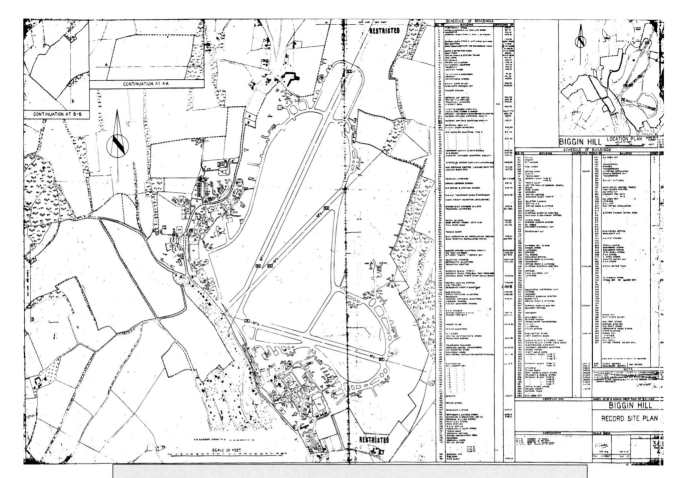

BIGGIN HILL

AP.3: TQ415605, on the east side of the A233, north of Biggin Hill, Kent.

The airfield first opened in February 1917 and in the mid-war period was used for ground-to-air radio experiments with the fighters defending London. It was a key Battle of Britain base being damaged many times by enemy action but remained operational. After World War 2, the airfield was transferred to RAF Transport Command, but reverted to Fighter Command in 1950 with a runway extension to the north end of the main runway. Fighter Command operated both regular and Royal Auxiliary Airforce squadrons with Meteors of 600 and 615 Squadrons and Hunters of 41 Squadron until 16 January 1958 when 41 Squadron disbanded, the RAF camp finally closing in 1979. The airfield is now a busy international airport operating business and commuter aircraft with strong general aviation and maintenance activities.

The airfield was split into two camps, South Camp and North Camp, and three hard runways were constructed connected by a perimeter track with aircraft dispersals around the edge. The South Camp was the original Wireless Testing Park in 1917. The North Camp was the main technical site with triple-bay Warren Truss girder Belfast hangars which were destroyed by the Luftwaffe. They were later replaced by 'T2' Type hangars, two of which remain in the North Camp, with another in the South Camp. An extensive building programme commenced in 1929 on the new technical site at North Camp with workshops, barrack blocks and administrative offices, with the officers' mess located in a large house on the Bromley to Westerham road opposite the main camp. As a permanent memorial to the battle, St George's Chapel of Remembrance was dedicated on 20 September 1954 with the entrance flanked by a Hurricane and Spitfire, now replaced by fibreglass replicas.

Left: Pilots gather around Spitfire I QJ-U of 92 Squadron at Biggin Hill. The 'trolley ack' is plugged in ready to start the Merlin engine. *(RAF Museum)*

Middle left: Ground crew assist a pilot climb into a Hurricane I of 79 Squadron at Biggin Hill. *(RAF Museum)*

Middle right: Taking a NAAFI break during a lull in operations the ground crew use the Hurricane tailplane as a snack table. *(RAF Museum)*

Bottom: A Hurricane I from 32 Squadron being refuelled at Biggin Hill on 16 August 1940. *(Imperial War Museum)*

Although these Defiants are from 264 Squadron, they illustrate the gun turret installation similar to the aircraft used by 141 Squadron at Biggin Hill. *(Imperial War Museum)*

It had been calculated that to make a successful attempt at invading Britain, the Germans would need at least 250 ships to move an armed force of 100,000 troops across the Channel, with the most likely landing area being the south coast between Dover and Brighton. Such a force would take a considerable resource to assemble without detection, and may well have been an impossible task, the invasion being an empty threat. Perhaps Hitler hoped that Goering would destroy the RAF on the ground and in the air, allowing Germany to sue Churchill for peace, and by removing an aggressor, Hitler could then continue unopposed with his domination of Europe by taking on the Soviet Union.

On 27 June, HM King George VI visited Biggin Hill to personally honour the gallantry of the fighter pilots. He awarded DFCs to Michael Crossley, 'Jack' Daw and 'Grubby' Grice of 32 Squadron, and Jimmy 'Dimsy' Stones of 79 Squadron. The DFM (Distinguished Flying Medal) was also awarded to Sergeants Whitby and Cartwright of 79 Squadron. The American volunteer pilot Jimmy Davies of 79 Squadron should have been awarded the DFC, but was posted missing, the second Hurricane pilot to be lost on that day.

The Boulton Paul Defiant was totally unsuitable for air-to-air combat with no forward firing armament, its only defence being a rearward firing gun turret behind the pilot's cockpit. On 12 July 1940, 141 Squadron brought its 12 Defiants south from Turnhouse to Biggin Hill. The squadron set up its headquarters at South Camp, although the aircraft were to operate from the forward satellite of West Malling. The initial success of the Defiant had been excellent, with 264 Squadron credited with 37 enemy aircraft on 29 May when the Luftwaffe must have mistakenly identified the aircraft as Hurricanes and approached from the rear. By the end of the month, Defiants had claimed 65 victories and were thought to be infallible, but it was not long before the Luftwaffe realised the inherent weakness of the aircraft with its blind spot below to the rear and no forward armament.

No 141 Squadron was declared ready for operations on 18 July in time for the first scramble the next day. Twelve Defiants flew to the forward airfield at Hawkinge where they were ready by midday. Just after 12.30 hrs, nine Defiants took off to patrol south of Folkestone at 5,000 feet, just as the air-raid sirens began to wail. The enemy were dropping bombs on

Dover Harbour with an escort of 20 Bf 109s and 141 Squadron was vectored towards Cap Gris Nez to catch the raiders on their return. The Bf 109s were spotted diving from out of the sun, and although the Defiants opened their formation to give beam attacks, the Bf 109 pilots were aware of the vulnerable area of the RAF aircraft. The Luftwaffe fighters dived below the Defiants and came up from below out of view of the power-operated gun turret. Within seconds two Defiants were shot down in flames with the loss of the crews. Soon after, another Defiant was shot down into the sea and the slaughter continued. A fourth Defiant was hit and the pilot was able to bail out before hitting the sea, but his gunner was lost. The Bf 109s regrouped for a second attack and a fifth Defiant was hit in the engine, but made a successful forced landing, both the crew surviving. A sixth Defiant was shot down over Dover, crashing in the town. A seventh Defiant was badly damaged and the pilot advised his gunner to abandon the aircraft while he attempted to reach land. He was able to reach Hawkinge, but his gunner was lost at sea. Only two Defiants made it back to Hawkinge after being rescued by 111 Squadron Hurricanes. One Bf 109 was damaged so badly by a Defiant that it crashed at St Omer on return to base, killing the pilot. In its first combat of the war, 141 Squadron lost six aircraft with four pilots and five gunners killed. The squadron was withdrawn to Prestwick to rebuild and retrain for night fighter duties.

During the long daylight hours of July 1940, both 32 and 610 Squadrons were deployed to the advanced satellite at Hawkinge, usually starting their days at 05.00 hrs and not finishing until 20.30 hrs, often fitting in up to four sorties a day. To the casual observer, the pilots were lounging around in deck chairs relaxing between sorties, but there were high tensions and anxieties when tempers could flare up. Sometimes a pilot would disappear behind the dispersal hut to be sick, but on the sound of the alarm, all pilots would sprint to their aircraft, often being airborne in two minutes.

Number 610 (County of Chester) Squadron, another member of the RAuxAF, was formed in February 1936 initially as a light bomber-bomber unit, but in January 1939, it was transferred to Fighter Command, and in the summer Hurricanes began to replace the Hinds. The squadron personnel were neither wealthy

nor from the aristocracy, but like the pilots of 601 Squadron, they were keen to prove that they were as good as the regular RAF officers. Before the squadron could see action the Hurricanes were transferred to 605 (County of Warwick) Squadron, and 610 received its first Spitfire on 28 September, by which time some of the pilots were being replaced by regular RAF officers.

After training at Prestwick in April 1940, 610 Squadron was moved to Biggin Hill when Germany invaded the Low Countries, and the aircraft were deployed to Gravesend to patrol the Dunkirk area during 'Operation Dynamo'. The first recorded victories for the squadron were on 27 May when a He 111 and six Bf 109s were either destroyed or seriously damaged with the loss of two RAF pilots. Two days later four Bf 109s were claimed but the Commanding Officer, Squadron Leader Franks and Sergeant Jenkins, had to bail out of their Spitfires. The squadron was left with only six serviceable Spitfires and therefore combined operations with the other units. After further action over the Channel, the squadron withdrew to Digby to rest and regroup.

On the return to Biggin Hill, Squadron Leader A T 'Big Bill' Smith took over command of 610 Squadron, and on 10 July, he made a crash landing at Hawkinge after his Spitfire was hit in the port wing by a Bf 109, fortunately without injury. Squadron casualties continued to grow when Sergeant Ireland lost control during dogfight practice and was killed on 12 July. On 13 July, Sergeant Watson-Parker failed to return from a routine patrol and on 18 July Pilot Officer Litchfield was shot down and killed over the Channel. Smith was killed in a

Following the withdrawal of Defiants from day combat they were adapted for night fighting with an overall matt black finish.

crash landing at Hawkinge on 25 July. On the same day, John Ellis, as temporary Commanding Officer, led seven Spitfires against a force of 20 enemy bombers and Bf 109s which were attacking a destroyer in the Channel. They were able to claim four Bf 109s destroyed, three German pilots being killed and one taken prisoner against no losses.

On 12 August, enemy action began to increase significantly with radar stations as primary targets, together with the airfields and coastal shipping, and both 32 and 610 Squadrons were ready for action. At 610 Squadron's dispersal the pilots were ordered to scramble at 07.31 to patrol the Dungeness area at 10,000 feet where they were warned of nine Do 17s with Bf 109 escorts approaching Dungeness. Just under an hour after take-off the Spitfires of 610 Squadron returned to Biggin Hill and Squadron Leader Ellis demonstrated their success by making a victory roll over the airfield, followed by three more squadron pilots. Their scores were uncertain, but two Bf 109s were destroyed with others unconfirmed or damaged, and two Spitfire pilots were posted missing. However, Flying Officer Fred Gardiner made it back to Biggin Hill in his damaged Spitfire with a leg wound, making a crash landing. The other pilot, Flight Lieutenant Smith, had managed to escape from his burning aircraft over the Channel and was saved by a rescue boat.

The Luftwaffe had achieved much of its planned objective, with four radar stations damaged, two convoys bombed and ships in Portsmouth Harbour burning. The Hurricanes of 32 Squadron were moved to Hawkinge ready for action to commence after midday, and while Squadron Leader Crossley and his pilots were outnumbered by a massive formation of Do 17s escorted by Bf 109s, Hawkinge was being bombed by Ju 88s. In need of fuel and rearming, 32 Squadron returned to a wrecked airfield, five Hurricanes landing carefully between the craters. On return to Biggin Hill in the evening, Crossley gave their account of the action which consisted of some 90 enemy aircraft faced by 12 Hurricanes, with 11 raiders claimed shot down, for the loss of one Hurricane from which the pilot bailed out safely. Meanwhile personnel at both Hawkinge and Manston worked through the night to return the airfields to operational condition for the next day.

The first attack on Biggin was at around 13.30 hrs on 18 August 1940, lasting for about an hour and resulting in little damage, but the second raid was more damaging, as one of the airfield defence Bofors gun installations was hit, killing one of the crew. The MT buildings were damaged and the landing area was covered in craters and unexploded bombs. WAAF Sergeant Elizabeth Mortimer was manning the Armoury switchboard surrounded by tons of high explosives, but stayed at her post relaying vital information around the defence positions. As the raiders departed, and before the all clear, she ran around the landing area placing the warning flags to identify the location of unexploded bombs, some of which had delayed fuses. When one of the delayed-action bombs exploded close to Mortimer she was knocked over and was unable to walk for a short while. When Mortimer recovered, she continued to plant the warning flags which would allow the fighters to land safely, and despite being ordered to leave the area, she carried on when the officer had walked away. For her brave actions, Mortimer was awarded the Military Medal with the citation 'This airwoman displayed exceptional courage and coolness which had a great moral effect on all those with whom she came into contact.'

The defending pilots were outnumbered by five to one in an action that lasted about ten minutes, during which the two squadrons claimed at least nine raiders and sent many others fleeing back home. Flight Lieutenant Russell shot down a Bf 109 but was hit in the leg by fragments of a cannon shell that exploded in the cockpit. This was his first combat sortie after joining 32 Squadron the previous day. Despite his serious wounds, he abandoned his Hurricane and managed to tie a tourniquet to stop the bleeding. Russell was taken to Edenbridge Hospital where his wounds were treated.

'Polly' Flinders, who was in charge of the training flight as well as converting Polish pilots to the Hurricane, almost missed the action. After the fighters had departed, Flinders took off and caught up with a Do 17, into which he emptied most of his ammunition. He then located another raider and fired off the remainder of his ammunition, and despite frantic manoeuvres, the enemy aircraft was shot down. John Ellis of 610 Squadron had been dealing with high altitude Bf 109 escorts at 31,000 feet until joining the low-level battle and shot down a He 111 into the sea. During the evening sorties, 32 Squadron Leader Michael Crossley was in combat with a Bf 109 which hit his glycol coolant tank, resulting in Crossley having to bail out. At the end of the day five pilots of 32 Squadron had bailed out of their stricken aircraft and a further pilot was killed. On 25 August 1940, 32 Squadron was posted to rest and recover at Acklington after nine busy years at Biggin Hill. The squadron was at the time the top scoring squadron in Fighter Command with 102 enemy aircraft claimed destroyed to the loss of three pilots killed and a POW. In the place of 32 Squadron came 79 Squadron from Acklington returning to Biggin Hill.

Over the next two weeks, German bombers made constant attacks on the airfield, destroying buildings and progressively reducing the efficiency of the base. All available personnel occupied themselves keeping the airfield operational in addition to the demands of their regular duties. On Friday 30 August, the first major raid on the airfield nearly knocked it out altogether. In reasonably good weather the first raid came at around midday, resulting in cratering of the landing areas and damage to local residential properties. Then at 18.00 hrs, the big raid came without warning as nine Ju 88s attacked at low level from the south. Although it lasted for only 30 minutes, most of the remaining buildings were destroyed or deemed unsafe to be used. Sixteen 1,000lb HE bombs

were dropped, six scoring direct hits on the technical site and all utilities were cut off with the telephone lines cut. Tragically, a WAAF shelter received a direct hit killing many of the girls inside. Total casualties were 39 killed and 26 wounded.

There was no respite or time to make repairs as the following day Biggin Hill was hit twice at 13.00 hrs and then at 17.30 hrs. Hangars were further damaged and the operations block received a direct hit, its concrete roof collapsing onto the ops table. The temporary repairs to the phone lines were again destroyed. On 1 September, more bombs were dropped from high altitude but few buildings were still standing. The operations room was moved to a new dispersed temporary site and later relocated to a more suitable location for the remainder of the war. The airfield was only capable of operating a single squadron with very basic facilities with most of the aircraft being dispersed. Biggin Hill shared with Hornchurch the dubious honour of being the most bombed airfield in Fighter Command.

West Malling in Kent was designated as an advanced landing ground for both Kenley and Biggin Hill, but bombing of the airfield began on 10 August 1940 and continued throughout the Battle of Britain, rendering the site unserviceable for the majority of the battle.

During the Battle of Britain, the Sector D station of Hornchurch was commanded by Wing Commander Cecil Bouchier. Originally

An Anson takes off over a 222 Squadron Spitfire Ia at Hornchurch on 15 September 1940 – the 'Hardest Day'. (RAF Museum)

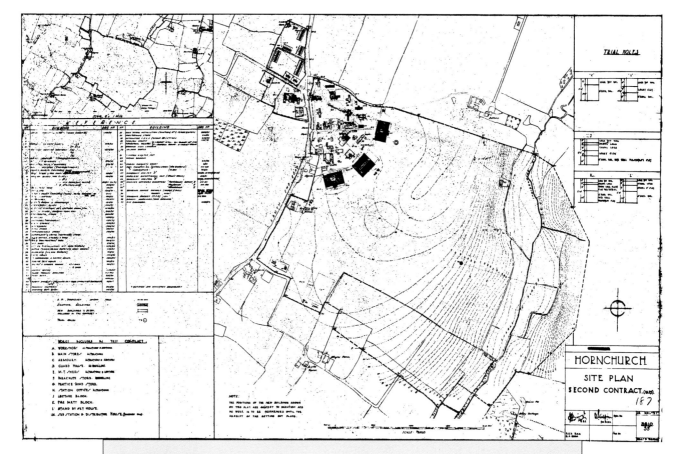

HORNCHURCH

AP.5: TQ530845, by the A125, two miles south-east of Romford, Essex.

Opened as Sutton's Farm in October 1915, the airfield was part of the air defence of London, its major targets being the Zeppelin bomber airships. A well-known success was when Lt Leefe-Robinson brought down Zeppelin SL.11 at Cuffley, Hertfordshire, in the early hours of 3 September 1916, for which he was awarded the Victoria Cross. Initial accommodation comprised wooden hangars, workshops and living quarters, but military flying ceased in December 1919, following which the site was cleared of all the main buildings. However, with the need for accommodation for RAF squadrons for the air defence of London, Sutton's Farm was re-requisitioned and construction of the new station began, including one 'C' Type and two 'A' Type hangars in a semi-circle with the workshops, barrack blocks and offices behind, all located in the north-west corner and with the grass landing ground in front. The station reopened on 1 April 1928 with the arrival of 111 Squadron led by Squadron Leader Keith Park and the name was changed to Hornchurch on 1 June 1928.

In 1936, Hornchurch became part of 11 Group Fighter Command as an important sector station and the first offensive patrol was by 12 Spitfires from 54 and 74 Squadrons over France on 21 May 1939. Hornchurch was bombed at least 20 times during the Battle of Britain. After the battle, it went on to offensive operations until May 1944 when the station was relegated to ground duties, which was just as well due to the many V1 flying bombs in the area. In June 1945, the station transferred to Technical Training Command and was reduced to Care & Maintenance in 1947. The airfield reopened on 1 July 1948 for flying training with Tiger Moth and Anson-equipped 17 RFS until it disbanded on 31 July 1953. The station then became the home of the Aircrew Selection Centre until it moved to Biggin Hill and the site closed on 1 July 1962. The airfield was sold off, the landing ground being used for the extraction of gravel and the technical site demolished and replaced by a housing estate.

Left: Spitfire Ias from 222 Squadron take off from Hornchurch on 15 September 1940 over a parked 610 Squadron Spitfire. *(RAF Museum)*

Middle: Newly delivered Spitfire Mk.Is lined up for inspection at Hornchurch in the spring of 1939. (*Vickers from BAE Systems*)

Below left: Pilots of 65 Squadron in a practice scramble at Hornchurch on 18 May 1939 with early Spitfire Mk.Is. (*Unknown copyright via BAE Systems*)

Below right: Spitfire I X4711 KL-D of 54 Squadron on a snow-covered dispersal in the winter of 1940. *(RAF Museum)*

known as Sutton's Farm, the airfield was first established in October 1915 as a defence against German airships over Britain, the first success being by Lieutenant W Leefe-Robinson when he brought down SL11 near Cuffley. Following the armistice in November 1918, the site was cleared of all buildings and returned to the farmer. However, within four years of the end of World War 1, the Air Ministry realised the need for a viable defence of London and made a compulsory purchase of the land and the erection of new buildings. The new RAF station was opened on 1 April 1928 and the first unit to arrive was 111 Squadron commanded by Squadron Leader Keith Park, later to fight the Battle of Britain at the HQ of 11 Group. The airfield was renamed Hornchurch in January 1929 and remained a grass surface for the whole time it was used by the RAF.

The first offensive patrol from Hornchurch was mounted by Spitfires of 54 and 74 Squadrons on 21 May 1940 and by 1 June eight squadrons had operated from Hornchurch achieving 122 confirmed victories with the loss of 26 of their own aircraft. Squadrons based at Hornchurch during the Battle of Britain included 54 from 8 August to 3 September, 65 from 5 June to 27 August, 74 from 26 June to 14 August, 41 from 26 July to 8 August, 222 from 29 August to 10 November and 266 from 14 to 21 August, all equipped with Spitfires.

There were at least 20 bombing attacks against Hornchurch during the battle, the most serious occurring at lunchtime on 31 August when a large enemy formation at 15,000 feet dropped about 60 bombs across the airfield, although the landing area remained serviceable. Eight Spitfires of 54 Squadron were able to take off as the first bombs were falling, but the remaining section had just become airborne when the explosions caused the aircraft to crash without any losses to the pilots. Meanwhile 222 and 603 Squadrons were defending the airfield, 603 claiming 14 enemy aircraft for the loss of one pilot and two Spitfires. The second attack came at 18.00 hrs when German bombers penetrated the defences, but the bombs fell inaccurately and Hornchurch remained operational. On 20 September, two land mines were dropped, one of which failed to explode, and on 15 October, the Operations Room (which had suffered a near miss on 9 September) was moved to a dispersed site at Lambourne Hall in Romford where it remained for the remainder of the war.

Hawkinge was a satellite for Hornchurch and was located on the cliffs overlooking the Channel close to Folkestone. The site was first used for military flying in October 1915 when 12 Squadron operating Be.2cs landed on their way to France, the airfield serving as a stopping-off point for the RFC throughout World War 1. The original aircraft accommodation was Bessoneaux hangars, but they were replaced by Belfast hangars from 1917 and single-storey barrack blocks replaced tented accommodation. Following the armistice, the airfield was the UK base for mail flights by 120 Squadron to the Continent, and in

Hurricane I P3522 GZ-V of 32 Squadron taxies ready for take-off at Hawkinge on 31 July 1940 with other Hurricanes in the background.

HAWKINGE

AP.6: TR213395, two miles north of Folkestone, Kent, by the A260.

The first official use of Hawkinge was by 1 Squadron in March 1915 as a staging point on the way to France. By the autumn the airfield was established, with three Bessoneaux canvas hangars and other tented accommodation which were gradually replaced by more permanent structures in 1916, later to include Belfast hangars. The airfield became inactive in October 1919, but became a fighter station on 20 April 1920 when 25 Squadron re-formed. In 1932, a programme of building commenced with barrack blocks, NAAFI, officers' mess, sergeants' mess and airmen's dining hall and married quarters. The main camp and technical site was on the north-west side of the grass landing ground, with a perimeter track around three sides giving access to a number of dispersal pens. During the Battle of Britain, the station was used as an advanced satellite with Hurricanes and Spitfires based there from early morning to late afternoon before returning to their bases. Being so close to the front line the station received considerable damage from enemy attacks, the hangars being virtually destroyed. In 1941, the station went on the offensive with fighter sweeps across the continent until April 1944 when the fighters departed to be replaced by an air sea rescue unit. On 7 November 1945, the site was reduced to Care & Maintenance with gliders operating from the airfield.

In the spring of 1947, Hawkinge was transferred to Technical Training Command, and on 1 June, was reopened as the WAAF Technical Training Unit, later part of the WRAF (Women's Royal Air Force). Hawkinge was closed on 8 December 1961 and reduced to Care & Maintenance in January 1962, with the technical site auctioned in the autumn of 1963. The last flying from the airfield involved Hurricanes and Spitfires for the making of the *Battle of Britain* film in June 1968, after which the airfield reverted to agriculture.

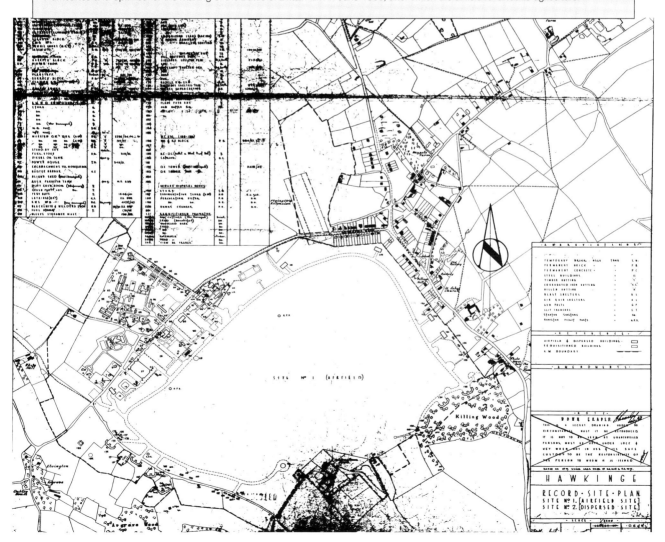

Pilots of 610 Squadron
Royal Auxiliary Airforce at
Hawkinge relax between
sorties in July 1940.
(Imperial War Museum)

April 1920, 25(F) Squadron arrived. Further permanent buildings were added in 1931.

On 29 September 1938, the station was put on a war footing with all ranks recalled from leave and the first attempts made at camouflaging the buildings. 25 Squadron began to receive Blenheims from December with little enthusiasm. However, after a stay of 19 years, 25 Squadron moved out to Northolt as the grass surface of the airfield was unsuitable for the operation of the heavier twin engine aircraft. With the declaration of war on 3 September 1939, Hawkinge became the home of No 3 Recruit Training Pool, an unusual role for what was a frontline fighter station. In the third week of December, 3 Squadron arrived with Hurricanes on the heavily camouflaged airfield, the Recruit Training School closing and the site becoming part of Fighter Command, the airfield being shared with 16 Squadron operating Army Co-operation Lysanders.

Following the Dunkirk evacuation the airfield saw many emergency landings due to a lack of fuel, the base being used mainly for the rearming and refuelling of RAF fighters as well as recovering damaged aircraft and injured pilots.

The anti-aircraft defences were inadequate for such an advanced airfield and Hawkinge never had a conventional control tower, a long, low brick building serving as a combined flying-control and operations building. Squadrons using Hawkinge regularly as a satellite included 32, 64, 72, 79, 501 and 610. 79 Squadron was sent to Turnhouse near Edinburgh for a well-earned rest on 10 July.

The first attack on the airfield was on 12 August. Hawkinge was quiet, with a few aircraft awaiting repairs in the hangars, and the dispersals were empty. At about 07.40 hrs, large formations of enemy aircraft were reported by the Observer Corps at Dover Castle. 610 Squadron was scrambled from Biggin Hill with 32 Squadron on standby. The initial target was the radar station at Rye with 610 engaging the enemy fighter bombers and at noon 32 Squadron was ordered to Hawkinge to refuel while 610 patrolled overhead. At 14.30 hrs, a scramble was signalled by the ringing of a bell, and as 32 Squadron departed, 610 Squadron came into land to refuel. With five of the radar stations out of action, tracking of the enemy was mainly undertaken by the Observer Corps. After an uneventful patrol 32 Squadron returned and within 15 minutes all the serviceable Hurricanes were ready for departure.

At around 16.45 hrs, 15 Ju 88s had been observed forming up over the French coast and 32 Squadron were patrolling the Margate area when enemy bombers were approaching Dungeness at 5,000 feet, splitting into two groups. The first group headed towards Lympne, while the second group headed for Hawkinge, which was undefended by fighters, and approached the airfield without a warning having been sounded. The first three raiders dropped their bombs inaccurately in the centre of the landing area, but the second wave was more accurate, hitting a large workshop which blew up with a terrific explosion while No 3 hangar received a direct hit. The main equipment stores were destroyed by a direct hit and two nearby houses were flattened. Fires in the hangar caused stored ammunition to explode, adding to the hazards. Despite considerable overall damage, the watch office remained serviceable. 32 Squadron was out of ammunition and low on fuel, most of the pilots making for Biggin Hill, but five appeared over the burning airfield. Although the telephone system was cut, the RT was operational and Squadron Leader Crossley was unable to divert to either Manston or Lympne as they were too badly damaged, so he landed at Hawkinge with caution. The ground crews and other personnel were busy dealing with the chaos and helping to rescue their trapped colleagues as the pilots climbed out of their Hurricanes when the Ju 88s suddenly returned. The first indication was fire from their nose guns, followed by bombs which completely destroyed No 5 hangar, although the Hurricanes were undamaged. Parties of airmen spent the night clearing rubble and shoring up buildings, the task of filling the craters beginning the following day in time for flying operations to commence for 13 August – Eagle Day – when the Luftwaffe planned to use every fighter, bomber and dive bomber available to destroy the RAF in the air and on the ground.

The day started fine and warm with 501 Squadron Hurricanes at standby. At 11.00 hrs, the enemy armada, consisting of 60 Ju 87 Stuka dive bombers armed with 250 and 500 kg bombs with a large escort of Bf 109s, left the coast of France and was detected by radar, the targets being Lympne and Hawkinge. 501 Squadron was scrambled to meet the raiders and as one wave of the dive bombers commenced their attack the airfield's Bofors guns fired in anger. Some bombs fell short, cutting the vital electricity supply to the Dover radar, and E Block used by the sergeant pilots went up in flames, showering nearby slit trenches in rubble. The airfield defences failed to hit any of the attackers, but both 54 and 501 Squadrons, having attacked the fleeing raiders from Lympne, were heading for Hawkinge. It was impossible for them to stop the raids, but their timely arrival helped to minimise damage and destroyed five Stukas for the loss of one Hurricane that ditched in the sea off Folkestone.

In the afternoon, the radar plots were so numerous that it was difficult to define a picture of the approaching attack. Some 130 Hurricanes and Spitfires from 11 RAF fighter squadrons were scrambled to intercept enemy formations with 32 Squadron ready to go at Hawkinge. The Luftwaffe force consisted of He 111, Ju 88, Do 17 and Bf 110 bombers ranged over a wide area at various heights and escorted by a large force of Bf 109s. 32 Squadron was scrambled to intercept the Bf 109s over Harwich, leaving Hawkinge undefended against attack when the next load of bombs was dropped. No additional damage was caused to buildings and there were no casualties, but the landing area was cratered further and was quickly repaired. By 18 August, the airfield was able to accommodate 615 Squadron with 12 Hurricanes who were able to operate Channel patrols when Hawkinge received its third attack.

At 13.15 hrs, a call came from the Observer Corps at Dover warning of a small enemy raid approaching the airfield, the Tannoy warning all non-essential personnel to take cover. The sector controller alerted 615 Squadron to return to Hawkinge to intercept the raiders, while 32 and 610 Squadrons were on stand-by at Biggin Hill and 501 was patrolling the coast near Margate. Within five minutes six Do 17s, escorted by a similar number of Bf 109s, approached the airfield at 100 feet, spraying the site with bullets and cannon shells. The airfield defence Bofors engaged the departing bombers but were attacked by Bf 109s. Meanwhile, 501 Squadron engaged a mass of Bf 109s near Canterbury, losing five Hurricanes and a pilot. Following this attack a temporary roof was erected over No 2 hangar.

On 7 September, Bf 109s and Bf 110s strafed and dropped bombs on and around the airfield. A total of 18 bombs were dropped killing one soldier with 12 personnel wounded, and six civilians were killed by a direct hit on a shelter outside the boundary. The station HQ was destroyed and No 1 hangar and the officers' mess were both damaged. The airfield surface was further damaged and had become a dust bowl due to the dry weather and many repairs to the surface.

The 'Hardest Day', 15 September, was comparable with the previous attacks on 15 August with large formations of enemy aircraft crossing the coast at several places during the day and night, but Hawkinge was spared any further damage. By October, Goering decided that his bomber losses, at some 1,650 aircraft, had not achieved air superiority, and with the deteriorating weather in the autumn, the invasion was shelved. Consequently, Luftwaffe tactics changed to employing roving packs of fighter-bomber Bf 109s and six attacked Hawkinge on 9 October at low level, but no serious damage was inflicted and the departing raiders were intercepted by 222 Squadron, one aircraft being forced to crash-land. This raid was followed by another on 27 October when fighter bombers destroyed much of the 1920s Officers' Mess as well as other buildings. Throughout the Battle of Britain, most of the buildings were destroyed by German bombs, but the station continued to operate large numbers of fighters, either as regular squadrons on advanced detachment from their home bases or stragglers in need of fuel, armament or repairs. The airfield site has now been returned to agriculture.

Another airfield used as a satellite in the Hornchurch Sector was Gravesend which was located on high ground in north Kent overlooking the Thames. It was established as a civil aerodrome with a grass landing area in June 1932. The RAF arrived in late 1937, setting up No 20 Elementary and Reserve Flying Training School (ERFTS) to train pilots for both the RAF and Fleet Air Arm (FAA) and the site was requisitioned by the Government in September 1939 as a satellite to Biggin Hill in 11 Group. The ERFTS moved out shortly after the declaration of war and 32 Squadron arrived in January 1940 with Hurricanes, replaced three months later by 610 Squadron Spitfires, which subsequently covered the Dunkirk evacuation. When 610 Squadron moved to Biggin Hill in July, they were replaced by 604 Squadron operating Blenheim

fighters mainly at night, but with no success.

With the Battle of Britain about to start, 501 Squadron arrived on 27 July with Hurricanes. The first major contact with the Luftwaffe was on 29 July when they engaged a large formation of Ju 87s escorted by Bf 109s, claiming six destroyed and six more damaged. The squadron continued to defend intensively against the raiders, sometimes operating from Hawkinge, and on 2 September, the first bombs fell on Gravesend injuring two soldiers. 501 Squadron moved to Kenley on 10 September, replaced the next day by 66 Squadron equipped with Spitfires, also operating from the advanced base at Hawkinge. Subsequently, enemy raids were switched to night bombing with 66 Squadron moving to West Malling on 30 October. Meanwhile, 421 Flight had been formed with a number of pilots from 66 Squadron to fly high over the Channel to report on the build-up of raids to complement radar information. Losses from Gravesend during the battle totalled 14 pilots and the airfield site is now covered by housing.

The airfield at Manston in north-east Kent near Ramsgate was another satellite in the Hornchurch Sector, which was about as exposed and vulnerable as Hawkinge with its location on the frontline. Military flying began in May 1916, the airfield being ideally located to combat the Gotha bombers approaching London during World War 1. Work started on establishing a permanent base with hangars, workshops and accommodation for over 3,600 officers and men, as well as a network of underground air-raid shelters. With the amalgamation of the RFC and RNAS to form the RAF on 1 April 1918, Manston became a bomber training establishment, and with the end of the war in November 1918, the base was also used as a demobilisation centre. Although Manston has a huge runway built in 1943-44 for the emergency recovery of damaged Allied bombers, the landing area was made of grass during the Battle of Britain.

On the declaration of war, the established School of Technical Training was dispersed to other sites and 3 Squadron arrived to be joined by 235 and 253 Squadrons which were formed on the base, although they were all soon replaced by 79 and 600 (City of London) Squadrons, the latter being equipped with Blenheim fighters. The base was mainly used in the classic satellite

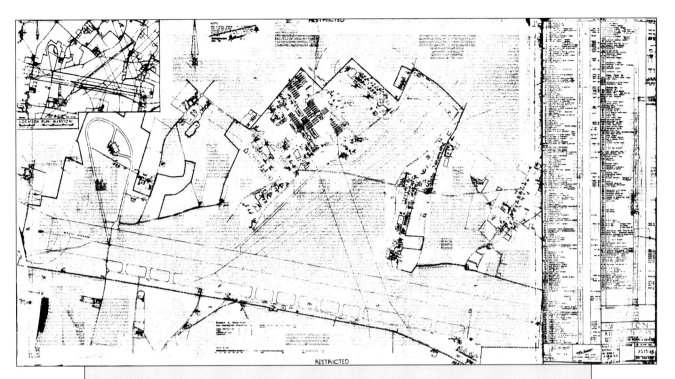

MANSTON

AP.8: TR333662, three miles north-west of Ramsgate, Kent, off the A253.

Manston first opened to flying in 1915 with building work starting in February 1916. The station was tasked with training of bomber crews, the RNAS taking over in 1917 and accommodated in very basic wooden huts. Upon the formation of the RAF on 1 April 1918, Manston became a day bomber training unit, later to be joined by an observers' school. By the end of September 1918, the construction of the station was almost complete, with one small and eight large aircraft sheds, two MT sheds, three large workshops and masses of single-storey wooden huts covering 100 of the 680-acre airfield. With the signing of the armistice in November 1918, the station reverted to a peacetime role and became a permanent RAF base in 1919 with a training role continuing. Flying operations continued until the outbreak of World War 2 when the training units were evacuated and preparations were made for hostilities. Manston was transferred to Fighter Command on 15 November 1939 and welcomed 79 Squadron Hurricanes and 600 Squadron Blenheims as the first combat aircraft since World War 1. The station, an advanced satellite for Hornchurch, was attacked and damaged by the enemy on a number of occasions.

Following the Battle of Britain, Manston was used for offensive operations from the grass surface with the unorthodox technical site located on the north-west side of the triangular landing ground. With increasing numbers of aircraft seeking a safe haven in emergencies there was a need for an additional runway, which was not provided until 1944. 825 NAS, led by Lt Commander Eugene Esmond and flying six Swordfish torpedo bombers, was tasked to attack the German battle cruisers *Scharnhorst* and *Gneisenau* when they broke out of Brest into the English Channel on 12 February 1942. There were only five survivors from the gallant crews and none of the torpedoes reached their targets. Esmond was awarded a posthumous VC.

On 15 June 1943 work started on a massive 9,000ft (2,743m) runway that was 750ft (229m) wide with a dispersal loop and 12 crash bays to accept the many aircraft in distress, with completion on 5 April 1944. In the first two weeks, 56 emergency landings were made on the new runway. In July 1950, Manston was handed over to the USAF to be used initially by F-84 Thunderjets. In April 1956, it became a master diversion airfield, remaining open 24 hours a day all year round to accept emergencies. The USAF moved out in May 1958 and it was reduced to Care & Maintenance by the RAF on 1 August 1958, not being reopened as a master diversion airfield until 28 March 1959. Commercial use commenced in April 1959, and the RAF finally moved out in 1999. The airfield is now mainly used by freight and charter operators.

Right: Spitfire Ias of 92 Squadron taking-off from Manston in March 1941 on an offensive patrol over occupied Europe. *(RAF Museum)*

Below: The pilots of 92 (East India) Squadron display their score at Manston on 6 February 1941 after the Battle of Britain when they were flying on offensive operations over Europe. *(Imperial War Museum)*

role for dispersing squadrons to a forward airfield during the day for refuelling and rearming, one of its early tasks being to provide air cover for the Dunkirk evacuation. The first bombs were dropped on the station at the beginning of June 1940, but no damage was done and preparations of the defences of the base continued.

On 12 August a strong force of enemy aircraft bombed the radar stations and Manston came in for its first major attack as well as Lympne and Hawkinge. As the bombs fell, Spitfires from 65 Squadron were in the process of taking off, most of them successfully, but two hangars were damaged and the workshops were destroyed with the loss of one civilian. Despite some 100 bomb craters on the landing field, 54 and 65 Squadrons managed to land, although repairs to

the surface were not completed until the next day. The next attack was on 15 August at just after midday by nine Bf 110s, two of which were destroyed by the ground defences, but four hangars were damaged. Manston was attacked anew the following day, this time by eight Bf 109s which destroyed a Blenheim and Spitfire on the ground, but there were no casualties. The attacks continued on 18 August when a dozen He 111s raked the airfield with machine-gun and cannon fire in a surprise attack, killing one airman, injuring 15 others and destroying two Spitfires. Further attacks were made on 20 and 22 August, causing further damage to hangars, but without casualties.

A much more severe attack was made on 24 August by 20 bombers with fighter escort, isolating the station, killing seven men and destroying buildings and aircraft and covering the landing area with more craters and unexploded bombs. As a result of this raid, all non-essential personnel were evacuated, and when Winston Churchill inspected the airfield on 28 August, it was barely serviceable, with craters and unexploded bombs, as attempts to try to return the station to normal operations were being made. No other recorded damage from bombing occurred during the remainder of the battle, no doubt the Luftwaffe believing that the base had been wiped out. Having continued in RAF service for many years after the war, the airfield is now a commercial airport with cargo flights as the main source of business.

The final satellite airfield under the control of Hornchurch in Sector D was Rochford, now Southend Municipal Airport, established in 1914 for Home Defence squadrons against Zeppelin

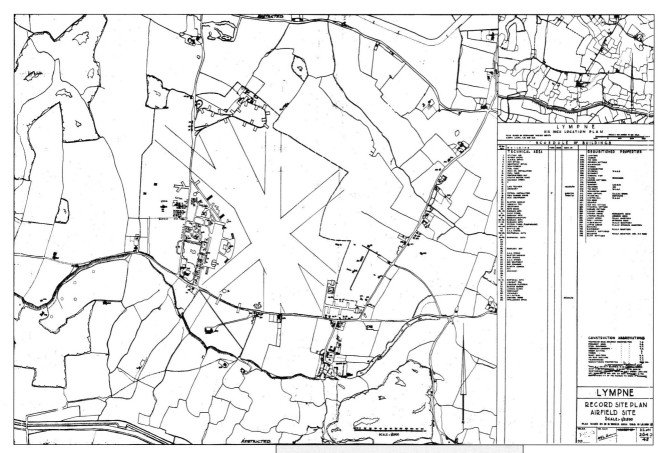

and Gotha raids on London. After World War 1 the land was returned to farming until 1933 when it was bought by Southend Corporation for develop-ment as a commercial airport. In November 1939, following Rochford's adoption as a satellite to Hornchurch, 54 Squadron arrived with Hurricanes, which also operated from Hornchurch alongside 74 Squadron during the Dunkirk evacuation as well as the Battle of Britain.

The first German attack on Rochford was on 28 August when 20-30 bombs were dropped in the general area of the airfield, cratering the grass landing ground, destroying buildings and cutting all services and telephone lines. After this particular raid, the airfield was spared any further attention from the enemy.

In Essex to the north-east of London was the Sector E station of North Weald that was first established in August 1916 with a flight of Be.2cs of 39 (Home Defence) Squadron, the duties of the flight being to combat the threat of Zeppelins and Gothas bombing London. Following the armistice, the resident 75 and 44

LYMPNE

AP.4: TR115355, three miles west of Hythe in Kent, near the A20.

The airfield was opened in late 1916 as the Machine Gun School, initially with canvas Bessoneaux hangars and the ambryonic technical buildings, and as well as gunnery training the airfield was used in preparing aircraft for transit to France. Three double-bay Belfast hangars were built to provide more permanent accommodation for the aircraft. The airfield was released to civil flying in March 1920 and later used by Short Brothers for test flying of a number of their landplane prototypes until May 1929 when they moved to Rochester. The RAF returned at the start of World War 2, initially with Lysander-equipped 16 and 26 Squadrons, and in the Battle of Britain, the airfield became a forward satellite for Biggin Hill, during which the technical site was destroyed by enemy action but the grass landing ground remained operational. Offensive operations commenced in 1941 with Typhoons arriving in 1943 and the RAF ceased flying in May 1945. Civilian aircraft returned in April 1946, but the airfield had closed to flying by 1989.

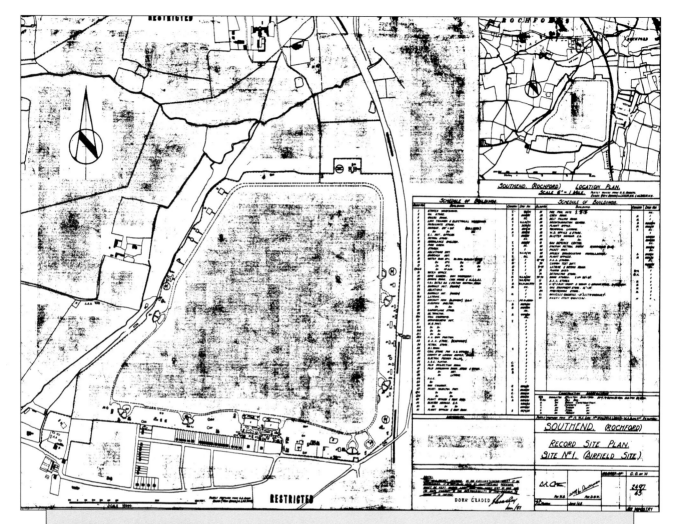

SOUTHEND / ROCHFORD

AP.9: TQ870895, two miles north of Southend, Essex, by the B1013.

Rochford was first used for air defence of London as a landing ground (LG) in May 1915 against German Zeppelins. The site was adopted by the RFC on 4 June 1916 and work started on the construction of hangars and hut accommodation. By the end of World War 1, there were four large hangars, four MT sheds and sufficient living and working accommodation for around 600 men. After the armistice the station closed in 1920 and returned to farmland. With the formation of Southend Flying Services in December 1932, Southend Council purchased a large field to allow commercial operations to start, but by the time the airport was officially opened on 18 September 1935, only flying clubs and private owners were in occupation.

With the start of World War 2, Rochford became an advanced satellite for Hornchurch, with the initial occupants being Spitfires of 54 and 74 Squadrons. The landing ground was a grass surface with a perimeter track around the boundary giving access to a number of dispersals. On the night of 18/19 June 1940, while operating from Rochford, Flight Lieutenant 'Sailor' Malan became the first day fighter pilot to destroy an enemy aircraft at night. In October 1940, the station was upgraded and became a night fighter base as RAF Southend, the initial unit being 264 Squadron Defiants. However, they moved out in November and the station became an advanced base for offensive fighter operations over Europe, later supporting the D-Day landings. All combat flying ceased with the arrival of V1 flying bombs and a balloon barrage was set up as protection, the station reverting to being a Hornchurch satellite. Southend was reduced to Care & Maintenance in February 1945, closing at the end of May, and the site was released in 1946. Southend Airport was relicensed on 1 January 1947 with commercial flying starting four days later and since then the site has been developed into a major airport with commercial operations, aircraft engineering, flight training and general aviation. While much of the original perimeter track remains, two runways have been constructed, one of which is now disused, but plans exist to extend the 24/06 main runway.

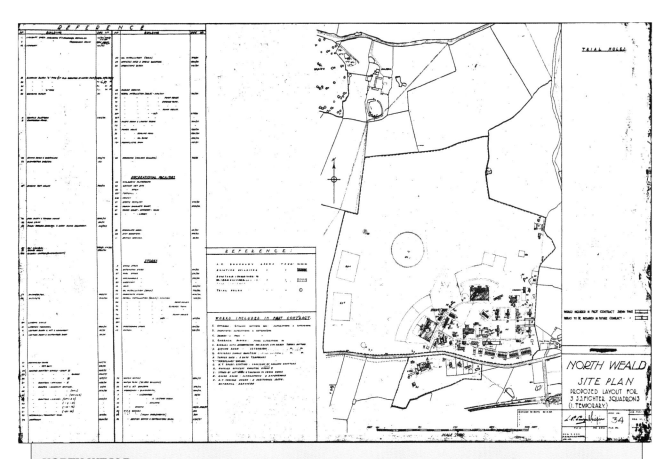

NORTH WEALD

AP.10: TL488044, alongside the M11, three miles north-east of Epping, Essex.

The airfield was first operational with 39 Squadron from August 1916 for home defence, and on 1 October 1916, 2nd Lt Tempest shot down Zeppelin L.31 over Potters Bar. After the armistice the airfield was abandoned until reconstruction commenced in 1926 for a reopening on 27 September 1927. The landing ground remained a grass surface and the camp was constructed in the south-east corner with two 'A' Type hangars widely spaced to allow another to be built if required. The third hangar was never erected. The first operational unit was 56 (Fighter) Squadron equipped with Siskins, arriving on 11 October 1927, and joined by 29 Squadron on 1 April 1928. In preparation for war, a perimeter track was constructed with aircraft dispersals, some of which still exist on the boundary, and two paved runways were laid, the main north-south runway, 2,800ft long, being one of the first hard runways to be laid on a fighter airfield. The airfield was a sector station within 11 Group Fighter Command, and amongst additional accommodation were four Blister Hangars and four larger Extra Over Blister Hangars. Two satellite land grounds were allocated at Hunsdon and Stapleford Tawney.

From December 1940, the squadrons commenced offensive fighter sweeps across occupied France, and in June 1941, the American volunteer 71 (Eagle) Squadron arrived at North Weald, one of many fighter units to be based at the station until early 1945 when it became relatively inactive until 1949. On 27 March 1949, 601 (County of London) Royal Auxiliary Airforce arrived, followed the next day by 604 (County of Middlesex), both equipped with Spitfire LF.16s, which were soon replaced by Vampire F.3 jet fighters. In March 1950, 72 Squadron arrived with Vampire F.3s, and in 1951, the runways were extended to make the operation of jet fighters more effective. Additional T.2 hangars were also erected. Meteors replaced the Vampires in 1952, and on 2 December 1953, 111 Squadron arrived with Hunters, which under the leadership of Squadron Leader Roger Topp became the famous 'Black Arrows' aerobatic team, one of their specialities being a 22 all-black painted Hunter loop. The Royal Auxiliary Airforce squadrons were disbanded in March 1957, and with the departure of 111 Squadron in November 1958, the station was reduced to Care & Maintenance, becoming inactive in September 1964. The site was gradually developed for general aviation and was the venue for many air shows including the start of the International Air Tattoo, as well as a location for the making of the *Battle of Britain* film. In August 1979, the site was bought by Epping Forest District Council and is now a mixture of general aviation with an interesting selection of historic aircraft, warehousing and heavy goods vehicle driving instruction. One of the 'A' Type hangars was destroyed by fire, but the other remains, together with a number of the original RAF buildings.

Above: An early production Hurricane I recently arrived at North Weald in 1938 having a wheel change and the 17 Squadron UV-S painted on the fuselage. (*RAF Museum*)

Above right: Hurricane I GG-D of 151 Squadron at North Weald in May 1939 with the pilot and ground crew running the Merlin engine. (*RAF Museum*)

Above: Based at North Weald in 1939 and 1940 were Blenheims of 604 Squadron. These aircraft were ineffective in air-to-air combat but were useful against soft ground targets such as troops and light vehicles, provided there was air superiority. (*RAF Museum*)

Below: While some Hurricanes taxi on returning from a sortie, a flight of three 32 Squadron Hurricanes depart for another patrol. (*Imperial War Museum*)

Squadrons were disbanded, the last leaving on 31 December 1919 after which the site was abandoned. Reconstruction began in 1926 ready for the formal reopening on 27 September 1927, 56 Squadron arriving from Biggin Hill on 11 October equipped with Siskin IIIas.

By November 1938, both 56 and 151 Squadrons were operating Hurricanes, ready for the challenges of combat with the facilities being progressively improved and additional ground acquired for the airfield. Two hard runways were constructed with additional areas of grass also used for flight operations. Amongst the buildings were two C Type hangars with dispersed blister hangars and a flying control tower. A third C Type hangar was later added together with accommodation for station personnel and usual functional structures. In October 1939, 56 Squadron was moved to the advanced satellite of Martlesham Heath, while 151 Squadron remained at North Weald. In January 1940, Wing Commander Victor Beamish was appointed station commander and led by example during the Battle of Britain.

56 and 151 squadrons were involved in the Battle of France, followed by the Dunkirk evacuation, and when the Luftwaffe commenced attacks on coastal convoys, both were heavily engaged in protection duties.

On 10 July, B Flight of 56 Squadron dispersed early in the morning to the satellite at Manston, going into action over a convoy, to be followed by almost daily battles over the slow-moving ships by both 56 and 151 Squadrons.

On Saturday 24 August, the Luftwaffe commenced their attacks on airfields with North Weald one of the targets. At 15.40 hrs, eight Hurricanes of 151 Squadron were scrambled to intercept a raid approaching from the east. As the pilots climbed they were confronted by massed formations of He 111 and Do 17 bombers escorted by Bf 109 and Bf 110 fighters

Above: Hurricane I N2479 of 56 Squadron at North Weald in 1940. In the foreground is a 'trolley ack' or mobile battery starter trolley.

Below: Three 56 Squadron Hurricanes climb away from North Weald in July 1940. *(Imperial War Museum)*

at altitudes from 15,000 feet upwards. As 151 Squadron went into the attack, they were joined by Hurricanes of 111 Squadron making a head-on attack. Many of the enemy bombers jettisoned their loads and turned for home, but others pressed on and dropped some 200 bombs on North Weald. The officers' and airmen's married quarters were severely damaged as was the power house, with damage to the water and gas mains. An air-raid shelter received a direct hit, killing nine members of the Essex Regiment with ten other personnel injured. The defending pilots claimed three He 111s destroyed with two Bf 109s as probable, losing one Hurricane.

On Sunday 1 September, the depleted 56 Squadron with only seven Hurricanes remaining left for Boscombe Down to reform and rest, and was replaced by 249 Squadron. On the same day 151 Squadron departed to Digby, replacing 46 Squadron, which came south and took up residence at the North Weald satellite of Stapleford. 25 Squadron operating Blenheims also arrived at North Weald with a flight detached to Martlesham. At 09.40 hrs on Tuesday 3 September, a force of 30 Do 17s escorted by 50 Bf 110s flew up the Thames Estuary at 20,000 feet and turned north towards North Weald. 249 Squadron had just landed and was refuelling when the alarm sounded. Those Hurricanes which were ready raced to become airborne before the bombs began to fall. Others with only partly refuelled tanks followed, the station's serviceable aircraft becoming airborne before the hostile force appeared at 15,000 feet from the north-east. With a disadvantage in height, 249 Squadron attempted to distract the bombers but their loads were already being released. Both 25 and 151 Squadron hangars were hit and burned out and the MT yard was badly damaged. The old operations room was partly destroyed and the new Operations Block survived a direct hit. Many other buildings were damaged including living quarters and main stores, with communications also disrupted. Over 200 bombs had been dropped, and although some fell on the landing area, the airfield was still useable during the day.

On 5 September, the Operations Room, station HQ, sick quarters and MT section were all dispersed in the local area. Wing Commander Victor Beamish was awarded the DSO by King George VI at Buckingham Palace on 5 September and continued to fly operationally during the battle. With the Luftwaffe concentrating their attacks upon London relieving the pressure of the station defences and allowing time to make repairs where possible, 257 Squadron, led by Squadron Leader Bob Stanford Tuck, arrived from Martlesham on 8 September, with the Blenheims of 25 Squadron departing to Debden. The final enemy attack on the station during the Battle of Britain was on 29 October just as 249 Squadron was airborne followed by 257 Squadron. A formation of Bf 109 fighter-bombers came low over the camp without warning, dropping 100 kg bombs and firing their guns. The first 'vic' of three Hurricanes was about 40 feet over the end of the runway, at their most vulnerable, when one of the bombs burst below; one Hurricane took the full blast under the wing, sending it into a roll towards Tuck's aircraft before it passed inverted over the top and nose-dived into the ground, bursting into flames. Some 45 bombs were dropped, of which 27 landed on the camp, killing 19 with 42 injured. Only the leader of the attack was shot down and the recently-rebuilt guard room was demolished with damage to other buildings and the landing area, the latter remaining serviceable for daylight operations. North Weald remained with the RAF after the war as a jet fighter base and is now a general aviation airfield with a number of warbirds.

A few miles south of North Weald is the grass airfield of Stapleford Tawney located inside the M25 and close to the M11 junction. The airfield was originally opened as a base for Hillman Airways on 23 June 1934 operating D.H.84 Dragons for what was the first budget airline, but by the spring of 1936, all commercial services were moved to Heston and the airfield left to a few private owners. With the RAF expansion programme fully established in 1938, the airfield was reopened as a base for 21 ERFTS for the training of RAFVR pilots initially on Tiger Moths. Soon after the start of World War 2, the airfield was taken over by the RAF and the training unit reallocated. Additional land was acquired and a concrete perimeter track was constructed around the grass landing area. Six double dispersal pens were constructed, together with buildings to accommodate pilots and ground crews for a fighter squadron. On completion the airfield was handed over to 11 Group and the first recorded use of the airfield was by 56 and 151 Squadrons

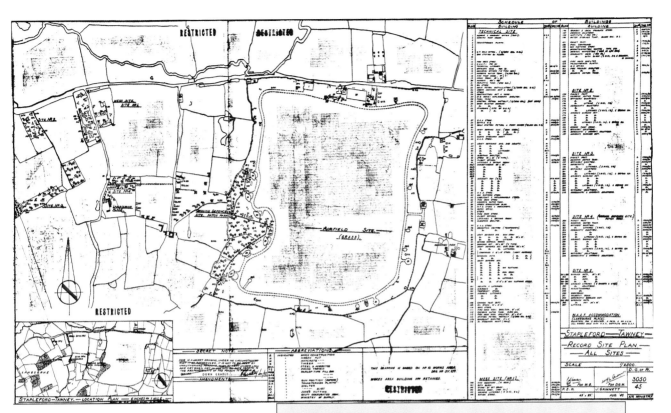

in late March 1940, where they were dispersed overnight in case of enemy attacks on North Weald. 151 Squadron moved into Stapleford from Martlesham on a more regular basis on 29 August, but moved for a rest to Digby on 1 September, to be replaced by 46 Squadron, the pilots being in regular combat with the enemy and sustaining increased losses. The airfield largely escaped enemy attention possibly due to its rural nature, as a number of incendiaries and two bombs were dropped during the night of 7 October cratering the surface, but not damaging any buildings or aircraft. The airfield turned to offensive operations after the Battle of Britain and was disused after the war. Flying operations commenced in 1953 and the airfield is now used for general aviation.

Martlesham Heath, the other North Weald satellite, was located a few miles east of Ipswich. The RAF first took possession on 16 January 1917 when the RFC Testing Squadron moved from Upavon. It became the Aeroplane Experimental Station in October 1917, later to gain the title Aircraft & Armament Experimental Establishment (A&AEE) and moved to Boscombe Down on 1 September 1939. The grass-surface airfield was prepared for war as a

STAPLEFORD TAWNEY

AP.11: TQ493970, by the A113, five miles north of Romford, Essex.

The airfield was first opened in June 1934 for the operations of Hillman Airways, a coach operator turned budget airline, but they moved out a year later. The grass airfield also had three small hangars built with a passenger terminal. With the departure of Hillman Airways in June 1935, the only occupants of the site were a few private aircraft, but in 1938, the airfield was reopened for RAF flying training. At the outbreak of World War 2, the site was requisitioned and the airfield enlarged with the construction of a 2.25-mile perimeter track plus six double dispersals and accommodation/administrative buildings. With accommodation for one fighter squadron it was handed over to 11 Group in early 1940 where it became a satellite for North Weald, the first arrivals being Hurricanes of 56 and 151 Squadrons in March 1940.

Owing to the poor airfield surface during the winter of 1940/41, the site had no flying units, but for a short period while in May 1941, 242 Squadron operated offensive fighter sweeps over France. In December 1941, the site became an air-sea rescue base and in the New Year eight Blister hangars were erected together with a number of billets and messes. In March 1943, the airfield was transferred to Army Co-operation as a satellite to Sawbridgeworth. The station became a ground support base for the invasion of Europe and two V2 rockets hit the site, the second killing 17 people. The site was reduced to Care & Maintenance on 11 May 1945, being used as a parachute drop zone before falling into neglect until the Herts and Essex arrived in 1953 and renovated some buildings. The airfield is now used for general aviation, training and maintenance with commercial developments.

Above: With the outbreak of World War 2 imminent, ground crews wear their tin hats during exercises with an 87 Squadron Hurricane I at Debden in August 1939.

Right: Blenheim IFs L1507 YB-A, L1509 LB-E and others of 29 Squadron were based at Debden in 1939, but moved to Digby for the start of the Battle of Britain. *(RAF Museum)*

Bottom: Hurricanes of 17 Squadron at readiness at Debden on 25 July 1940 with the pilot's parachute ready to be grabbed from the tailplane. *(Imperial War Museum*

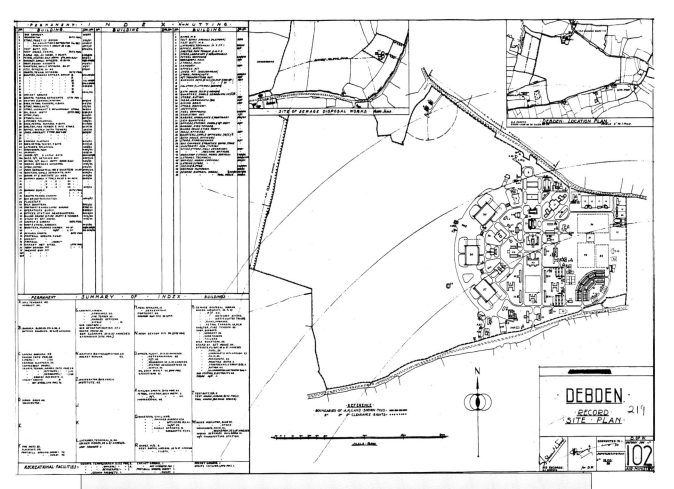

DEBDEN

AP.13: TL565340, three miles south-east of Saffron Walden, Essex, by the B184.

The station was opened for operations on 22 April 1937 as part of the RAF Expansion Scheme with a grass landing ground and the main camp in the eastern corner. Aircraft accommodation was in three 'C' Type hangars built in a semi-circle, with the workshops, station HQ, administration and accommodation buildings behind. The first flying units to arrive were 80 and 73 Squadrons with Gladiators, and when World War 2 started, 85 and 87 Squadrons with Hurricanes and 29 Squadron with Blenheims were in residence, but the two Hurricane squadrons were posted to France and replaced at Debden by 17 and 504 Squadrons, also with Hurricanes.

Construction work continued after the start of World War 2, including the laying of two runways and connecting perimeter tracks with fighter dispersals around the boundary. In the spring of 1941, the station was home to 52 OTU to prepare pilots to fight with Hurricanes, and in April 1942, 71 (Eagle) Squadron arrived at Debden to be followed in September by the remaining two Eagle squadrons to form the USAAF 4th Fighter Group, the Spitfire-equipped units being renumbered 334, 335 and 336 Squadrons. The Spitfires were replaced by P-47 Thunderbolts in the spring of 1943 for long range escorts of the 8th AF day bombers. In February 1944, the P-47s were replaced by P-51 Mustangs, which in June were supporting the D-Day Allied landings in Normandy. After the departure of the USAAF fighters, the station became part of RAF Technical Training Command as a division of the RAF Technical College until 1960, the final aircraft being operated from the airfield being Vickers Varsities and de Havilland Chipmunks. The RAF finally withdrew from Debden on 25 April 1975 and the site was taken over by the Army. The runways still remain, but the hangars have gone to be replaced by new military structures, and much of the original accommodation remains in use in the barracks.

Above: Flt Lt R R 'Bob' Stanford Tuck with 92 Squadron at Duxford in June 1940. *(RAF Museum)*

satellite for North Weald with the Hurricanes from North Weald and Debden using the airfield during the spring of 1940. Martlesham was bombed at the start of the Battle of Britain with an attack at 05.15 hrs on 10 July 1940 when a number of unidentified aircraft dropped bombs at the edge of the landing area without causing damage or casualties. On 12 July, 17 Squadron A Flight with Hurricanes arrived at Martlesham from Debden, later to be joined by 85 Squadron. 'Adler Tag', 13 August, brought 17 Squadron to Martlesham on a regular basis and 85 Squadron left for Debden. Two days later, as 17 Squadron was taking off, 16 Bf 110s and nine Bf 109s swept across the station at low level, firing their guns and dropping bombs. In four and a half minutes the enemy had departed, leaving serious damage, with two hangars wrecked and buildings damaged including the guard room plus a parked Fairey Battle. Of the seven casualties, two were seriously injured.

At the beginning of September the leaderless 257 Squadron arrived at Martlesham after suffering from low morale and many losses over the previous weeks. Their new Commanding Officer was Bob Stanford Tuck DFC, already one of the top-scoring fighter pilots, who had the task of restoring the squadron as an effective fighting unit. During the late afternoon of 7 September, the Germans mounted the largest raid to date on London, and in the company of the other squadrons of Fighter Command, 257 Squadron attacked the northern flank of the enemy formations, losing two of their pilots. On 15 September, Martlesham's fighters returned after three exhausting patrols totalling more than seven hours in the air with claims for five enemy aircraft destroyed for two Hurricanes damaged. In the first two weeks of October, 257 Squadron moved to North Weald and was replaced by 17 Squadron from Debden, but the action was beginning to diminish. On 27

Above left: Hurricane I P2754 YB-W of 17 Squadron after a landing mishap at Debden on 27 July 1940. *(Imperial War Museum)*

Above: Hurricane I of 504 Squadron having its machine guns rearmed at Debden in 1940. Great care had to be taken to feed the belts of ammunition into the wings to avoid jamming at a critical moment during combat. *(RAF Museum)*

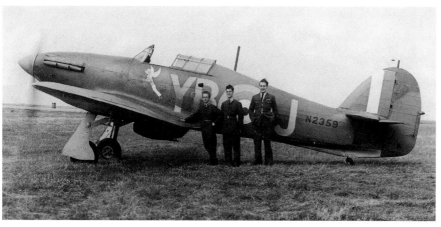

Left: With Merlin running and no chocks, pilot P/O Stevens, rigger LAC Jaques and mechanic LAC McEvoy pose by Hurricane I N2359 at Debden in August 1940.

October, the station was attacked by 20 Bf 109 fighter-bombers at 7,000 feet, leaving little damage. On 9 April 1963, the airfield was finally closed, the site being developed for industrial and residential use.

The most northerly 11 Group sector station was Debden, three miles south east of Saffron Walden. The airfield was built in the pre-war RAF expansion period and intended as a fighter base with a grass landing area and three C Type hangars. The station opened on 22 April 1937 with 73, 80 and 87 Squadrons equipped with Gladiators. In 1938, 85 and 87 Squadrons arrived with Hurricanes and 29 Squadron

Hurricane I VY-X of 85 Squadron in overall matt black ready for night fighting duties at Debden in 1940. *(Imperial War Museum)*

Squadron Leader Peter Townsend (centre of group) with walking stick after sustaining an injury.

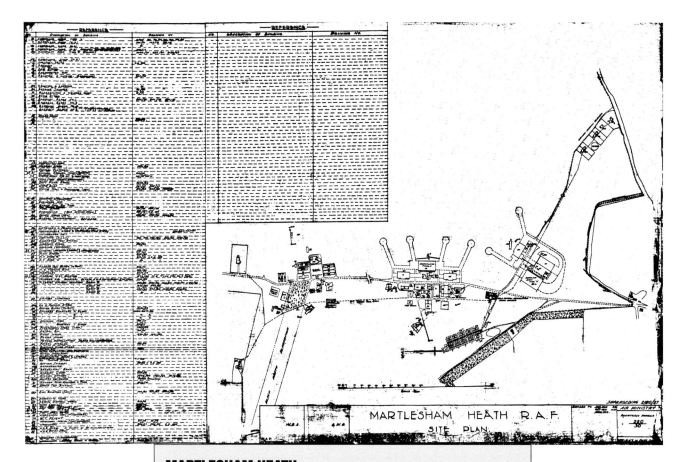

MARTLESHAM HEATH R.A.F.
SITE PLAN

MARTLESHAM HEATH

AP.12: TM245455, by the A1093, east of Ipswich, Suffolk.

Opened as the Aeroplane Experimental Unit in January 1917, Martlesham was redesignated the Aeroplane & Armament Experimental Establishment (A&AEE) in 1924 for the operational testing of military aircraft and certification of new civil types. The landing ground was a grass surface and a number of specialist buildings were erected for the test units including one 'A' Type hangar, workshops and accommodation. The A&AEE moved to Boscombe Down on 1 September 1939 and the first combat unit to arrive was 264 Squadron with Defiants, the airfield being a satellite to Debden. During the summer of 1940, the visiting squadrons were busy on coastal convoy protection duties, and on 11 November 1940, the Italians made their one and only attempt to attack Britain, which failed dismally. The planned target was Harwich Harbour, the defending fighters claiming seven enemy aircraft destroyed and four damaged without loss. A bonus was wine salvaged from a Fiat BR.20 bomber brought down on Bromswell golf course. In the autumn of 1943, two runways were laid and the station was prepared for the arrival of the P-47 Thunderbolts of 356th Fighter Group of the USAAF 8th AF, which would remain at Martlesham for two years. The first mission was flown on 15 October. The P-47s were replaced by P-51D Mustangs, flying their last mission on 7 May 1945, but a USAF presence remained until March 1992. After the end of World War 2, Martlesham returned to testing duties mainly concerned with armament with nearby Woodbridge as a satellite. The site closed on 25 April 1963 with many of the original buildings used for commercial purposes. The control tower houses a museum.

Left: Hurricane Is of 56 Squadron were based at Martlesham Heath in 1939 and are practising echelon to starboard, a formation that had no tactical value at all. *(RAF Museum)*

Below: F/O C I R Arthur on a 242 Squadron Hurricane dispersed to Martlesham Heath. *(RAF Museum)*

arrived with Blenheim fighters in 1939. Debden had originally been part of 12 Group but was transferred to 11 Group, becoming a key station in the Battle of Britain. At the start of the Battle of France, 85 and 87 Squadron were sent to France with 17 and 504 Squadrons taking their place. Two runways were built, linked by perimeter track with dispersals in the surrounding countryside, and in June, nearby Castle Camps was made the first satellite to Debden, with a weakened 85 Squadron led by Squadron Leader Peter Townsend to be the first to occupy Castle Camps.

Ready for the start of the Battle of Britain, the station was equipped with Hurricanes under the overall command of Wing Commander J L F Fuller-Good. On the first day of the battle, 10 July 1940, Debden suffered slight bomb damage from a solitary Do 17. Both 17 and 85 Squadrons were in constant action against the Luftwaffe over the next few weeks operating around East Anglia, the Thames Estuary and Kent. For the last two weeks of August, 17 and 85 Squadrons moved south and were replaced by 111 and 601 Squadrons which joined the newly arrived 257 Squadron. With the Luftwaffe concentrating attacks on major fighter stations, Debden became a target on 26 August. The approaching raid had been plotted by the Observer Corps but was then lost; the first

knowledge of an enemy attack on Debden was when bombs rained down on the station. More than 100 HE and incendiary bombs were dropped, scoring direct hits on the Sergeants' Mess, NAAFI, WAAF and airmen's accommodation and other buildings and on the landing ground. Four RAF personnel and

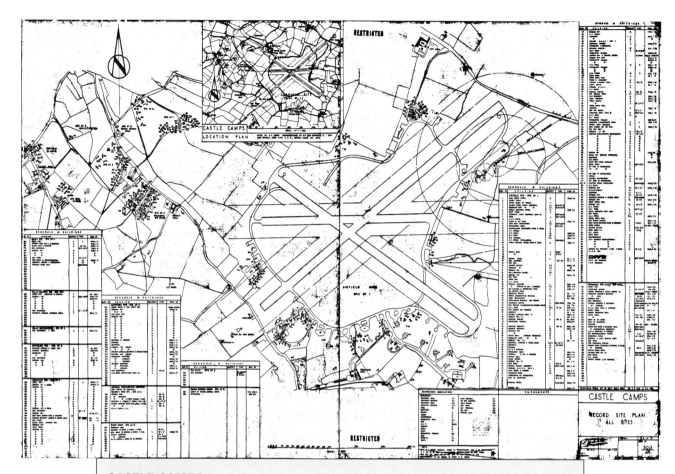

CASTLE CAMPS

AP.14: TL630425, in Cambridgeshire, six miles north-east of Saffron Walden.

Preparation of the rather exposed and bleak satellite for Debden at Castle Camps commenced in September 1939, the first Hurricanes of 85 Squadron arriving on 27 June 1940. Accommodation was mainly under canvas. In September, 73 Squadron replaced 85 Squadron and participated in the Battle of Britain until November 1940, when work commenced to upgrade the airfield with the construction of three runways, a perimeter track and a Bellman hangar in preparation for the introduction of the de Havilland Mosquito in RAF night fighter operations. The first example of the 'Wooden Wonder', a dual control T.III trainer, arrived on 26 January, but due to technical delays the first operation by 157 Squadron was not until 27 April 1942, with the first success on 30 May when a Do 217 was shot down.

In March 1943, 605 (County of Warwick) Royal Auxiliary Airforce replaced 157 at Castle Camps, the Mosquito being used for night intruder operations over occupied Europe. In July, the change from Mosquito NF.IIs to FB.VIs commenced, which continued night intruder and night bomber support operations. In late December, 410 (RCAF) Squadron arrived with Mosquito night fighters for the defence of the north-east approaches to London against enemy night bombers, claiming a number of successes before moving to Hunsdon in April 1944 to provide cover for the D-Day landings. The Mosquitos were replaced by Griffon-powered Spitfires and then Typhoons and Tempests supporting the preparations for the invasion of Europe. In June 1944, Mosquito night fighters returned with 68 Squadron to combat the V1s, the first of which was destroyed on 9 July, with other squadrons following on bomber support duties. With the end of the war, the station began to wind down, flying ceasing in January 1946. The airfield was finally declared surplus in July 1948, returning to agriculture, and now very little evidence remains of its wartime activities.

Castle Camps was the satellite to Debden and was occupied by B Flight of 85 Squadron with Hurricane Is in July 1940 used for night fighting with a metal shield forward of the cockpit to reduce the glare of the engine exhaust. The pilots are taking a welcome break with pints of beer. *(RAF Museum)*

one civilian were killed. On 31 August, Debden was attacked again, the first enemy wave dropping bombs in the distance to the north. The second formation of 30 Do 17s with a Bf 110 escort released their bombs from 15,000 feet at around 08.40 hrs, straddling the station, before circling the airfield. At this point 111 Squadron Hurricanes arrived from Castle Camps and engaged the raiders, claiming two destroyed, three probable and three damaged. The Hurricanes of 601 Squadron were airborne when the raiders arrived, and destroyed two enemy aircraft with one probable and one damaged. Meanwhile, 257 Squadron was airborne from Martlesham and engaged the raiders, accounting for five victories and three damaged. The enemy dropped around 100 HE and incendiary bombs, badly damaging a barrack block and the sick quarters. A hangar, the Sergeants' Mess, NAAFI and the cookhouse were also damaged. The Operations Room continued to function and the station remained operational. One airman and one civilian were killed and 12 RAF personnel were injured. As a result of this raid, the Operations Room was dispersed off base.

In early September, 17 Squadron returned and was joined by 73 Squadron. With the Luftwaffe changing to night bombing, 73 Squadron was allocated to night duties and was joined by the more effective Beaufighter-equipped 25 Squadron. The Defiants of 264 Squadron and the rejuvenated 85 Squadron were also based at Debden on night fighter duties until the end of 1940. During the period from August to November 1940, the fighter pilots based at Debden claimed 110 enemy aircraft destroyed, 33 probable and 60 damaged for the loss of 33 aircraft and 11 pilots killed. Both Debden and Castle Camps were to become Mosquito bases after the Battle of Britain, and while Castle Camps has been returned to farmland, Debden is now home of the Army Carver Barracks.

To the west of London the 11 Group Fighter Command Sector Station was Northolt and is the longest continually serving RAF station with flying units, having first opened in March 1915 when No.4 Reserve Aeroplane Squadron arrived from Farnborough. The main duties of the airfield during World War 1 were the training of single-seat fighter pilots and with the end of the war, the training requirement reduced considerably. In May 1919, when the training role ceased, it became the base for the South Eastern Communications Flight. The airfield continued to house more communications units and the use by commercial organisations was encouraged for the operation of training and charter operations as well as some aircraft manufacture.

During 1925, a programme provided permanent buildings, replacing the earlier temporary structures. In addition to barrack blocks and airmen's mess, an Operations Block and Station HQ were added in the late 1920s. In 1930, three of the flight sheds were replaced by a more suitable A Type hangar, and in 1925, the Auxiliary Air Force had formed its first two units at Northolt – 600 (City of London) and 601 (County of London) Squadrons to provide reserve pilots for the regular RAF.

On 12 June 1934, 111 Squadron arrived at Northolt to become the first Hurricane unit in the RAF when the first aircraft were delivered in December 1938. On 1 May 1936, the station became part of 11 Group, and in 1939, Northolt

No 111 Squadron at Northolt was the first RAF unit to take delivery of Hurricanes, the first arriving in December 1937 from nearby Brooklands. These early aircraft had fixed pitch wooden propellers and the early rudder shape which was improved for better control when recovering from a spin.

Technicians working on the Rolls-Royce Merlin in an early Hurricane I of 111 Squadron at Northolt in 1938. (*RAF Museum*)

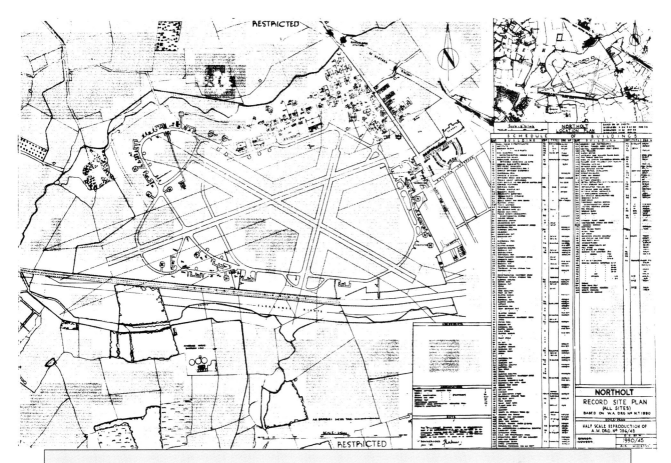

NORTHOLT

AP.15: TQ100850, three miles east of Uxbridge, Middlesex, north of the A40 by the B455.

Northolt claims to be the longest continuously operating RAF base in Britain, construction having commenced at the beginning of 1915. Six flight sheds and a twin hangar were erected, plus workshops and barrack accommodation, in time for the official opening on 1 March 1915, the main camp being located along the northern boundary of the airfield. The station was designated as a home defence night landing ground with operations starting on 4/5 June against Zeppelins. Northolt soon took on the training role, but with the signing of the armistice, flying reduced until training was withdrawn altogether in May 1919. The airfield then became a communications base with joint military/civil operations. Expansion commenced in the late 1920s with the demolition of three of the original wooden hangars to be replaced by an 'A' Type hangar and new barrack blocks and messes. In 1925, 600 and 601 Auxiliary Squadrons were formed at Northolt in the light bomber role, while communications flying continued. As recounted elsewhere, 111 Squadron became the first RAF Hurricane squadron in January 1938 and with the preparations for war, a 'C' Type hangar and five 'H' barrack blocks were built in the north-east corner of the site. Northolt became one of the first RAF airfields to have hard runways when two were laid in 1939.

After the Battle of Britain, the station went on the offensive, and by mid-1941, it was the base for three Polish squadrons until April 1944. In November 1943, Northolt was designated 131 Airfield in the newly formed 2nd Tactical Air Force to provide close support to the ground forces in the invasion of Europe. With the formation of RAF Transport Command in March 1943, it became the main London airfield and work commenced on extending the main northeast-southwest runway. As the year 1944 progressed, transport movements increased rapidly with improvements to the runways and the creation of passenger and cargo terminals on the south side of the site.

During the preparations for Heathrow to become London Airport, Northolt was used as the main London air terminal with regular services from 1 February 1946, and in October 1954 the airport reverted to RAF control. In the mid-1950s, further improvements were made to the runways and buildings with the removal of the World War 1 hangars. Today Northolt is still in joint military and civil use with RAF and other military communications on the north side and the civil business terminal on the south alongside the A40.

Top: A pair of Hurricane Is of 303 (Polish) Squadron based at Northolt in September 1940. Northolt had been declared operational on 2 August. *(J B Cynk Photo Archives)*

Middle: New Zealand Sergeant Pilot Mitchell wearing his 'Mae West' life jacket, standing by Hurricane I with 615 Squadron at Northolt. *(J G Millard)*

Bottom: Hurricanes Is of 615 Squadron on finals to land at Northolt in October 1940.

Pilots, and the mascot of 615 Squadron, being briefed for their next sortie from Northolt. *(J G Millard)*

became one of the first RAF airfields to have hard runways, two being constructed with connecting perimeter tracks. At the outbreak of war the resident units were 111 and 601 Squadrons, but these were replaced by a number of other squadrons in the lead-up to the Battle of Britain. The Station Commander during the battle was Group Captain S F Vincent, who insisted that the airfield buildings were camouflaged. The landing ground was painted to represent the original fields with a stream down each runway, and a pond where they joined. It was so effective that visiting pilots had difficulty finding the airfield.

On 18 May, 609 Squadron arrived and experienced their first action on 30 May over Dunkirk. The remnants of 1 Squadron arrived at Northolt from France on 20 June with the surviving Hurricanes to rebuild its operational strength. On 4 July, 609 moved to Middle Wallop and was replaced by 257 Squadron from Hendon. 2 August was a significant day for Northolt with the formation of 303 (Kosciuszko) Squadron, the second Polish RAF fighter squadron, but the first to go into action. The association with Polish pilots was to continue for the next four years and is commemorated by the nearby Polish War Memorial just outside the south-eastern boundary of the airfield. The

contribution of the Allied pilots to the Battle of Britain was key to the final victory, and although the Polish pilots were experienced, they had to be trained to operate the Hurricane and undertake a basic English language course. The Commanding Officer and flight commanders were Poles, but duplicated by regular RAF officers. While the Polish pilots were training on 30 August, a large enemy formation was spotted and a pilot broke away and claimed a Do 17. As a result 303 Squadron was declared operational and on the following day in their first scramble engaged six Bf 109s, claiming four destroyed and two damaged.

By the middle of August, 257 Squadron had lost four pilots and eight Hurricanes, and the unit was moved to Debden to regroup. Two days later 1 (RCAF) Squadron arrived at Northolt, 1 Squadron RAF having returned on 1 August. The station's strength now consisted of three squadrons from three nationalities. The RCAF squadron was an example of the pilots from the British Commonwealth who volunteered to fight against Nazi tyranny. They had arrived in Britain with Canadian-built Hurricanes in late June, working up at Middle Wallop and Croydon before moving to Northolt.

No 1 Squadron moved out to Wittering on 9 September and was replaced by 229 Squadron

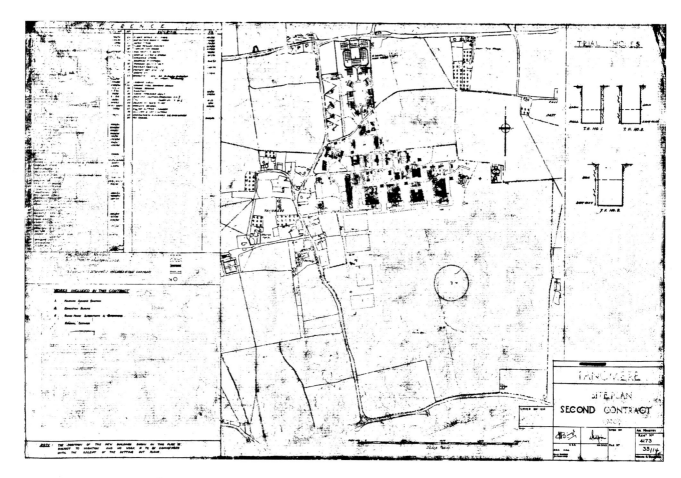

flying Hurricanes who lost three aircraft within two days, although the pilots survived. The Canadians lost two aircraft on the same day with the pilots bailing out, and the Poles lost three Hurricanes with two of the pilots killed, all within a period of 20 minutes in dogfights with Bf 109s. On 15 September, all three squadrons were in action losing a total of eight aircraft with three pilots killed. On 25 September, Northolt was bombed for the first time by a solitary aircraft causing little damage and no casualties. A more damaging attack was made on 6 October by a Ju 88 that roared over the airfield at 200 feet firing at buildings. Two bombs were dropped between the hangars, killing a lookout on the hangar roof and a Polish pilot taxying his Hurricane, before shooting up 229 Squadron's dispersal. Two of 229's Hurricanes were in the air at the time and damaged the bomber sufficiently for it to crash near Leatherhead.

On 9 October, the RCAF squadron went to Prestwick for a rest and was replaced by 615

Squadron Hurricanes. A few days later 303 Squadron went to Leconfield in Yorkshire, changing places with 302 (Polish) Squadron. The total claim by 303 squadron during its six weeks in battle was 126 enemy aircraft destroyed for eight Polish pilots killed. The remainder of October was relatively relaxed apart from the 18th when 302 Squadron became lost in poor weather and four pilots were killed in landings. The station had remained fully operational throughout the battle and Northolt is still in use today by the RAF who once again share the runways with general aviation.

The most westerly sector in 11 Group and bordered by 10 Group was Sector A, with Tangmere as the Sector Station, located three miles east of Chichester on the south coast of England. Construction of the airfield commenced in 1917 initially as a training station, but 91, 92 and 93 Squadrons arrived in March 1918, leaving for France in July. The airfield was closed early in 1919, but the site was retained by the Air Ministry. Tangmere was reopened in

Opposite: Spitfire IIa P7753 QJ-X with 616 Squadron in the protection of a dispersal with more Spitfires taxying in at Tangmere in 1941. *(RAF Museum)*

TANGMERE

AP.16: SU910060, three miles east of Chichester, West Sussex, by the A27.

The site that was to become Tangmere airfield was requisitioned in September 1917, following which work commenced on clearing the ground and flying by 92 Squadron RFC commenced between March and June 1917. The Americans took over the base in September 1918, by which time one single-bay and three twin-bay Belfast hangars and a Handley-Page assembly shed had been constructed, with wooden hut accommodation on the north side of the site. With the signing of the armistice, the American troops returned home and Tangmere was declared surplus, closing in 1920. However, the land and buildings were retained by the Air Ministry, and on 1 June 1925, the base reopened for storage but returned to flying as a fighter base when 43 Squadron arrived in December 1926, joined by 1 Squadron on 1 April 1927. Work began in June 1928 on the construction of permanent barrack blocks, messes and married quarters on the north side of the airfield behind the hangars. With the RAF Expansion Scheme in 1937, additional buildings were constructed including workshops, MT yard and more living accommodation. In 1938, the airfield was extended to the east, giving a maximum length of 4,500ft/1,327m. Hurricanes were delivered to 1 Squadron in October 1938, with 43 Squadron receiving theirs the following month. The station was extremely active during the Battle of Britain and suffered major damage from the Luftwaffe, two hangars being destroyed and three badly damaged. Also wrecked were the station workshops, sick quarters and officers' mess amongst other major damage.

From early 1941, fighter squadrons went on the offensive, the resident Spitfires operating over the Channel and Northern France. During 1941-1942 there was a degree of reconstruction, the wrecked hangars being replaced temporarily by 16 Blister hangars dispersed around the airfield. The station was extended to the south-east and west with two runways built, the longest being 5,850ft/1,783m, and the taxiways were extended. Tangmere was a key 2nd TAF station in the build-up for D-Day, Typhoons being joined by Canadian squadron Spitfires who were tasked with the destruction of the *Noball* sites, the codename for the V1 launching ramps. With the invasion of Europe, the aircraft gradually moved out as advances were made in France, the last combat units departing at the end of August. In October 1945, a refurbishment programme was started with three 'T2' hangars erected on the bases of the original hangars, and the Blister hangars were removed. The High Speed Flight was formed on 14 June 1946 at Tangmere with specially modified Meteor IVs flown by Group Capt Donaldson and Squadron Leaders Waterton and Duke, Donaldson achieving a new speed record of 616 mph/991 km/h. The following month 1 Squadron began to re-equip with Meteor IIIs, and was joined by 222 Squadron to form the Tangmere Wing, with 85 Squadron responsible for night defence. In April 1947, 266 Squadron replaced 85 Squadron, 266 being renumbered 43 Squadron in February 1949. Neville Duke returned to Tangmere in August 1953 with the red prototype Hunter, and on 7 September, raised the air speed record to 727.63 mph/1,171 km/h, the equivalent of Mach 0.92 at sea level. The Meteors were replaced with Hunters which in turn were replaced with Signals, Canberras and Varsities in August and September 1958. The flying units moved out in late 1963 and the station was finally closed on 16 October 1970, the site being sold in 1979. The three 'T2' hangars were used for grain storage and many of the other buildings were demolished to make room for commercial buildings, the runways being removed and the airfield returned to agriculture. An aviation connection remains with the Tangmere Military Aviation Museum, which amongst other aircraft houses the Meteor and Hunter speed-record holders.

Hurricane I L2124 SD-H of 501 Squadron at Tangmere being prepared by ground crewmen in the autumn of 1940. *(RAF Museum)*

June 1925, the first unit to arrive being 43 Squadron in December 1926 from Henlow. In February 1927, they were joined by the newly reformed 1 Squadron, both units being equipped with Gamecocks, which were progressively replaced by Siskins and the Hawker Fury over the next 11 years. Three double and one single Warren Truss girder hangars provided accommodation for the aircraft, in addition to a long non-standard hangar.

Modernisation of the station began in 1937 with new station workshops, MT building and barracks and the grass surface of the landing ground was replaced by two runways although these were not completed until the autumn of 1939. No 1 Squadron went to France in August 1939, 92 Squadron formed at the station with Blenheim Fighters and 43 Squadron moved to Acklington in November, leaving 501 and 605 Squadrons in residence for the first winter of the war. From July 1940, the Tangmere squadrons consisted variously of 1, 43, 145 and 601, who were providing some protection for the coastal convoys leading up to the direct attacks on Britain by the Luftwaffe from 8 August onwards. On this day, 145 Squadron in particular achieved many successes against the raiders, with additional victories scored by 43 and 601 Squadrons. On the same day the satellite at Westhampnett was made operational and became the home for 145 Squadron.

At 13.00 hrs on Friday 16 August, the station was the target for a large force of Ju 87s. Although many were intercepted before reaching the airfield, enough got through to inflict serious damage in a very short time. Two hangars were destroyed and the other three damaged while the station workshop and fire hydrant pump-house received direct hits. Severe damage was caused to the Officers' Mess and sick quarters, and an air-raid shelter received a direct hit. Aircraft destroyed or damaged included seven Hurricanes and six Blenheims. The pilot of one Hurricane from 601 Squadron, Pilot Officer Billy Fiske, crash-landed his burning Hurricane on the airfield and died the following day from his wounds. (Fiske was possibly the first American volunteer airman to die in the Battle of Britain and was to be the subject of a proposed Tom Cruise movie.) Despite considerable damage to the landing area, the remaining Hurricanes of 43 and 601 Squadrons returned safely and Tangmere was never out of operation for a single hour. During the Battle of Britain, 17, 213, 602 and 607 Squadrons operated from Tangmere, and in early 1941, the Tangmere Wing was formed to go on the offensive across the continent. Three new hangars were built and the runways extended for the jet age until final closure on 16 October 1970 when most of the site was returned to agriculture and the runways removed. Now the only aviation connection is the excellent Tangmere Military Aviation Museum.

Two miles north-west of Tangmere was the satellite of Westhampnett, now better known as Goodwood. The airfield at Westhampnett

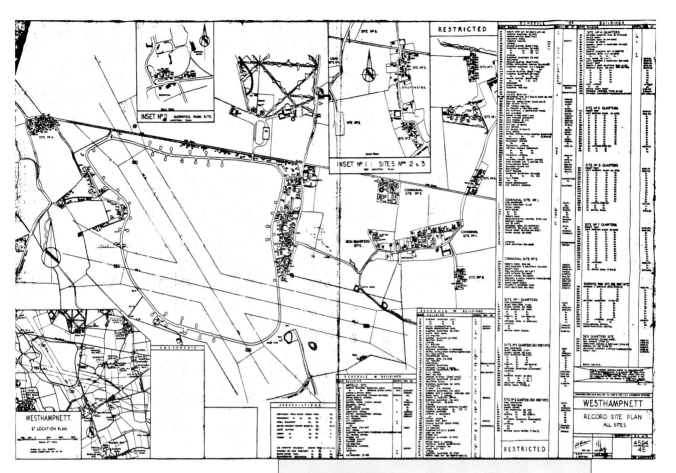

began its existence as an emergency landing ground for Tangmere, but during the month of July 1940, it was developed into a full satellite accommodating its own squadron. The landing ground was of a grass surface with tarmac perimeter track. Aircraft were sheltered in blister hangars and air and ground crew accommodation was initially under canvas until the erection of barracks and Nissen huts, the Officers' Mess being located in a nearby manor house. As already mentioned in the account of Tangmere, the first unit to take up residence was 145 Squadron with Hurricanes, and was tasked with flying daily on convoy protection patrols during the month of July. 145 Squadron's greatest day was on 8 August when during three separate actions they destroyed seven Ju 87s and four Bf 109s, with five Ju 87s and two Bf 110s damaged. This was not without a high cost as five of the squadron pilots were lost over the Channel. The shattered remains of the squadron returned to Westhampnett and congratulatory telegrams

WESTHAMPNETT

AP.17: SU875075, two miles north-east of Chichester, West Sussex, off the A285.

The airfield was first opened as a satellite to Tangmere in July 1940 and had a grass landing area with a paved perimeter track around the boundary giving access to dispersals. The main camp was located on the eastern boundary and the first residents were Hurricanes of 145 Squadron, which operated as part of the Tangmere Wing during the Battle of Britain. Nissen huts replaced the original tented accommodation and Blister hangars gave some protection for aircraft maintenance and repair. No 302 (Polish) Squadron arrived on 23 November 1940 for a short period to return in early 1941, joining 601 Squadron on coastal patrols and escort for daylight raids over France and Belgium. There followed short stays by a number of Spitfire squadrons, the last of which departed on 25 September 1944. Westhampnett reopened for flying in July 1945 with the arrival of the Naval Air Fighting Development Unit from Tangmere, which stayed until 27 November, and the site was closed on 13 May 1946. The perimeter track was then converted into the Goodwood motor racing track and flying operations returned in 1958 from a grass airfield, with new buildings erected on the old RAF technical site for general aviation.

Westhampnett from the air, showing the two grass take-off and landing strips connected by a concrete perimeter track, now used for racing cars.
(RAF Museum)

were received from the Secretary of State for Air, the Chief of the Air Staff, and Air Vice-Marshal Keith Park in addition to a personal visit by HRH the Duke of Gloucester.

Three days later 145 Squadron joined other units in a battle with 100-plus hostiles approaching Portland naval base. Four Hurricanes were lost with two of the pilots bailing out. The following day saw more action against some 150 hostile aircraft which attacked the Royal Naval Dockyard at Portsmouth and three more pilots were lost in the Channel. On 14 August, the remaining four pilots of 145 Squadron were replaced by 602 (City of Glasgow) Squadron equipped with Spitfires. On 16 August, when Tangmere was heavily bombed, 602 flew in the defence of the parent station attacking the Bf 109 escorts, leaving the

home-based units to deal with the Stukas.

On 18 August, the Luftwaffe attempted raids on the FAA bases at Ford and Gosport and the RAF Coastal Command base at Thorney Island, with a fourth formation heading towards the radar station at Poling. The squadrons were alerted in plenty of time and were patrolling above their bases ready to face 85 Ju 87s and 25 Ju 88s, escorted by two groups of Bf 109s. The Ju 88s successfully carried out an unopposed attack on Gosport before returning to France. However, the remaining raids faced strong opposition with 234 Squadron Spitfires concentrating on the escorts while 152, 601 and 602 Squadrons attacked the vulnerable Stukas. A total of 18 were shot down, making it the last appearance of the type over Britain. Squadron 602 claimed four destroyed and four damaged for the loss of one Spitfire that successfully ditched. Westhampnett was never bombed by the Luftwaffe and 602 remained based there until December 1940, the replacement units taking up the offensive. The final military use of the airfield was to accommodate fighter units in support of D-Day, and after September 1944, all combat operations ceased at the satellite.

However, the landowner, the Duke of Richmond and Gordon, who was a keen motor racing enthusiast, recognised the value of two and a half miles of surfaced perimeter track and on Saturday 18 September 1948, the Goodwood Circuit was opened. However, with the increased performance of racing cars, the track closed in 1965, although it is still used for driver training and development. In 1958, aviation returned to the site in the form of training and general flying which continues to this day, many of the surviving RAF buildings still remaining amongst the new structures.

STANFORD TUCK

Wing Commander Roland Robert Stanford Tuck took over 257 Squadron in September 1940 with the task of returning the squadron to an effective fighting unit after it had suffered major losses in the battle. Bob Stanford Tuck joined the RAF on a short service commission in 1935 and following flying training joined 65 Squadron in September 1935. He remained with the squadron until May 1940 when he was posted to Spitfire-equipped 92 Squadron at Croydon as a flight commander. His first combat experience was over Dunkirk on 23 May 1940 when he claimed three victories against German fighters with two bombers destroyed the following day. His score continued to increase over the next two weeks, resulting in the award of a Distinguished Flying Cross (DFC) by HM King George VI at Hornchurch on 28 June.

In June 1941, Tuck was shot down over the English Channel and was fortunate to be rescued by a Gravesend coal barge. In July 1941, he was promoted to Wing Commander and led the Duxford Wing on fighter sweeps across France. After a tour of the USA, he was posted to Biggin Hill as Wing Leader. It was while flying an offensive sortie over northern France on 28 January 1942 that his Spitfire was hit by anti-aircraft fire, forcing him to crash-land near Boulogne where he was taken prisoner, serving the next couple of years in Stalag Luft III at Sagan. He made a number of abortive escape attempts from other POW camps and finally succeeded on 1 February 1945 where he joined the advancing Russian army and reached the British Embassy in Moscow before returning to Britain. He retired from the RAF as a Wing Commander on 13 May 1949, his final score being 27 victories with two shared destroyed and one shared unconfirmed destroyed, six probable and six and another shared damaged. Tuck continued flying as a test pilot, including working on the Canberra jet bomber, before retiring to his mushroom farm in Kent. He died on 5 May 1987 at the age of 70.

CHAPTER 5
12 GROUP AIRFIELDS

Hurricane I of 229
Squadron being refuelled
at Digby and ready for
rearming as the fabric
patches over the gun ports
have been breached.
(Imperial War Museum)

The primary stations within 12 Group in the Battle of Britain were Duxford and its satellite at Fowlmere. Both airfield sites date back to World War 1, Fowlmere being the oldest, built early in 1917 as a landing ground for 75 (Home Defence) Squadron. Visiting the two sites today it is difficult to appreciate that both airfields were almost identical in layout with three double Warren Truss girder hangars and a single hangar between two of the pairs. Although Duxford exists almost as it was conceived, Fowlmere has returned to agriculture with a World War 2 T.2 hangar and a private airstrip. Both stations opened in March 1918 before they had been completed and the first flying units were 31 and 35 Training Depot Stations, but within seven months the war was over and both airfields were more concerned with the demobilisation of squadrons returning from Europe. At the end of March 1920, Fowlmere was put up for disposal and five years after the site

development had commenced, the buildings were demolished and the site cleared, leaving no trace of its past occupancy.

Fortunately Duxford was selected as a post-war training station with 2 FTS opening in May 1920. However, 2 FTS moved to Digby and three new fighter squadrons – 19, 29 and 111 – took up residence. In 1928 both 29 and 111 Squadron departed, leaving 19 Squadron as the resident unit. They were progressively equipped with Grebes, Siskins and Bulldogs and became the first to introduce the Gloster Gauntlet in 1935. With the formation of 12 Group Fighter Command with its HQ at Watnall in 1937, Duxford became the most southerly base in the Group.

Probably the most significant date in Duxford's history was 4 August 1938 when Jeffrey Quill delivered the first Spitfire to 19 Squadron. By the end of the year both 19 and 66 Squadrons were fully equipped with the new fighter, their initial duties to undertake trials of

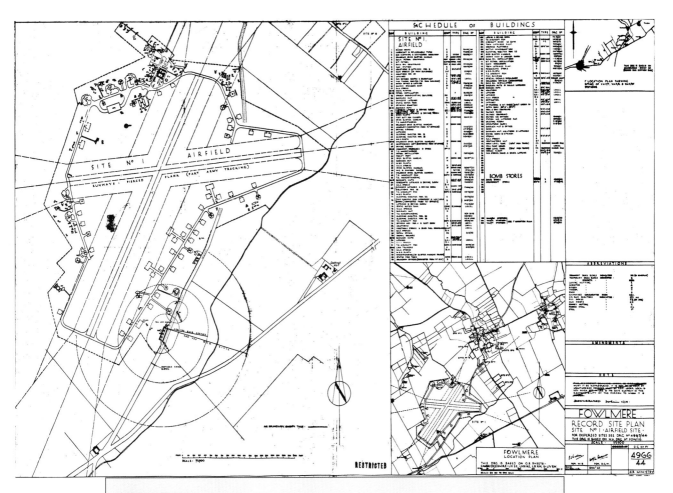

FOWLMERE

AP.19: TL415440, by the B1368, four miles north-east of Royston.

Fowlmere, first opened in 1918, was built in an identical pattern to nearby Duxford. Like Duxford it was used by American squadrons from March 1918, the last units departing in February 1919. The original plans for the station had been as a flying training base but with the reduction in the RAF after the end of World War 1, Fowlmere was closed in 1922, the buildings demolished and the site cleared in 1923. A second Fowlmere on a different site was prepared as a Duxford dispersal site which came into use in the spring of 1940; some of 19 Squadron Spitfires were based there in July. The airfield continued to be used during the Battle of Britain to accommodate squadrons which were part of the 12 Group Wing. After the battle, Fowlmere was generally located too far from offensive operations but was used for the forming up of new units. From March 1943 improvements were made to the base with a pair of PSP metal runways laid, a concrete perimeter track built with fighter dispersals and a T.2 hangar on the technical site. This configuration is shown in the plan.

In April 1944, P-51B Mustangs of the USAAF 339th Fighter Group flew their first operation on 30 April, providing forward support for US fighter-bombers attacking targets in France. Earlier Mustangs were gradually replaced by P-51Ds with 8th AF bomber escort duties being the main task. The 339th's final sortie was on 21 April 1945 and the unit began to wind down until the last personnel left for home in October 1945. On 15 October the USAF returned the airfield to the RAF and in January 1946, it was put up for disposal, although it was not sold until 1957. The site is still used by light aircraft and the T.2 hangar survives, having been reclad.

new systems, and by September 1939, both squadrons were ready for war. Because of the distance from the coast, both squadrons deployed in turn to advanced airfields at Watton and Horsham St Faith operating convoy protection patrols.

Early in February 1940, Flying Officer Douglas Bader was posted to 19 Squadron, having been discharged from the RAF at Duxford seven years previously as permanently unfit after a flying accident in which he lost both legs. In March, 222 Squadron began to exchange its Blenheims for Spitfires, Bader joining them as a flight commander, but they moved in May and were replaced by 264 Squadron flying Defiants. On 26 May, 19 Squadron claimed 13 enemy aircraft over Dunkirk for the loss of four pilots, including the Commanding Officer Squadron Leader Geoffrey Stephenson, who was taken prisoner. 66 Squadron ended its four-year association with Duxford when it moved to Coltishall in May and in the next month 19 Squadron moved to the newly opened satellite at Fowlmere with basic facilities and a grass surface landing area. At the same time, 19 Squadron was the first unit to be equipped with the more effective cannon-armed Spitfire, although early teething problems made the aircraft practically non-operational during the early stages of the Battle of Britain.

The first Hurricanes arrived at Duxford in July with the formation of 310 (Czech) Squadron, crewed by pilots who had fled the Nazis and were eager for revenge. The Czech pilots replaced the 264 Squadron Defiants.

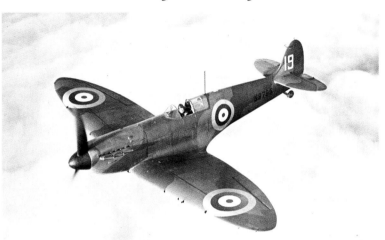

Above: Spitfire I K9795 of 19 Squadron which operated from Fowlmere close to Duxford in October 1938. Note the early-style roundels and the squadron number on the fin. (*Vickers via BAE Systems*)

Right: Early Spitfire Is lined up at Fowlmere in 1938 when it was not necessary to disperse them due to anticipated enemy action. (*Vickers via BAE Systems*)

Although mainly a 11 Group unit, three 92 Squadron Spitfire Is are ready for take-off from Fowlmere. *(Unknown copyright via BAE Systems)*

Being some distance from the frontline, Duxford did not see much action until the third phase of the Battle of Britain when the Luftwaffe attacked the 11 Group sector stations. By the end of August, Douglas Bader, now a squadron leader, was Commanding Officer of 242 Squadron which moved from Coltishall to Duxford, joining 19 and 310 Squadrons. On 30 August, 242 Squadron claimed 12 enemy aircraft that attacked North Weald for no losses.

It was unfortunate that Douglas Bader did not possess the experience of the air fighting and control in 11 Group, as without this knowledge he devised the 'Big Wing' and persuaded Air Vice-Marshal Leigh-Mallory to let him organise the Duxford squadrons to mount mass attacks against the Luftwaffe. The initial formation of the Wing was 19, 310 and 242 Squadrons, with Bader leading. By this time, 19 Squadron had reverted to machine-gun armament as the cannons were not fully developed. The problem with the 'Big Wing' was that it took too long to form up, especially with a mix of Spitfires and Hurricanes, and while waiting to create the 'Balbo', or massed formation, aircraft were draining valuable fuel, thereby reducing their fighting time. In addition, by the time the fighters had arrived in the combat sector, the Luftwaffe had bombed their targets and were on their way home.

The Duxford Wing was not effective until 9 September (by which time the Luftwaffe had switched its attention to the bombing of London) when it claimed 20 enemy aircraft destroyed for the loss of four Hurricanes and two pilots. However, this high claim was difficult to confirm following the battle. On the strength of this engagement, two more squadrons were added to the Wing, making it even more unwieldy, these being the second Polish squadron, 302, with Hurricanes and 611 Squadron with Spitfires. Ready for each day's action, some 60 Hurricanes and Spitfires were dispersed around the airfields of Duxford and Fowlmere. On 15 September, the 12 Group Wing, as it had become known, went into action three times against the Luftwaffe raiders of London. The claim of the Wing at the end of the day was 42.5 victories for the loss of four RAF fighters and one Polish pilot killed.

Being remote from the battle area, neither Duxford nor Fowlmere suffered damage during the Battle of Britain although some bombs fell close to Fowlmere and a delayed-action bomb hit Duxford but was removed and exploded safely. Duxford suffered more damage during the making of *Battle of Britain* (1968) when a single-span hangar was blown up. Following RAF use, the station was handed over to the USAAF until it was returned to the RAF on 1 December 1945. A 6,000ft runway was built between 1949 and 1951 to allow the operation of jet fighters, including Meteors, Hunters and Javelins, until it finally closed on 1 August 1961. Following the making of the *Battle of Britain* movie, Duxford was taken over by the Imperial War Museum and now houses one of the largest collections of historic aircraft in the world. Meanwhile, Fowlmere returned to agriculture; the only major addition during the USAAF stay was a single T.2 hangar which still stands and has been reclad, the site being used for light aviation.

At the start of the battle, 12 Group had sector airfields as far north as South Yorkshire. In addition to Duxford and Fowlmere, commanded by Wing Commander A B Woodhall, 12 Group was commanded by Air Vice-Marshal Trafford Leigh-Mallory with the HQ situated at Watnall

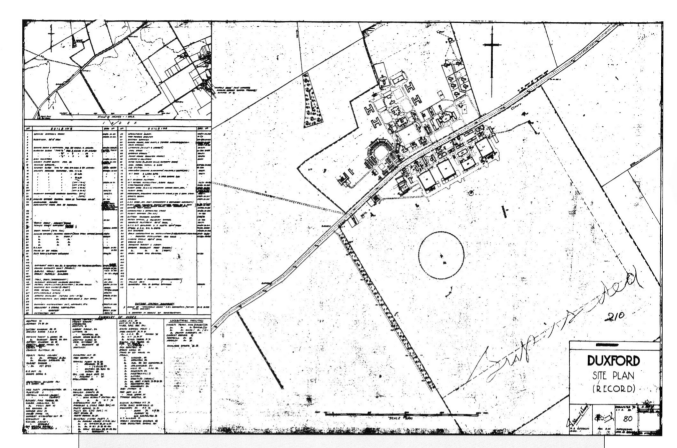

DUXFORD

AP.18: TL460460, in Cambridgeshire, seven miles east of Royston, by the A505.

Duxford opened under HQ 26 Wing on 1 March 1918, the first arrivals being 119 and 129 Squadrons, which were preparing to fight in France. Duxford was put under Care & Maintenance on 1 June 1919, but flying returned at the end of the year and construction of the single-bay and three double-bay Belfast hangars commenced on the northern boundary of the airfield, with many of the other buildings dating from the early 1920s. While the technical site was located on the south side of what is now the A505, the administration and living accommodation including the classic officers' mess were built on the north side of the road. At the entrance, the traditional guard room is on the left, facing the station HQ. After World War 1, Duxford was a flying training base. However, it became a fighter station on 1 April 1923, one of the resident units being 19 Squadron, which on 30 July 1938 became responsible for the introduction of the Spitfire into RAF service.

With the end of the Battle of Britain, Duxford was located a considerable distance from the front line and its role changed to that of operating a variety of aircraft with the Air Fighting Development Unit (AFDU). In October 1942, the USAAF 354th Fighter Squadron arrived with Bell Airacobras for a short period, to be replaced by P-47Ds of the USAAF 78th Fighter Group at the beginning of April 1943. The P-47Ds were used for long-range day bomber escort, followed by beach cover of the D-Day landings. P-51D Mustangs replaced the Thunderbolts from December 1944 until their final operation on 25 April 1945. The airfield was then put under Care & Maintenance but reopened for flying in January 1946. A metal PSP runway had been laid but was inadequate for the operation of jet fighters. In 1950, work commenced on a 2000-yard 24/06 concrete runway and Meteors arrived with 64 and 65 Squadrons in August 1951. The Meteors were replaced by Hunters with 65 Squadron in early 1957. From August 1956, 64 Squadron became a Meteor night-fighter unit and converted to Javelins from September 1958. With the reduction of Fighter Command, 65 Squadron disbanded in March 1961 and the Javelins of 64 Squadron moved to Waterbeach in July, the station closing at the end of the month. Duxford became the main flying base for the *Battle of Britain* film and is now the home of the Imperial War Museum's extensive collection of aircraft with regular flying displays during the summer season.

Top: The layout of Duxford shown in this 1918 view changed little up to World War 2 apart from additional concrete hard-standings. The single Warren Truss girder hangar was destroyed in the making of the *Battle of Britain* film and the domestic part of the station is on the other side of the main road which separates the camp. *(RAF Museum)*

Middle: A Spitfire Ia of 19 Squadron being rearmed and refuelled at Duxford. *(Imperial War Museum)*

Bottom: Hurricane I P3707 NN-A of 310 (Czech) Squadron force-landed near Duxford on 29 October 1940 after a mid-air collision with another Hurricane from the same squadron during an operational patrol.

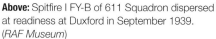

Above: Spitfire I FY-B of 611 Squadron dispersed at readiness at Duxford in September 1939. (*RAF Museum*)

Above right: Exhausted 19 Squadron pilots discuss the last sortie with the squadron intelligence officer. Left to right: S/L Lane, F/O Crastor, F/L Lawson and Sgt Lloyd. (*Imperial War Museum*)

Right: Ground crew of a 66 Squadron Spitfire I at Duxford after preparing the aircraft for flight. (*RAF Museum*)

Below: The Czech President, Dr Edvard Benes, with Squadron Leader Alexander Hess of 310 (Czech) Squadron during an official visit to Duxford on 14 December 1940.

Below right: A 310 (Czech) Squadron Hurricane I undergoing maintenance in one of the Duxford hangars in early 1941.

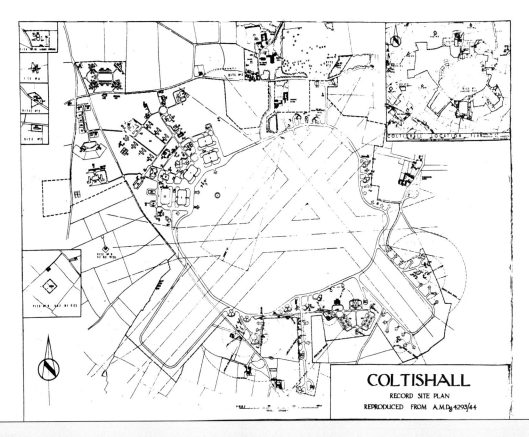

COLTISHALL
RECORD SITE PLAN
REPRODUCED FROM A.M.D₈4293/44

COLTISHALL

AP.20: TG270225, nine miles north of Norwich, Norfolk, near the B1150.

The construction of a bomber airfield began in February 1939, but before completion was designated as a fighter base. In May 1940, the first Spitfires of 66 Squadron arrived for coastal shipping protection. The main technical site was located in the north-west corner with four 'C' Type hangars and workshops, MT bay, station HQ and seven 'H' barrack blocks. The landing ground was initially grass-surfaced with a paved perimeter track giving access to dispersals including a number protected by earth banks. As the plan shows, there were later additional landing ground extensions to the south-east and south-west. Coltishall was declared a fully operational Sector Station as part of 12 Group on 23 June 1940, by which time the remnants of 242 Squadron were in residence from France and Squadron Leader Douglas Bader was given the task of commanding and rebuilding the unit. The station was largely out of range of the Battle of Britain until the squadrons were involved in the 12 Group 'Big Wing' operations from Duxford, which usually consisted of up to 72 fighters from six squadrons. During the Battle of Britain, the resident squadrons were responsible for the defence of Norwich against enemy bombing, the station also being hit from time to time. By the end of 1940, Coltishall squadrons had claimed 83 enemy aircraft destroyed.

Night fighting duties began at Coltishall with Defiants of 151 Squadron arriving in March 1941, a role which was a speciality for nearly 30 years. Offensive operations commenced in June 1941, but the distance of the airfield from the enemy required landings at advanced airfields both out and return for refuelling, a process which continued throughout the war. Also in 1941, an ASR flight was formed due to the close proximity of the station to the North Sea, the crews being kept busy recovering downed airmen. In mid-1943, Summerfield track runways were laid due to the high usage of the landing area, and in the closing months of the war 307 (Polish) Squadron arrived at Coltishall with Mosquito NF.30s, to be joined by Mustangs of 303 and 316 (Polish) Squadrons. In peacetime the station continued its night fighting role, initially with Mosquitos, and a concrete runway was laid from November 1949, being completed by September 1950. No 23 Squadron re-equipped with Vampire night fighters in the summer of 1951 and Meteor night fighters equipped 141 Squadron from July. The improved Venom night fighters replaced the earlier aircraft, and in 1957, both squadrons received Javelins, which remained until March 1963 when the night fighting role ceased. Extensive improvements were made to the station in preparation for the arrival of Lightnings, the first being delivered to 74 Squadron on 2 August 1960. When 74 Squadron moved to Leuchars, 226 OCU arrived on 20 April 1964 as the Lightning training unit to be replaced by Jaguars in 1974, the first unit being 54 Squadron in early August 1974, followed by 6 and 41 Squadrons. The station remained with Jaguars until their premature withdrawal and the closure of the station. The base is now used for commercial development and includes a prison.

near Nottingham. From north to south the
sector airfields were Church Fenton,
commanded by Group Captain C F Horsley;
Kirton-in-Lindsey, commanded by Wing
Commander S H Hardy; Digby, commanded by
Wing Commander I Parker; Wittering,
commanded by Wing Commander Harry
Broadhurst; and Coltishall, commanded by
Wing Commander Beisiegel.

Coltishall in Norfolk was originally intended
to be a bomber base with construction starting in
1939 to a more economic design and
construction than the earlier permanent RAF
bases. The main aircraft accommodation was

four C Type hangars, instead of the regular five,
and in May 1940, with increased build-up of
enemy activity against shipping in the Channel,
the decision was made to allocate the base to 12
Group Fighter Command. Although
construction was still underway, the first unit was
66 Squadron with Spitfires using the airfield as a
forward base from 29 May 1940. On 20 June
1940, the remnants of 242 Squadron had arrived
at Coltishall from France, and their new
Commanding Officer was Squadron Leader
Douglas Bader. There was a certain element of
surprise from the battle-weary pilots at being
commanded by a 'legless' pilot, but Bader soon

Right: Pilots of 257
(Burma) Squadron at
Coltishall in January 1941
with the Commanding
Officer, Bob Stanford
Tuck, on the right.
(Imperial War Museum)

demonstrated his powerful leadership capabilities. The station officially opened for combat operations on 23 June and 66 Squadron arrived in full strength on 10 July.

The first enemy action against Coltishall was on 19 August when a He 111 emerged from clouds without warning and dropped six bombs on an unfinished hangar. No 66 Squadron took the challenge and claimed the raider. With its location in the north of East Anglia, Coltishall did not see much action until the launch of the Big Wings, by which time 242 Squadron had moved to Duxford with their Hurricanes and 66 Squadron moved to Kenley on 3 September. No 616 Squadron arrived at Coltishall from Kenley on 3 September and was replaced by 74 Squadron on 9 September, the latter unit joining the 12 Group Wing operating from Duxford. On 20 October, 72 Squadron arrived at Coltishall and a week later another He 111 bombed and strafed the base, but was shot down by ground defences, the final enemy attack being on 8 November when 11 bombs were dropped, damaging the watch office. Following the Battle of Britain, the Coltishall squadrons went on the offensive, and despite being destined as a bomber base, Coltishall retained the fighter role into the jet age, finally ending its days as a RAF base for the Jaguar strike fighter. When the Jaguar was withdrawn from service, Coltishall was declared ineffective and closed on 1 April 2006 with vacation by the RAF on 1 November the same year. The site now includes a prison and residential development.

Wittering, close to the A1 road, three miles south of Stamford, was first used for military aviation in December 1916 when it was the home of A Flight of 38 Home Defence Squadron flying Fe.2bs. At this time the base was known as Stamford and also was designated as No.1 Training Depot Station until May 1919. At the end of 1919, the site became a storage depot until being put under care and maintenance in January 1920. Following the defence reviews of the early 1920s, the base was designated as RAF Wittering in May 1924 as the new home of the Central Flying School (CFS). Reconstruction began when the first sections of the CFS arrived on 21 July 1926 from Upavon. However, Wittering was designated as a Fighter Sector station and the CFS completed its move back to Upavon on 2 September 1935. In the interim 11 FTS formed at Wittering on 1 October 1935, pending the fighter expansion programme, and left on 13 May 1938. Aircraft accommodation was one 1917 hangar to be retained and three C Type hangars to be erected, as well as a number of other support buildings and personnel accommodation.

On 16 May 1938, 23 Squadron with Demons arrived and were joined two days later by 213 Squadron's Gauntlets, which moved in from Church Fenton. While 23 Squadron temporarily re-equipped with Blenheim Fighters armed with four machine guns in a belly fairing, the first Hurricanes were delivered to 213 Squadron on 16 January 1939 with a full establishment of 16 aircraft received by 3 March. With mobilisation ordered on 3 September 1939, 213 Squadron detachments were moved forward to West Raynham to be better placed for convoy patrols off Norfolk. On 8 October, 610 Squadron joined 213 on convoy patrols. After a quiet winter period, flying increased at Wittering with the arrival of a detached flight of 264 Squadron equipped with Defiants and 610 Squadron moved to Prestwick on 4 April 1940. On 7 April, 266 Squadron arrived to replace 610 and joined the convoy patrol duties three days later.

With the start of the German advance into France and the Low Countries, a flight of 213 Squadron was despatched to France on 16 May, soon followed by the remaining squadron Hurricanes joining 3 and 79 Squadrons. After evacuating to Manston and then Biggin Hill to help provide cover for the evacuation of the BEF at Dunkirk, they returned to Wittering on 31 May. A move was made by 213 Squadron to Exeter in 10 Group on 18 June. Bombs were dropped in the area of Wittering at night on 18/19 June, 25 June and 26 June without damage and four He 111s were shot down.

During the battle, Wittering was too far north to be able to participate directly, but the squadrons could provide reinforcement support to 11 Group where 266 Squadron moved on 12 August. As a replacement, 74 Squadron, whose Commanding Officer was South African 'Sailor' Malan, arrived for a rest from operations. On 21 August, 66 Squadron returned from Hornchurch and 74 Squadron moved further north to Kirton-in-Lindsey, while 23 and 229 Squadrons were dispersed to the satellite at Easton. Despite the distance from the battle, the Wittering squadrons remained on readiness to

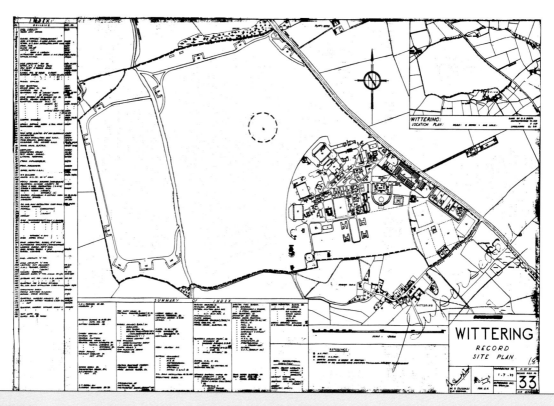

WITTERING

AP.21: TF045025, in Cambridgeshire, three miles south-east of Stamford, by the A1 Great North Road.

Wittering, initially known as Stamford, was first used by the RFC in December 1916 for home defence, the camp being located in the south-east corner alongside the Great North Road. At the end of 1919, the station became a storage depot until placed under Care & Maintenance in January 1920. Following a defence review in the 1920s, improvements were made with new buildings for the Central Flying School (CFS) to start the move into what was now named Wittering in May 1924. The station then had two World War 1 hangars but improvements to the site included new station HQ, sergeants' mess and four 'H' barrack blocks, officers' mess, married quarters and the guard room located by the A1. Aircraft accommodation was provided by three 'C' Type hangars arranged in a semi-circle, replacing the earlier structures. The training role continued until April 1938, when the station was allocated to Fighter Command as an operational base, with further improvements including a concrete perimeter track with ten dispersals. On 16 January 1939, 213 Squadron took delivery of the first of 16 Hurricanes, which shared the airfield with Blenheims of 23 Squadron. The major duty of the resident units was east coast patrols on convoy protection as the station was too far from the action to participate directly in the Battle of Britain without moving to forward airfields. On 14 March 1941, a German bomber dropped six 250kg bombs and 100 incendiaries which badly damaged a hangar and other parts of the station as well as setting another hangar and two barrack blocks on fire. Five men died and 15 were injured.

With the end of the battle, Wittering contributed to offensive operations from forward bases, but retained its night flying role. In another bombing raid on 7 May, five were killed and ten injured, with two more attacks the next day, another on 9 May and the last on 10 May. The station night fighters were able to make a number of claims against the raiders to compensate for the loss of life and damage. On 6 April 1942, the first Mosquito NF.II arrived for 151 Squadron and operations began on 29 May. In August 1944, Wittering became the centre of advanced fighter training, which was to result in the formation of the Central Fighter Establishment (CFE) in October, the station then being taken over by Flying Training Command in March 1945. Runways had been laid in 1941, but with the end of World War 2, it was decided to extend the airfield for jet operations, which included that of nearby Colly Weston airfield, a new runway being built for Fighter Command to return on 1 May 1946. Wittering was designated as a bomber base in 1950 when the runway was strengthened and a 'Gaydon' type hangar erected to replace the central damaged structure. Bomber Command took over in 1953, starting with Lincolns, followed by Canberras and 138 Squadron with Valiant V-Bombers arrived in July 1955. The Valiants were withdrawn due to metal fatigue by the end of September 1962. The replacement Victor V-Bomber was entering service with the formation of 139 Squadron in February 1962, later to operate the Blue Steel-armed Victor B.2s with both 139 and 100 Squadrons. Victors were withdrawn from the bomber role at the end of 1968 and converted as flight refuelling tankers. On 18 July 1969, 1 Squadron arrived with Hunters in preparation for the forming of the Harrier 233 OCU in October 1970, and the station continues the Harrier training task with the developed versions now in service with the Joint Harrier Force.

suppress enemy attacks within 11 Group. The long-overdue replacement of 266 Squadron's early Spitfires with Mk.IIs was achieved; they went into action on 7 September. On 9 September, 229 Squadron moved to Northolt to be replaced by 1 Squadron for a rest, but remained ready for action providing rear support for Duxford on 15 September. From November, the Wittering squadrons became part of the 12 Group Wing starting offensive patrols across occupied Europe.

Wittering's first runway was built in 1941. With the end of the war in Europe the station became the quietest it had been since the 1920s, allowing the runway to be extended for jet operations and including the nearby airfield of Colly Weston where a new runway was built in 1945-46. Following a brief period as a training airfield, Wittering was again taken over by Fighter Command with late-mark Spitfires and night fighter Mosquitos until Flying Training Command returned on 20 February 1948. On 6 April 1950 Wittering was earmarked as a bomber station. Bomber Command took over in 1953 and the first Lincolns arrived in early August, soon to be replaced by Canberra jet bombers of 76 Squadron which arrived on 12 December 1953, later to be joined by 40, 100 and 61 Squadron Canberras to form the Wittering Wing. This stage was relatively brief as

Wittering was selected as a V-Bomber base that required further development and the last Canberras of 100 Squadron left on 1 September 1959 when the unit was disbanded. In July 1955, the Valiants of 138 Squadron arrived from Gaydon, but due to metal fatigue in the wing spars the bombers were withdrawn and replaced by Victor B.2s armed with Blue Steel standoff missiles. Wittering is now home to RAF Harriers of 233 OCU under the control of Cottesmore, where the Joint Force Harrier is based with two RAF and two FAA squadrons, some having participated in the war in Afghanistan.

In Lincolnshire, the Sector Station of Digby, ten miles south of Lincoln, was commanded by

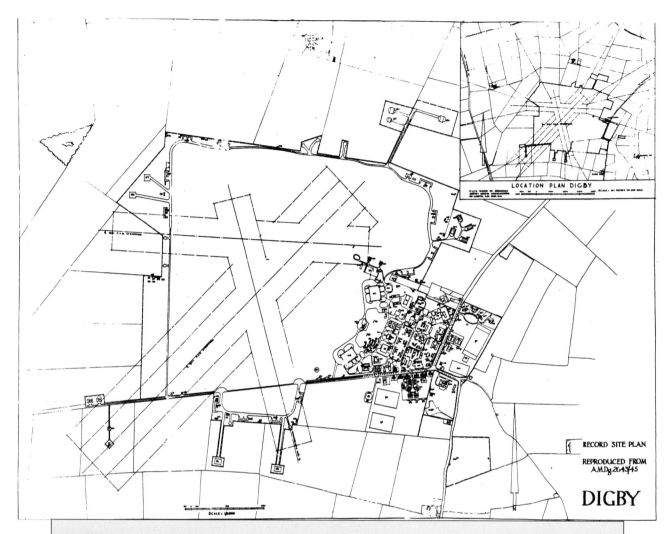

DIGBY

AP.22: TF045570, ten miles south-east of Lincoln, west of the B1191.

Initially known as Scopwick, the airfield was opened in March 1918 as a satellite to the RN Air Service Training School at Cranwell and construction commenced on one single and three double Belfast hangars, plus single-storey barracks, messes and other accommodation. These were completed in October 1918, although the airfield had been officially opened on 28 March. The base continued in the training role and was renamed RAF Digby in July 1920. Digby was placed under Care & Maintenance in 1922 but returned to training use in June 1924, following which there was further development of the station with expansion of the airfield and the building of married quarters. During 1935/36, the original hangars were demolished and replaced with barrack blocks, and two new 'C' Type hangars were built with space for a third between them. The technical site and main camp were located in the south-east corner of the station with provision for three grass runways. Digby was transferred to 12 Group Fighter Command and 46 Squadron with Gauntlets and 73 Squadron with Gladiators arrived in November 1937. During 1938, Hurricanes replaced the biplane fighters, and in August 1939, 504 (County of Nottingham) Squadron Royal Auxiliary Airforce arrived, the duties being local fighter defence and convoy patrols. During the Battle of Britain, there were many changes of squadrons and 112 (City of Winnipeg) arrived on 11 December 1940 to become 2 Squadron RCAF, later to be joined by 1 Squadron RCAF, the pilots being trained on Hurricanes and Spitfires. These squadrons were renumbered 401 and 402 and in June 1941 409, 411 and 412 RCAF Squadrons arrived. As the tide of the air war ebbed, Digby became a training station from late 1943, leading to the formation of a RCAF Spitfire Wing that departed for operations in March 1944. In May 1945, the last Canadians left and the station reverted to RAF control. In July, Digby was allocated to Technical Training Command with some flying training from the airfield. The RAF still occupies Digby, although there are no flying activities as the station is now a signals unit.

The officers of 504 Squadron at Digby with early Hurricane Is. (*RAF Museum*)

Wing Commander Ian Parker and at the start of the Battle of Britain housed 46 Squadron with Hurricanes, 611 Squadron with Spitfires, and 29 Squadron with Blenheim fighters.

RAF Digby first opened as a bomber station on 28 March 1918, then known as RAF Scopwith, although it had been used as a satellite to Cranwell from late 1917. After the armistice in 1918, the airfield was used for flying training from 1920 until 1937, apart from between 1922 and 1924 when it was under care and maintenance. It was named RAF Digby in April 1920. In August 1937, the training role was transferred out and preparations were made for the airfield to become a Sector Station in 12 Group Fighter Command ready for the arrival of 46 and 73 Squadrons equipped with Gauntlets and Gladiators. 73 Squadron re-equipped with Hurricanes in July 1938, followed by 46 Squadron in February 1938 and 504 (County of Nottingham) Squadron joined them on 27 August 1939, also equipped with Hurricanes, although they stayed only until 9 October.

The Spitfires of 611 (County of Lancashire) Squadron became long-term residents on 10 October staying until 14 December 1940, and 229 Squadron was formed with Blenheims in December 1939 to be used on convoy protection, but in March 1940, they were rearmed with Hurricanes and transferred to Wittering on 16 June. 46 Squadron was tasked with the defence of Norway and sailed on HMS

Glorious – initially on 14 May with a second attempt on 26 May – when ten Hurricanes landed at Bardufoss to provide cover for Narvik. With the German invasion of France, British forces were withdrawn from Norway and the Hurricanes returned to the carrier despite the pilots never having deck landed and the aircraft lacking arrester hooks. Unfortunately, this gallant action was wasted as the German battleship *Scharnhorst* sank HMS *Glorious* on 8 June 1940 with the loss of the aircraft and over 1,500 men perished. Three weeks later a number of personnel returned to Digby to reform 46 Squadron which departed for Stapleford on 1 September 1940, to be replaced by 151

Hurricanes of 46 Squadron were lifted aboard HMS *Glorious* on 25 May to participate in the defence of Norway following the German invasion. (*RAF Museum*)

Top: HM King George VI visits the pilots of 611 Squadron at Digby in the winter of 1939. *(RAF Museum)*

Middle: Spitfire I FY-Q of 611 Squadron dispersed at Digby ready to go with other Spitfires flying overhead. *(RAF Museum)*

Bottom: Pilots of 402 Squadron RCAF were still active in early 1941 at Digby and are seen running to their Hurricanes, with the ground crew ready to assist in a rapid scramble.

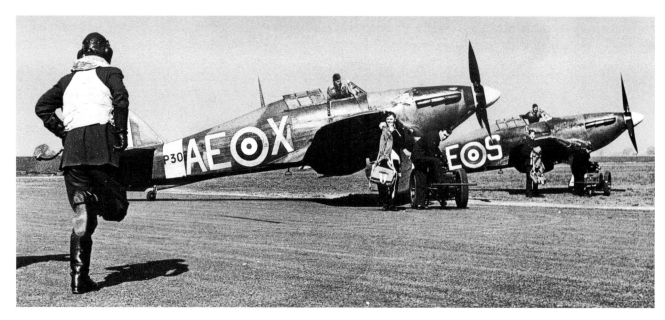

Squadron's Hurricanes. The station was not attacked during the battle due to its remoteness from the frontline, and on 11 December 1940, the first group of Canadian officers arrived to man 112 (City of Winnipeg) Squadron which was re-designated 2 Squadron (RCAF), followed by more Canadian personnel. After World War 2, Digby returned to the training role linked with the RAF College at Cranwell until 1 October 1954 when flying ceased and the station became part of 90 Group with Signals duties which continue to the present day.

Perched up on the Lincolnshire Wolds, 16 miles north of Lincoln, is the grass surface airfield of Kirton-in-Lindsey. The site was used for Home Defence squadrons from around

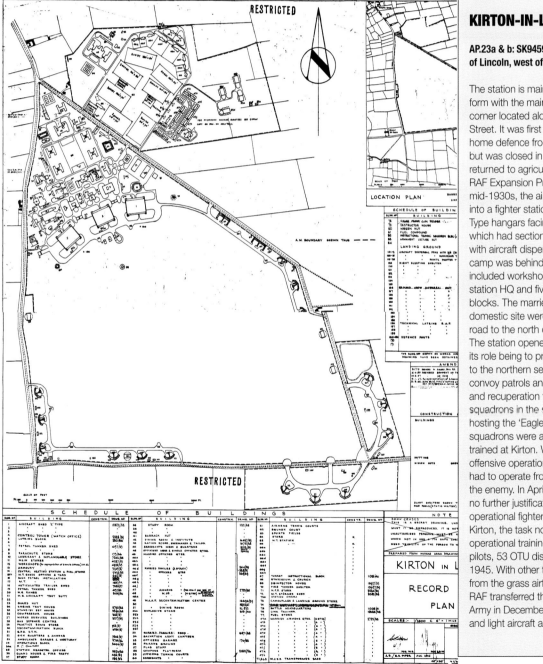

KIRTON-IN-LINDSEY

AP.23a & b: SK945972, 16 miles north of Lincoln, west of the A15.

The station is mainly triangular in plan form with the main camp in the north corner located alongside Ermine Street. It was first used for flying on home defence from December 1916 but was closed in June 1919 and returned to agriculture. During the RAF Expansion Programme in the mid-1930s, the airfield was developed into a fighter station with three 'C1' Type hangars facing a grass airfield which had sections of perimeter track with aircraft dispersals. The main camp was behind the hangars and included workshops, MT garage, station HQ and five 'H' barrack blocks. The married quarters and domestic site were across the B1400 road to the north of the camp.

The station opened in May 1940, its role being to provide fighter cover to the northern sector, undertake convoy patrols and provide rest and recuperation for the battle-weary squadrons in the south. In addition to hosting the 'Eagle' squadrons, RAAF squadrons were also formed and trained at Kirton. When tasked with offensive operations, the squadrons had to operate from bases closer to the enemy. In April 1943, there was no further justification for retaining operational fighter squadrons at Kirton, the task now changing to the operational training of Spitfire fighter pilots, 53 OTU disbanding in May 1945. With other flying training duties from the grass airfield post-war, the RAF transferred the station to the Army in December 1965, and gliders and light aircraft are still in residence.

Above: Flying Officer 'Red' Tobin, an American volunteer with 71 'Eagle' Squadron, in the cockpit of a Hurricane.

Right: Squadron Leader Peter Townsend leads 85 Squadron Hurricanes on a patrol from Kirton-in-Lindsey in late 1940. *(Imperial War Museum)*

Below: Kirton-in-Lindsey was significant as it was the base for 71 'Eagle' Squadron which was manned entirely by American volunteers before the USA came into the war. Hurricane I XR-J of 71 'Eagle' Squadron is being prepared for its next sortie. *(Imperial War Museum)*

Hurricane I V7118 UZ-V of 306 (Polish) Squadron at Church Fenton in August 1941. The Polish pilots provided a much needed resource not only for the defence during the Battle of Britain but also for the follow-on offensive operations over occupied Europe. *(Imperial War Museum)*

October 1916 as a night defence against Zeppelin raids, the last units moving out in June 1919 when the airfield was closed and returned to agriculture. However, during the RAF expansion in the 1930s, the land was re-acquired, the traditional camp being built with three C Type hangars. The station was allocated to 12 Group as a fighter base and three squadrons arrivied in May 1940, consisting of 65 and 222 with Spitfires and 253 with Hurricanes. With its remoteness from the frontline, there was regular rotation of squadrons at Kirton, providing an effective rest, recuperation and training base for the squadrons which had been in the thick of combat. After the Battle of Britain, units continued to rotate through the station, but were tasked with offensive operations over occupied Europe with fighter deployments reducing until the last departed in April 1943. The station then undertook the role of operational training until the end of the war with the OTU disbanding in May 1945. No 7 FTS arrived in April 1946 and the base carried out the flying training function in one form or another including gliders until October 1965. The RAF handed over the airfield to the Royal Artillery in December 1965, but glider flying continues, both military and civilian, at Kirton-in-Lindsey.

The most northerly sector station within 12 Group was RAF Church Fenton in Yorkshire, a few miles southwest of the city of York. It was constructed during the RAF expansion scheme as a Fighter Command sector station. The base opened in June 1937 with a grass landing area

and the first two units to arrive on the incomplete station were 72 Squadron with Gladiators on 1 June 1937 and 213 Squadron with Gauntlets on 1 July. When war broke out in September 1939, the base was transferred to 13 Group, while in August, 72 Squadron converted to Spitfires before moving out to Leconfield. In the place of 72 Squadron was a detachment of 245 Squadron and 242 Squadron reformed at Church Fenton with Hurricanes on 30 December 1939. During the first year of the war and the Battle of Britain the fighter units at the base were deployed in the defence of the east coast of Yorkshire and major towns. In May 1940, 242 Squadron moved to Biggin Hill to participate in the Battle of France and a number of other fighter squadrons passed through the station on rotation from the south of Britain. The first success claimed by a Church Fenton-based aircraft was a Ju 88 by 249 Squadron on 8 July north of Flamborough Head.

Church Fenton returned to the control of 12 Group on 10 August 1940, and on 15 August, a number of Yorkshire airfields were attacked by the Luftwaffe, 73 Squadron at Church Fenton claiming two Ju 88s. On 28 August, 306 (Polish) Squadron was formed as the first to be manned entirely by Polish nationals. 73 and 85 Squadrons exchanged places between Castle Camps and Church Fenton giving 85 Squadron a well-earned rest. On 19 September 1940, 71 Squadron formed as the first American Eagle Squadron made up of American volunteers who were keen to assist in Britain's victory before the USA entered the war. Unfortunately, the RAF was not ready for these volunteers as the only aircraft available was an unserviceable Magister trainer and some pilots left to join active regular RAF units until Brewster Buffalo fighters arrived on 25 October, though these turned out to be totally unsuitable. They were finally replaced by Hurricanes on 7 November, allowing 71 Squadron to become operational, but too late for the Battle of Britain. The main role of Church Fenton during 1940 was to support the combat squadrons in the south of Britain by providing a rest from combat and an opportunity to regroup and train new arrivals. During the remainder of the war, the station was used in the training role and night fighter operations with Beaufighters and Mosquitos, and by the beginning of 1944, the operational pace had reduced. At the end of the war Church Fenton was designated as a permanent RAF base and was one of the first to be operational with 263 Squadron Meteor jet fighters in June 1946 (the base also operated Mosquito fighter squadrons). Its role as a fighter station came to an end on 28 June 1959 when Hunters of 19 Squadron and Javelins of 72 Squadron departed for Leconfield. Church Fenton was then transferred to Training Command, duties which are still undertaken today as the base for the Yorkshire Universities Air Squadron, although some of the buildings have been demolished, including the Officers' Mess.

ADOLPH 'SAILOR' MALAN

Adolph Malan, known as 'Sailor' due to his service with Union Castle shipping line, was born in South Africa on 24 March 1910. He joined the RAF in 1935, starting his flying on 6 January 1936, and having completed his training, was posted to 74 Squadron on 20 December. He gained the rank of Pilot Officer in January 1937, followed by being made commander of A Flight, by then operating Spitfires. 74 Squadron was involved in fierce fighting over Dunkirk and was awarded the Distinguished Flying Cross (DFC) after achieving ace status with five successes. During the clear moonlit night of 19/20 June, Malan located and shot down two He.111s, being awarded a bar to his DFC. He and his colleagues abandoned the 'Vee' formation in favour of the more effective 'finger four' which had been previously adopted by the Luftwaffe.

Malan was older than most of his pilots and insisted on strict discipline. Although relaxed and sociable when off duty – he preferred to spend time with his wife and family – he would often hand over command of the squadron to an experienced colleague after the first sortie of the day to have a chance to keep up with the administration of the unit.

On 24 December Malan was awarded the Distinguished Service Order (DSO), and on 10 March 1941, was appointed leader of the Biggin Hill Wing for offensive operations across occupied Europe. He gained a bar to his DSO on 22 July 1941. In August, he finished his active combat career with 27 enemy aircraft destroyed, seven shared, two unconfirmed, three probable and 16 damaged, making him at the time the leading ace with the RAF.

In 1946, Malan left the RAF to return to South Africa where he became active in human rights, opposing the establishment of a police state, abuse of state powers, censorship, racism and other oppressive actions. Malan died in 1963 at the young age of 53 from Parkinson's disease. (RAF Museum)

DOUGLAS BADER

Group Captain Sir Douglas Bader joined the RAF as an officer cadet at the RAF College at Cranwell in 1928, making his first flight under training on 13 September. After 11 hours and 15 minutes' instruction, he went solo on 19 February 1929 and following his two-year course he was commissioned as a Pilot Officer, ready to join 23 Squadron on 26 July 1930, flying Gamecocks and Bulldogs from Kenley. Bader was an above average pilot and an outstanding sportsman in rugby and cricket.

When visiting Woodley airfield near Reading on 14 December 1931 in a Bulldog, he crashed while attempting low-level aerobatics when a wing tip hit the ground, and as a result both legs had to be amputated, one below and the other above the knee. In 1932, he was transferred to the RAF hospital at Uxbridge where with the use of artificial legs he tried to regain his former abilities, and after agonising and determined efforts he was able to drive a car, play golf and dance. His wish was to continue flying, and in June 1932, Bader flew an Avro 504 trainer and was passed fit for service. However, in April the following year, the decision was reversed by the RAF and Bader reluctantly took an office job with the Asiatic Petroleum Company, which later became Shell.

Upon the outbreak of World War 2, Bader reapplied to join the RAF. Despite some official reluctance his perseverance paid off and he passed his pilot's medical in November 1939. In February 1940, at the relatively advanced age of 29 compared to his colleagues, Bader was posted to 19 Squadron at Duxford, flying Spitfires. In April, he became a flight commander with 222 Squadron, also based at Duxford, and while on patrol near Dunkirk he claimed his first victory against a Bf 109, followed by a Do 17. After experiencing combat over Dunkirk, Bader was posted to Coltishall to command 242 Squadron which was suffering from high losses and low morale. It was Bader's job to bring them back to operational readiness, despite their reluctance to have a legless Commanding Officer. When he had succeeded in rebuilding the squadron, it was posted to become part of the Duxford Wing operating Hurricanes.

In 1941, Bader was promoted to Wing Commander as leader of the Tangmere Wing including 616 Squadron, flying Spitfire missions across France. On 9 August, he was flying a Spitfire Mk.Va over the French coast when he was shot down by a Bf 109 and taken prisoner (records suggest that Bader could have been shot down by another 616 Squadron Spitfire in error). Bader made numerous escape attempts, the Germans threatening to take away his false legs to convince him otherwise. In August 1942, Bader escaped from Stalag Luft III at Sagan, but was recaptured and on 18 August sent to Colditz Castle, where he remained until liberated by the US Army on 15 April 1945.

On his return to Britain, Bader was given the honour of leading the victory flypast over London in June 1945 and was promoted to Group Captain, leaving the RAF in February 1946. In 1976, Bader was knighted for services to the disabled and flew as a pilot for the last time on 4 June 1979, having amassed a total flying time of 5,744 hours and 25 minutes. Bader died of a heart attack on 5 September 1982 at the age of 72. *(Imperial War Museum)*

CHAPTER 6
10 GROUP AIRFIELDS

Hurricane I of 601 Squadron with F/O Whitney and ground crew at Exeter. *(RAF Museum)*

With its headquarters in Rudloe Manor at Box, Wiltshire, 10 Group Fighter command was commanded by Air Vice-Marshal Sir Christopher Brand. No 10 Group was tasked with the defence of the southwest of England and to provide support when required to 11 Group.

Early in the Battle of Britain the situation within 10 Group was as follows. Closest to 11 Group was the grass airfield of Middle Wallop, commanded by Wing Commander David Roberts with 152 and 609 Squadrons equipped with Spitfires, 238 Squadron with Hurricanes and 604 with Blenheim night fighters. The forward satellite airfield was at Warmwell close to the south coast by Weymouth where many of the Middle Wallop units dispersed during the daylight hours. Moving west, the next Sector Station was at Filton, north of Bristol, which used Exeter as a satellite (with Group Captain Robert Hanmer as station commander) and was the base for 87 and 213 Squadrons with

Hurricanes. One of their tasks was the defence of the Bristol Aircraft and Engine Companies. In South Wales, Pembrey was the Sector Station commanded by Wing Commander J H Hutchinson and home for 92 Squadron Spitfires which moved to Biggin Hill on 9 August. The most westerly Sector Station was St Eval in Cornwall shared with Coastal Command, the Fighter Section HQ being commanded by Group Captain L G le B Croke. The main fighter units based here were 234 Squadron with Spitfires and 247 Squadron with one flight of Gladiators operating from the small grass airfield at Roborough north of Plymouth and tasked with the protection of the RN Dockyard.

RAF Middle Wallop was originally conceived as a bomber station but was initially used for flying training by 15 FTS. The landing area was surrounded by a perimeter track and five C Type hangars were built as well as the usual facilities. The station was still under

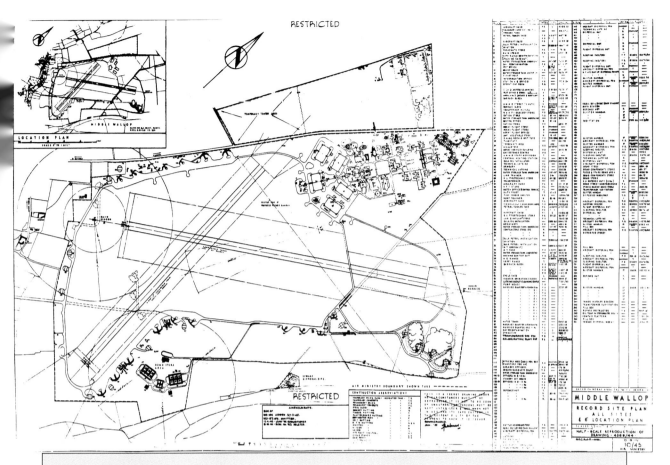

MIDDLE WALLOP

AP.24: SU305393, six miles south-west of Andover, Hampshire, by the A343.

Middle Wallop was planned as a two-squadron bomber station with a grass operational area and concrete perimeter track and dispersals. While under construction the site was transferred to 11 Group Fighter Command but the first occupation was by 15 FTS who arrived in April 1940. At that time one of five 'C' Type hangars was fit for occupation, together with stores, guard room, station HQ and three of the six 'H' block barracks. The main camp was located in the north-east corner of the station with the A343 running along the western boundary. The Hurricanes of 601 Squadron arrived by the end of May 1940 and the FTS moved out in June.

As work continued on the preparation of the station, a number of fighter units passed through and the newly formed 10 Group took over control in time for the first major assault by the Luftwaffe on 13 August. In addition to day fighter operations, 604 Squadron with AI-equipped Blenheims and Beaufighters was tasked with night fighting, led by Squadron Leader John Cunningham. His first of 20 successes was on 20 November 1940 against a Ju 88 which was the first victory with AI-fitted Beaufighters. Once fully equipped with Beaufighters 604 Squadron remained at Middle Wallop until December 1942.

From 1943, the station was used for night intruder operations across Europe, an example being 456 Squadron with Mosquito F.IIs from March, until the end of August when the USAAF moved in, the station being formally transferred to American control in January 1944. The USAAF units were responsible for photo reconnaissance of the French coastline in preparation for D-Day, with the flying units moving out on 2 July and 10 Group regaining control with two Mosquito night fighter units, mainly responsible for *Anti-Diver* patrols, the hazardous task of intercepting V1s. During September, the base was used for servicing aircraft returning from operations in France, followed by the RN who took over in February 1945 until April 1946 when the RAF returned.

Although under RAF control, the station became involved with Army Air Observation training so that it became the Army Air Corps Centre on 1 October 1958. The derelict fifth hangar was rebuilt, and in 1970, the station became the HQ of the Directorate of Army Aviation. The airfield is now used for the training of Army helicopter pilots following their basic training at Shawbury, and located on the airfield boundary is the excellent Museum of Army Flying.

Hurricane IIc BD936 ZY-S
of 247 Squadron based
at Middle Wallop on night
fighter duties after the
battle. *(Imperial War
Museum)*

Spitfire Mk.Is of 609
Squadron operated from
the grass airfield at Middle
Wallop and are ready to
scramble in the summer
of 1940. *(Unknown
copyright via BAE
Systems)*

construction when it was declared operational on 12 June 1940 with only one hangar completed and much temporary accommodation for the personnel. As 15 FTS left for Brize Norton, 601 Squadron flew its Hurricanes into Middle Wallop and the Operations Record Book was opened at 09.00 hrs on 12 June 1940. A number of squadrons rotated through the base, the squadrons mainly involved for the duration of the Battle of Britain being 234 and 238 with Hurricanes and 609 with Spitfires, while 152 Squadron with Spitfires operated from the advanced satellite at Warmwell. All the Middle Wallop squadrons used the satellite as an advanced airfield, usually flying early in the morning and returning at dusk.

The battle began in earnest on 8 August when a large convoy was attacked by a sizeable force of German aircraft off the Isle of Wight. 609 Squadron claimed three Bf 110s and two Ju 87s, and 238 Squadron claimed two Bf 110s and four unconfirmed with a loss of two pilots. For the next three weeks the battle was continuous with many attacks made against south coast targets and Middle Wallop was bombed with varying degrees of success. On 13 August, the first raid on the station was by a force of Ju 87s without Bf 109 escort as they had to return to France due to a lack of fuel. 609 Squadron shot down six of the nine dive bombers in one unit, and one Ju 88 from a larger group located Middle Wallop and dropped its bombs on a nearby village. By the end of the day the two squadrons were able to claim 18 destroyed and three probable without loss. The next day another heavy attack consisted of He 111s and Ju 88s, but only one Ju 88 bombed successfully with four hits on the 609 Squadron hangar. Three Blenheims of 604 Squadron and a number of Spitfires were destroyed. Three airmen were killed when a hangar door fell on them and three civilian contractors also died. However, a 609 Squadron Spitfire was close by and shot the Ju 88 down, making a total tally for the day of four Ju 88s and one He 111 destroyed without loss.

On 15 August, there was a further attack on the base with many near misses although two hangers were damaged with one aircraft destroyed and five damaged, but without any casualties. The defending pilots claimed 13 victories and six probables, but for the loss of one pilot killed and two posted missing. On 16 August, German heavy attacks continued but mainly on coastal targets where the bombers enjoyed the protection of Bf 109s. On this date, 249 Squadron was operating from Boscombe Down in the Middle Wallop sector and Flight Lieutenant James Nicholson attacked three Ju 88s that led to the only award of the Victoria Cross to a pilot of Fighter Command. Nicholson was leading three Hurricanes against an air-raid building up over Gosport when, as they were about to attack Ju 88s, they were bounced by Bf 109s. Two of the Hurricanes were set on fire with one pilot bailing out, but Nicholson stayed with his burning aircraft to press home his attack on a Ju 88, following which he bailed out with extensive burns to his face and hands. Both pilots were fired on by local Allied land forces as they descended by parachute, the other pilot being killed while Nicholson was further injured. After a long stay in hospital to recover from his injuries Nicholson was awarded the VC, but was later to die fighting in Asia.

There were no further attacks on Middle Wallop and by the end of the battle a squadron was dispersed to each of Boscombe Down and Chilbolton, with 152 still resident at Warmwell. Meanwhile 604 Squadron with night fighter Blenheims had been developing

On 16 August, while flying with 249 Squadron based at Boscombe Down, Flt Lt John Nicholson attacked three Ju 88s after which he bailed out of his stricken Hurricane. As a result he was awarded the Victoria Cross, the only one to a pilot in Fighter Command.

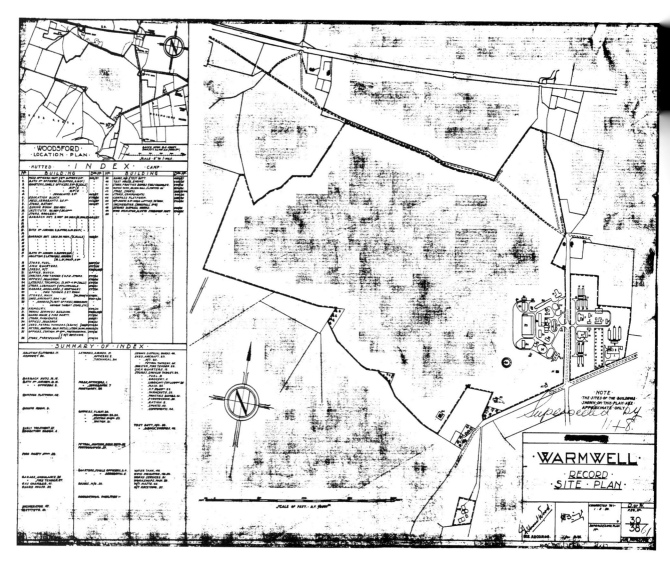

the detection of enemy night raiders using the secret Airborne Interception (AI) radar. Led by John Cunningham, known as 'Cats Eyes' Cunningham because of the security surrounding the AI equipment, the squadron re-equipped with the more potent Beaufighters during the long winter nights, and Cunningham was later to become the top scoring night fighter pilot with 20 kills.

Middle Wallop was used by the USAAF from December 1943 as part of the preparations for the invasion of Europe and the station was returned to RAF Fighter Command on 19 April 1946, reverting to the training role. On 1 October 1958, the station was formally passed to Army control and is now the training centre of the Army Air Corps

who use the grass airfield for the training of Lynx and Apache crews. It is also the home of the fine Museum of Army Flying.

Warmwell first opened in May 1937 as the home of No 6 Armament Training Camp, the landing area being grass surface, and the original hangar was later replaced by two T2 hangars. The airfield was used for air firing and summer camps by a variety of units for two years, the target area being over Chesil Beach, the resident unit becoming known as the Central Gunnery School. With the threatened invasion of Britain, Warmwell took on a more aggressive role when it was transferred to 10 Group Fighter Command and the Spitfires of 609 Squadron moved from Northolt to Middle Wallop on 4 July 1940 with 152 Squadron with Spitfires

WARMWELL

AP.25: SY760885, four miles south-east of Dorchester, Dorset.

Warmwell was opened as an armament practice camp (APC) in May 1937 and the Chesil Bank ranges used for gunnery practice. On 1 November 1939, the camp was renamed 10 Bombing & Gunnery School (B&GS) with a fleet of around 60 aircraft of many different types. On 13 November, it was re-designated as the Central Gunnery School (CGS). In March 1940, Warmwell was chosen as a forward operating base for Middle Wallop and declared operational on 4 July with 609 Squadron arriving the following day, one of the tasks being the defence of the Portland naval base. Accommodation was under canvas and coverage was reduced to a flight each day on 15 minutes' readiness. The first engagement was on 9 July when three Spitfires of B Flight were vectored on to a formation of Ju 87 Stukas with one destroyed for the loss of one Spitfire to the escorting Bf 109s; however, the attack on Portland had been broken up. No 10 Group took over Middle Wallop and Warmwell, and the B&GS moved out to make way for 152 Squadron.

Warmwell was a grass airfield; the technical site was on the eastern boundary with one hangar and a small collection of workshops and MT compound. The domestic and administration site was on the other side of a public road. The first enemy raid was on 25 August when a 30-strong formation of Ju 88s approached Warmwell: only seven got through causing damage but no casualties. 152 Squadron claimed three victories. 609 Squadron moved to Warmwell in November 1940 and were still living under canvas in miserable conditions until replaced by 234 Squadron in February 1941. With the switch to offensive operations, the CGS moved out in June and the first fighter sweep was made over France with 12 bombers and three fighter squadrons, the target being radar installations. No 175 Squadron was formed at Warmwell in March 1942 with fighter-bomber Hurricanes, joining 402 (RCAF) Squadron who also used Hurricanes for fighter ground attack operations. The base was designated USAAF Station 454 of the IXth AF in March 1944 and housed the 474th FG with three squadrons equipped with P-38 Lightnings, the task being to prepare occupied France for the planned invasion, the Group moving to France on 6 August. By mid-1945, the station was starting to run down and was reduced to Care & Maintenance. In 1952, the watch tower was converted into a large house, the domestic site becoming a housing estate and the airfield used for the extraction of gravel.

The RAF Warmwell hangars in 1938 included a 'T2' Type on the left. *(RAF Museum)*

arriving on 12 July as resident for the defence of the RN base at Portland. In the early stages of the battle, the 609 Squadron pilots had little success against overwhelming odds, losing three Spitfires and pilots for the destruction of three Ju 87s in early July, a fourth pilot being lost on 27 July. Meanwhile, the facilities at the airfield were basic and meals were served at fixed times whether the pilots were airborne or not. No 152 Squadron had a slow start with no victories in the first month despite taking part in a number of operations, but on 11 August lost its first pilot, with two more killed the next day.

On 13 August, there was a welcome change when a large raid was detected by 609 Squadron approaching the coast. The raid was estimated to consist of around 60 aircraft, comprising Ju 87s escorted by Bf 109s and followed by Bf 110s. The Bf 110s were attacked by a Hurricane squadron who were in an ideal position above the enemy at 20,000 feet. Diving down on the enemy, the Spitfires claimed 13 destroyed and six damaged with no losses. The claims continued to grow and then on 25 August, Warmwell was attacked for the first time.

During the day the two Warmwell squadrons had been in action with 152 Squadron claiming three destroyed and one probable for the loss of two pilots. Meanwhile, 609 Squadron was patrolling in the Swanage area and attacked a large enemy formation, destroying at least six aircraft for no loss to themselves. The raid on Warmwell commenced at 17.30 hrs with some 20 bombs dropped on the airfield, destroying the station sick quarters and damaging the two hangars and other buildings with some craters on the landing area. Fortunately there were no casualties. The remainder of August was relatively peaceful with some contacts with the enemy but no pilot losses. During much of September, 609 Squadron moved out of Warmwell to assist in the defence of London, while 152 remained at Warmwell in the defence of the local dockyards and gained a number of victories with help from radar at Worth Matravers near Swanage. The air battles continued throughout the month with some successes and seven victories claimed for the loss of three pilots.

Warmwell was bombed again on 1 April 1941, killing ten personnel and due to the heavy damage the station was evacuated at night except for essential defences. 152 Squadron departed on 9 April and in June, the Central Gunnery School moved in with many squadrons making use of the range facilities. Active units with ground-attack 'Hurribombers' and Typhoons moved to the airfield in November 1941, flying offensive sweeps against ground targets in occupied France. The USAAF arrived in March 1944 in the form of 474th Fighter-Bomber Group, US 9th Air Force, equipped with P-38 Lightnings in preparation for the invasion of Europe, leaving in August 1944 as the ground forces advanced across France. The airfield returned to an armament practice camp until October 1945 when the duties of Warmwell were concluded and the station reduced to care and maintenance. It was disposed of in 1973 for gravel extraction, the whole area of the airfield being excavated leaving the watch office to be converted into a residence and a housing development on the original camp area.

Filton, four miles north of the centre of Bristol, was an early aviation manufacturing site which opened in February 1910 as the British & Colonial Aeroplane Co Ltd and by November Bristol Boxkites were in production. Following the start of World War 1, the facilities were expanded considerably and the RFC used the airfield from December 1915 to form new squadrons before they went to France. After the armistice military use of the airfield reduced, although the company ran the Reserve Training School for the RAF and 501 (County of Gloucester) Squadron formed at Filton on 14 June 1929. The RAF camp was constructed on the north side of the airfield while the manufacturing activities of what had become the Bristol Aeroplane Company continued to expand on the south side of the site and up the hill. The main RAF aircraft in production when war was declared was the Blenheim and at the end of 1938, 501 Squadron was declared a fighter unit and equipped with Hurricanes. There was little action for them at Filton, so they were moved to Tangmere and replaced 263 Squadron flying Gladiator biplanes who departed for Norway in April 1940, leaving Filton without air defence.

With both production of aircraft and aero engines at Filton it was not long before the Luftwaffe started taking an interest in the site, and the first night bombing of Bristol took place on 24 June 1940, without damaging Filton. This was followed by daylight raids in

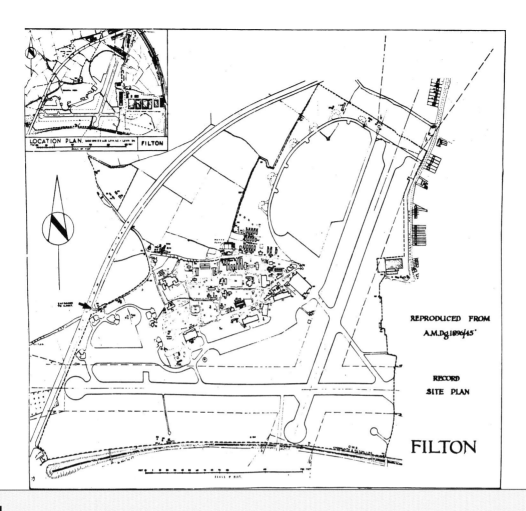

FILTON

AP.26: ST595802, four miles north of Bristol, by the A38.

Aviation first came to Filton in February 1910 when the British & Colonial Aeroplane Company began the production of Boxkites at what was later to become the Bristol Aeroplane and Engine Company. The RFC made use of the airfield from December 1915 to form and train new squadrons before they went to France. The South West Aircraft Acceptance Park was formed to process new aircraft produced by local manufacturers with 18 hangars being erected for the unit. No 501 Squadron (County of Gloucester) Royal Auxiliary Airforce was formed on 14 June 1929 as a reserve unit for local air defence equipped with Avro 504Ns. In 1930, work began on improvements to the site with new accommodation for one regular and one reserve squadron on the RAF site to the north of the airfield. The RAF camp consisted of Belfast hangars, workshops and administration and living accommodation. The Bristol Aeroplane Company factory was located on a hill on the south side with a railway line between the factory and airfield.

By the end of 1938, 501 Squadron had become a fighter unit, and in September 1939, it was merged into the regular RAF for war service. The squadron with its Hurricanes saw little action and moved to Tangmere. They were replaced by Gladiator-equipped 263 Squadron until they departed for the defence of Norway in April 1940. During World War 2, aircraft production consisted of Blenheims and Beaufighters. Following the first major bombing raid on the undefended factories on 25 September 1940 where 238 factory workers and civilians died, the RAF acted swiftly. The first RAF unit to be posted for local defence was 504 Squadron Royal Auxiliary Airforce which arrived with 17 Hurricanes the following day. No 504 Squadron left for Exeter in December 1940 and was replaced by 501, but action was slow, the unit being involved on convoy patrols until April 1941 when 263 Squadron arrived with Westland Whirlwinds. The Whirlwinds departed in August 1941, the last operational unit to be based at Filton during the war. Work began on the construction of two tarmac runways with a number of dispersals and hardstandings. In March 1946, work commenced on the construction of an 8,150ft / 2,484m lengthened and widened main runway for the flight testing of the Brabazon airliner. 501 Squadron returned the following May as a Royal Auxiliary Airforce unit until it was disbanded in February 1957. While the long main runway still exists and is used by Airbus Industrie, the remaining runway has been closed and much of it cleared for development of the land.

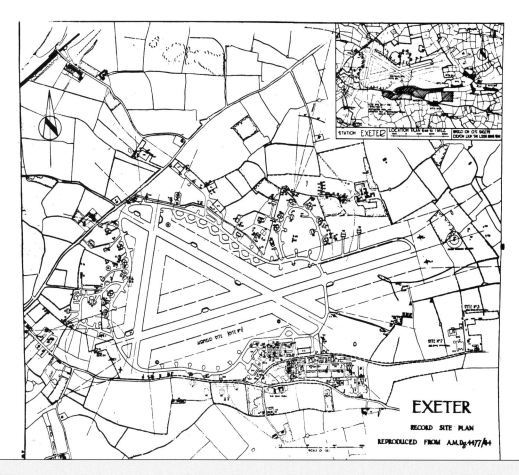

EXETER

AP.27: SY002938, four miles east of Exeter, Devon, by the A30.

Exeter Airport was first opened for commercial flying in May 1937; a terminal building was completed in 1938 and the airport formally opened on 30 July. Upon the declaration of war, civil flying ceased and the RAF took over the site as an advanced satellite for Filton with 213 Squadron arriving in June 1940, followed by 87 Squadron on 6 July when the airfield officially became RAF Exeter. The station was developed into a main fighter base with T.2 hangars on the north and south sides of the airfield, with the landing area extended to the east and north-west. Work commenced on the construction of three runways with an interlinking perimeter track incorporating aircraft dispersals.

No 601 Squadron replaced 213 in September and Whirlwinds of 263 Squadron arrived in November. During 1941, Exeter was used by a number of fighter squadrons for convoy protection while resting from other operations. The station was attacked by the Luftwaffe five times during the early part of the year, the worst damage being inflicted on 5 April with the main hangar being wrecked and 17 aircraft damaged. On 26 April, 307 (Polish) Squadron arrived bringing day and night defence to the area, but there was little contact with the enemy until November. Meanwhile, the No 2 Polish Fighter Wing was with 317 Squadron at Exeter and 302 and 316 at Church Stanton to provide defence for Exeter and the south coast ports. 307 Squadron left in April 1943, but offensive operations were operated by Typhoons over occupied France. In April 1944, the RAF was replaced by the USAAF with 45 C-47s and Hadrian Gliders for the carriage of paratroops into Normandy in the early hours of 6 June for the start of D-Day. The Americans departed on 20 November and the station was used for a number of second-line duties, and in June 1946, the Meteors of 222 Squadron arrived with the Mosquito Night Fighters of 151 Squadron. Their stay was short, leaving on 1 July, and the station was closed in October.

The airfield was reopened for civil flying on 1 January 1947. The RAF returned with Tiger Moths equipping 10 RFS from May 1949 and 3 CAACU which was civilian operated and flew Spitfires and Beaufighters, later replaced by Mosquitos, Vampire trainers and Meteors before it was disbanded at the end of 1971. Exeter Airport is now the base of Flybe, formally Jersey European, with the passenger terminal on the south side and many of the ex-RAF buildings in use by the resident companies.

July and August which were equally ineffective, but further night attacks during August caused some damage and casualties as well as interrupting production due to air-raid warnings. To reduce these delays, the company instigated its own warning system which was effective, but on 25 September, when all the employees had taken cover, two shelters received direct hits, killing 72 employees and injuring 166, of whom 19 subsequently died. Work then commenced improving the airfield with the construction of two runways, while production continued with aircraft and engines. The last attack on the site was on 11 April 1942, when a bomb destroyed an office building and a wind tunnel, fortunately without casualties. After the war the RAF presence continued when the Bristol UAS and 501 Squadron returned although disbanding followed in February 1957, along with all the other members of the RAuxAF.

When the Bristol Aeroplane Company was awarded the contract to build the Brabazon airliner in 1945, the main runway was widened and extended ready for the prototype airliner to make its maiden flight on 7 September 1949. The same runway was later used for the first flight of the Concorde supersonic airliner

on 9 April 1969, although the runway was not suitable for the full range of test flying which was undertaken from Fairford. Now only the main runway is in use with the remains of the RAF camp on the north side. The site is used by Airbus Industrie for design and development of the Airbus range of airliners, and the manufacturing activities have recently been taken over by GKN.

Exeter Airport was opened on 30 July 1938 with a grass surface which had been in use for about a year. The RAF presence was officially inaugurated on 6 July 1940 as a Filton satellite with 87 and 213 Squadrons in residence, who were later joined by 601 Squadron, all equipped with Hurricanes and all of whom operated from Exeter during the Battle of

Above: Squadron Leader Ian 'Widge' Gleed DFC, the officer commanding 87 Squadron in Hurricane I LK-A, leading the squadron from Exeter to Bibury in September 1940.

Left: Pilots of 601 Squadron relax between sorties at Exeter in muddy conditions around a Hurricane tail.

Britain. There was one enemy attack on the base, on 21 August, when bombs fell on Army tents killing two servicemen, two more who died later, and injuring a further 21. Following the end of the Battle of Britain the Fighter Command squadrons continued to provide an airborne defence of Exeter and Plymouth, the night fighters of 307 (Polish) Squadron defending during darkness, initially using Defiants, and progressing on to AI-equipped Beaufighters and later Mosquitos until April 1943 when 125 Squadron took its place. The station was bombed on two other occasions, one on 5 April 1941, when one hangar was destroyed, and again on 12 February 1942, when one of the raiders was shot down by local anti-aircraft defences. From 1941 until April 1944, a succession of Spitfire squadrons used Exeter and it became a forward base for attacks on Europe by the 9th Air Force. In April 1944, it was taken over by the USAAF to be occupied by C-47 glider tugs and Hadrians and Horsas ready for the D-Day landings in June. As the Allies advanced across Europe, the need for Exeter declined and the airfield transferred to the training role. Exeter was closed as an RAF base in July 1946 when it

reverted to commercial use, but from 1951, No 3 CAACU operated as a target facilities unit staffed by civilian personnel and operating Spitfires, Mosquitos, Vampires and Meteors over a period of time for the benefit of coastal guns. Exeter continues as a civil airport with a number of scheduled flights and is the home base for Flybe.

St Eval, above the rocky north coastline of Cornwall, is situated about six miles north-east of Newquay and was allocated to the newly formed RAF Coastal Command. As part of the RAF expansion scheme, work started on the site in 1938 and RAF personnel began to arrive at the incomplete station, which was officially opened on 2 October 1939 when the Ansons of 217 Squadron arrived from Warmwell. The aircraft were accommodated in three C Type hangars with all the usual accommodation for the personnel and operation of the station. A sector operations room was established on the station and enemy raids followed on 21 August 1940 when a hangar was destroyed. The following night the pyrotechnics store was hit causing rockets and flares to explode, creating the impression that the station had been destroyed. The defenders of St Eval at

A Spitfire Ia of 234 Squadron dispersed at St Eval. *(RAF Museum)*

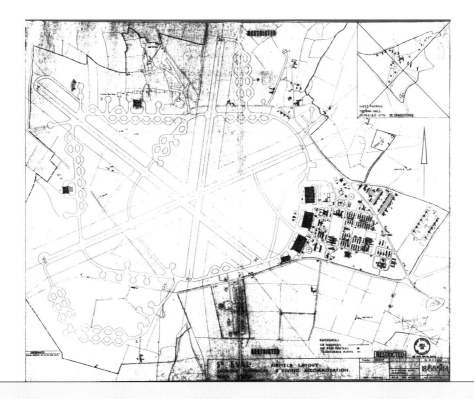

ST EVAL

AP.28: SW873685, six miles north-east of Newquay, Cornwall.

The RAF Expansion Scheme of the 1930s primarily concentrated on the construction of fighter and bomber stations, but the newly created Coastal Command required suitable airfields to base the new Anson general purpose reconnaissance aircraft on anti-submarine patrols off the coast of the West Country. After surveying a number of sites in Cornwall, St Eval was chosen to accommodate two general reconnaissance squadrons. Work began in 1938 on clearance of the site and the foundations of four 'C' Type hangars were laid on the eastern side of the landing ground with the administrative and technical buildings behind as well as barrack blocks and a large area for married quarters. Progress was slow resulting in temporary hut accommodation being supplied to allow the official opening on 2 October 1939 when Ansons of 217 Squadron arrived from Warmwell. With the fall of France, 234 Squadron with Spitfires was posted to St Eval for inshore convoy protection from enemy aircraft. With the need for night flying, the Spitfires were replaced by 238 Squadron Hurricanes and a lodger Sector Operations Room was established on the station. Soon after, St Eval gained the attention of the Luftwaffe, and on the night of 21 August, the hangar behind the front row of three was completely destroyed and never rebuilt.`

In the spring of 1940, work commenced on the laying of three concrete runways, the main 26/08 being 3,600ft/1,097m long and the other two 3,000ft/914m long, connected by a concrete perimeter track with bomber style dispersals and hard-standings. During the autumn, the station was used as an advanced base for attacks on the Biscay ports and against the invasion barges being assembled along the French coast. In December, 217 Squadron converted to the more effective Beauforts which were used for bombing, sea mining and anti-submarine patrols. In early 1941, enemy bombing attacks continued – one such raid on 25 January made a direct hit on a shelter and 21 personnel lost their lives.

As the attacks intensified accommodation in the area was requisitioned, allowing as many as possible to live off base. Maritime reconnaissance and photo reconnaissance continued throughout the war, the maritime operations being taken over by the long-range Liberators of 53, 224 and 547 Squadrons from the beginning of 1944. The airfield was extended and improved in 1943, the runways being lengthened to the north and west with many more hard-standings. As D-Day approached with increased operations, 206 Squadron joined the Wing in April, but by September they had moved out. Following the end of World War 2, the station continued in the maritime role using Lancasters and the Shackleton MR.1 with 220 Squadron in November 1951. With the introduction of the heavier Shackleton MR.3 maritime operations were transferred to nearby St Mawgan in December 1956 as St Eval was considered too small, resulting in its closure on 6 March 1959. Now only one hangar remains, the airfield site having been fenced off and allocated for Government use.

Below: Spitfire Ia R6597 GR-A of 92 Squadron after a forced landing at Pembrey on 22 July 1940. *(RAF Museum)*

Right: P/O Williams of 92 Squadron with a Pembrey-based Spitfire I on detachment at Gatwick in April 1940. *(RAF Museum)*

Bottom: Spitfire Is of 92 Squadron dispersed at Pembrey with rudimentary air and ground crew accommodation and a collection of various hangars in the background. *(RAF Museum)*

night were the Hurricanes of 238 Squadron, but they were not effective due to the lack of night fighting equipment. For day fighter defence the Spitfires of 234 Squadron arrived on 18 June 1940, staying until 14 August, and again from 11 September 1940 until 24 February 1941. Additional defence was provided by the Hurricanes of 247 Squadron on detachment from Roborough, starting in February 1941. Three runways were constructed in the spring of 1940 as heavier aircraft were having difficulty with the grass surface. In the autumn the airfield was used as a forward base for attacks on invasion barges situated at various point along the French coast, and then the station reverting to purely Coastal Command duties.

Shackleton Mk.1s arrived at St Eval from November 1951, with 220, 42 and 206 Squadrons to form the St Eval Wing. In December 1956, 220 Squadron moved to nearby St Mawgan to convert to the improved Shackleton MR.3 (which was considered too heavy for operations from St Eval), followed by 206 Squadron on 10 January 1958, hastening the rundown of the station, with final closure on 6 March 1959. The site is still MOD owned with the runways intact, but all the wartime buildings have been demolished, and a new administration facility is near where the original main gate was located with a residential development across the main road.

RAF Pembrey in South Wales became operational by 1939, and after the Battle of France became a 10 Group Fighter Command base to protect the approaches of the Bristol Channel and installations in Wales, including the local Royal Ordnance Factory. Amongst the units in residence was the Hurricane equipped 316 (Polish) Squadron which was not formed until 12 February 1941 and the Spitfires of 92 Squadron who arrived from Hornchurch on 18 June 1940 and left for Biggin Hill on 8 September. They were replaced by 79 Squadron flying Hurricanes until June 1941, by which time they had received Hurricane IIbs. In 1941, the base was used for training bomber gunners, but Pembrey was wound down by 1947 although there were Vampires and Hunters of 233 OCU based there until final closure in 1957. There were five C Type hangars, but these were removed in 1962 and only two T2 hangars remain with the runways and perimeter tracks, which are now used for motor racing. A section of one runway is used for general aviation. Nearby the RAF still retains a presence at the Pembrey Sands range used for air-to-ground firing of guns and rockets.

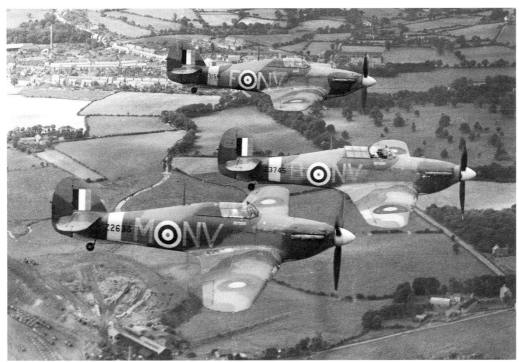

Hurricane Mk.IIs of Biggin Hill 79 Squadron in a 'vic' formation after the battle, ready for offensive operations over occupied Europe.

CHAPTER 7
13 GROUP AIRFIELDS

111 Squadron pilots with mascot relax at dispersal between operations with Hurricane IL1822 JU-K. The squadron was based at Acklington at the outbreak of war and had been equipped with the latest Merlin III-powered Hurricanes with three-blade variable-pitch propellers. *(Imperial War Museum)*

Formed for the defence of the north of England and Scotland, 13 Group Fighter Command provided bases for depleted squadrons to rest and regroup before returning to the battle in the south. The HQ of 13 Group was the Blakelaw Estate in Newcastle upon Tyne and the air officer in command was Air Vice-Marshal Richard Saul. The sector stations were Catterick in Yorkshire with Wing Commander G L Carter as the Commanding Officer (the station being the base for 219 Squadron with Blenheims and 41 Squadron with Spitfires); Usworth (commanded by Wing Commander Brian Thynne) where Hurricane-equipped 607 Squadron was based plus both 72 and 79 Squadrons with Spitfires; Wick – a Coastal Command base with Wing Commander Geoffrey Ambler as Commanding Officer of the Fighter Section HQ and operating 3, 232 and 504 Squadron Hurricanes; Dyce, another Coastal Command station with Group Captain F Crerar as Fighter Section

Commanding Officer and housing the Spitfires of 603 Squadron – and the Turnhouse sector station commanded by Wing Commander the Duke of Hamilton and Braden, housing the Hurricanes of 253 and 605 Squadrons, 602 Squadron Spitfires and the Defiants of 141 Squadron for night fighting. In addition, 245 Squadron was based at Aldergrove in Northern Ireland with Hurricanes.

The most southerly 13 Group sector station was RAF Catterick in North Yorkshire, situated between the A1 Great North Road on one side and the River Swale on the other. Catterick airfield, located near the Army barracks of the same name, was opened as an RFC airfield in 1914 for pilot training and defence of the northeast of England, initially with only modest numbers of aircraft. On 27 November 1915, No 6 Reserve Aeroplane Squadron arrived and 44 Squadron was formed at Catterick on 15 April 1916, the first of a number until the armistice in November

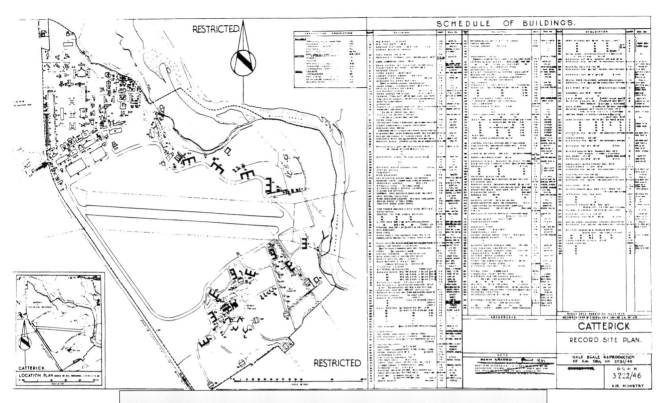

CATTERICK

AP.29: SE250968, south of Catterick, North Yorkshire, by the A1 Great North Road.

Catterick first opened in 1914 as a RFC flying training base for home defence duties and formation of a number of combat squadrons. It opened as a full RFC base on 1 December 1917, and after the end of World War 1, the station was used for flying training until flying ceased in March 1919. The site, which included ten hangars and a repair shed, was retained, and in the mid-1920s, five aircraft sheds replaced the hangars and more permanent buildings were constructed, including the watch office. Married quarters were built alongside what is now the A1, all the development being in the northern corner of the site. With limited flying taking place, mainly Army Co-operation due to Catterick Barracks being located nearby, it was decided to undertake further improvements, with two 'C' Type hangars built in front of the other remaining aircraft sheds. To the east of the new hangars a new watch office, control tower and fire tender shed were built. Other new buildings included barrack blocks, MT sheds, a fighter operations building, stores and workshops to accommodate three squadrons. Once complete, 41 (Fighter) Squadron arrived in September 1936 exchanging Furies for Spitfire Is in early 1939.

In September 1939, Catterick was designated a sector station in 13 Group and its main duty was to provide local air defence using squadrons resting from operations in the south, while also being used for the formation and training of new fighter squadrons. By early 1943, operations were slowing down, the last combat unit departing in February 1944. By this time there was a single short runway 3,330ft long, bounded by a perimeter track giving access to dispersals close to the River Swale and in the south-east corner of the site where Blister hangars had also been erected. As the runway was restricted at both ends by the river and Great North Road, it was unsuitable for the new high-performance aircraft entering service and the station was allocated to ground training for the RAF Regiment. The only aviation activity involved arrivals of aircraft for the RAF Fire School until November 1989 when it was moved to Manston and the station is now exclusively used by the Army.

Spitfire Is, including X4178 FB-K of 41 Squadron, operated from Catterick throughout 1940 when resting from combat duties at Hornchurch. *(Unknown copyright via BAE Systems)*

1918 when the airfield reverted to the training role and flying ceased in April 1919. The base was retained by the RAF in mainly non-flying duties, but many improvements were made including the construction of hangars and married quarters as well as the normal technical buildings. Even more buildings were added during the mid-1930s expansion period including two C Type hangars, a fighter operations building and workshops to cater for three squadrons.

The first fighter unit to arrive was 41 Squadron, in September 1936, which re-equipped with Spitfire Is in early 1939 and was joined by 609 Squadron in August also operating Spitfire Is. In September 1939, Catterick was designated a sector station within 13 Group Fighter Command and 219 Squadron was reformed on 4 October with Blenheim 1Fs, although all the squadrons were relocated to other bases for the Battle of Britain. The station was, however, busy providing a home for the battle-weary squadrons from the south, giving them a chance to rest and train replacements while also maintaining a local area defence.

On 28 May 1940, the Spitfires of 54 Squadron arrived from Hornchurch followed by 41 Squadron on 17 June, and both squadrons made a number of return visits to recuperate during the battle. During 1941 and 1942, the station was busy with the formation of a number of new squadrons ready for the offensive over Europe. However, activities were reduced during 1943 and after a stay by 222 Squadron fighters, before they moved to Acklington at the end of February 1944, the airfield was used by second-line units, the single 3,330 ft runway having restrictions at both ends making it too short for the operation of modern aircraft. The RAF Regiment moved to Catterick in 1946 for training activities and the base was also used for the training of RAF firefighters. In May 1994, the RAF Regiment moved to Honington and the RAF Ensign was lowered on 1 July, the base being handed over to become part of Catterick Garrison and named Marne Barracks, while the airfield is still used for light aviation and gliders.

Usworth airfield, located close to the northeast coast in what is now known as Tyne and Wear, was opened to flying in October 1916 for home defence, but all flying ceased after World War 1 and the site was returned to agriculture. On 17 March 1930, 607 Squadron was formed as a day bomber unit and it was allocated to the former site of Usworth, which was not ready for re-occupation until September 1932. 607 Squadron transferred to the fighter role in September 1936, moving to Acklington on 10 September 1939 and subsequently serving in the Battle of France equipped with Gladiators. The squadron returned to Usworth in June 1940 to re-equip with Hurricanes from Tangmere ready for the Battle of Britain.

On 'Adler Tag', 13 August 1940, a large force of He 111s with an inadequate escort of Bf 110s was detected approaching the east coast. They were met by Spitfires of 72 Squadron and although heavily outnumbered were able to claim some victories. The German formation split into two, one group heading for Tyneside and the other turning south. 79, the second Acklington squadron, attacked the escorts of the northern group off the coast and Hurricanes pursued the bombers approaching Newcastle where Usworth was presumed to be the target. With opposition from both ground defences and Hurricanes, the Heinkels scattered and departed, jettisoning their bombs to no effect. The southern force was met by 41 Squadron from

Above: Usworth became the base for 51 OTU in 1942 to prepare pilots for offensive ground-attack operations across occupied Europe. *(RAF Museum)*

Left: No 43 Squadron Hurricane I line-up at Usworth. The station was so far north that there was less risk of enemy attacks and therefore the aircraft did not need to be widely dispersed. *(RAF Museum)*

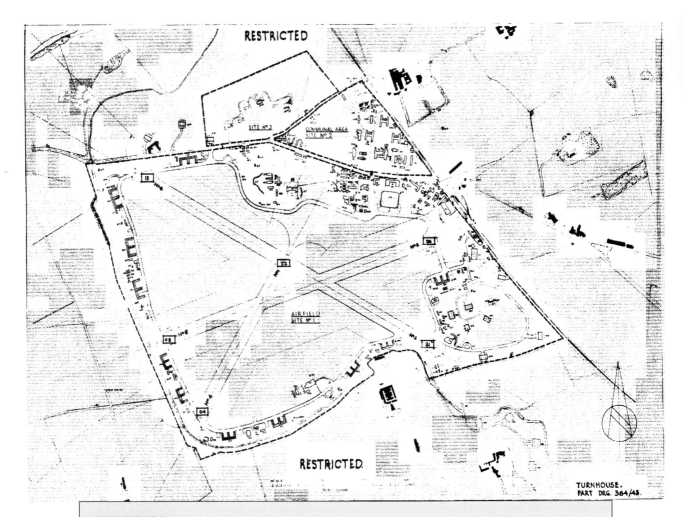

TURNHOUSE.
PART DRG. 384/45.

TURNHOUSE

AP.30: NT657954, five miles west of Edinburgh, by the A8.

Turnhouse first opened in May 1916 with the formation of 26 (Reserve) Squadron and was used for flying training until September 1917 when it was allocated as a Fleet Practice Station. In October 1925, 603 Squadron formed at Turnhouse as a bomber unit and was designated a fighter unit in October 1938, re-equipping with Spitfires in time to claim the first enemy aircraft to be brought down over Britain in World War 2.

Turnhouse was designated a sector station within 13 Group in September 1939 and was the transitional base for many squadrons on rest periods from combat in the south while they were also responsible for local air defence. From December 1939, three hard runways were laid with the main technical site in the north-east corner and a perimeter track around the boundary giving access to a number of blast pens. One 'C' Type hangar was erected with workshops, stores and station administration surrounding it and accommodation including barrack blocks on a communal site north of the technical site.

As well as rest and training, Turnhouse was used for the formation and training of new fighter units before they flew to the operational areas in the south. No 603 Squadron returned in March 1945 but disbanded on 15 August. It reformed in 1946, initially with Spitfires which were exchanged for Vampires in July until disbandment in March 1957. The airfield was transferred to civil operations, the main runway being strengthened for operations by BEA Vanguards. The airport was taken over by BAA in April 1971 and a new 2,560m runway was built to the north-west of the existing airport to avoid problems with frequent crosswinds. New terminal facilities and aprons were also added and the airport now provides domestic and international flights for the city of Edinburgh.

Catterick and 607 Squadron from Usworth, the enemy jettisoning their bombs and the RAF squadrons claiming eight He 111s and seven Bf 110s with no losses.

Following the Battle of Britain, Usworth took on the duties of operational training with Hurricanes and later specialised in night fighter observer training until June 1943 when all flying ceased at the base. In July 1963, the site became Sunderland Airport and is now home to the North East Aircraft Museum. The airfield closed on 31 May 1984 and the site was taken over by Nissan for the manufacture of motor vehicles.

Turnhouse Airport is located five miles west of Edinburgh and is now the aerial gateway for the city. The site was first used for flying in 1916, when it was used for RFC training, and was then transferred to Fleet Practice and Fleet repair in 1917. It reverted to RAF use in the 1930s when 83 Squadron reformed as a day bomber unit on 4 August 1936, before 83 Squadron moved to Scampton in March 1938. The first enemy aircraft to be shot down in World War 2 was shared between 602 and 603 Squadrons. 603 Squadron had formed at Turnhouse on 14 October 1925 as a bomber unit, but was re-designated as a fighter unit in October 1938, initially equipped with Gladiators, soon to be replaced by Spitfires. Turnhouse became a Sector Station in September 1939 and 141 Squadron was reformed here on 4 October and equipped with Defiants which went south in July 1940. After the vulnerability of the aircraft was highlighted, the squadron returned to Turnhouse in September to retrain in the night fighter role. 603 Squadron left in mid-December 1939 to allow the construction of runways and the next fighter unit to arrive was 245 Squadron, with Hurricanes, on 5 June 1940, remaining until 20 July when they moved to Aldergrove for the air defence of Belfast. They were replaced in turn by 253 and 65 Squadrons, the latter unit being withdrawn from the battle for a chance to rest while undertaking local air defence duties. The Hurricanes of 3 Squadron were at Turnhouse in September and October and 65 Squadron flew south to Tangmere at the end of November. During 1941, a number of fighter squadrons were formed at Turnhouse and then moved south for the action, the station continuing to be allocated to fighters and Fleet

The air and ground crews of 501 Squadron Royal Auxiliary Air Force pose for a group photo at Turnhouse in 1938. Behind them is a 'C' Type hangar which was common to many pre-war permanent RAF stations. *(RAF Museum)*

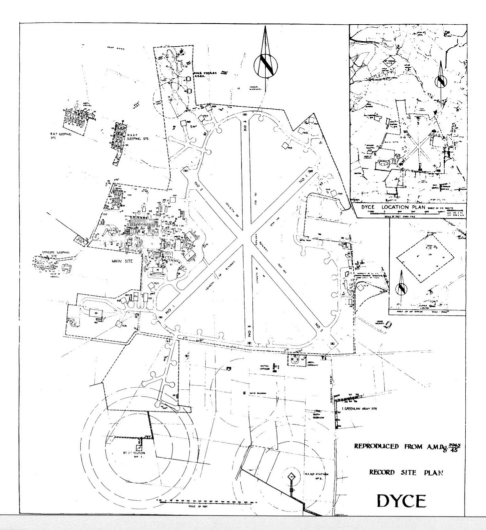

DYCE

AP.31; NJ880215, six miles north-west of Aberdeen, by the A947.

A civil airport was established at Dyce and opened on 4 July 1934 for local services by de Havilland Dragons of Gander-Dower-operated Aberdeen Airways. Military operations commenced with the formation of 612 Squadron in June 1937 as an Army Co-operation unit with Hectors. With the cessation of civil flying at the start of World War 2, Dyce was taken over by the RAF on 16 October 1939 and 612 Squadron became responsible for convoy escort duties. Three runways were built in the spring of 1940 with the technical site on the western boundary, including four Bellman hangars, workshops, stores and administration buildings with sleeping accommodation on detached sites. Aircraft dispersals were located off a perimeter track which also included Blister hangars. The air defence of Aberdeen was initially the responsibility of 603 Squadron Spitfires, but was shared by a number of combat squadrons resting and retraining from combat in the south. The airfield was also used by Coastal Command shipping strike squadrons in the early war years, attacking targets off Norway and flying convoy patrols.

The airfield was unsuitable for major military development due to poor approaches caused by surrounding high ground, Dyce becoming the home of 8 OTU with responsibility for the training of photo-reconnaissance pilots to operate Spitfires and Mosquitoes, later to be joined by 540 Squadron. With the end of the war in Europe military flying reduced with a gradual transition to civil operations from October 1945, although 612 Royal Auxiliary Air Force Squadron operated Spitfires and Vampires until disbandment in March 1957. With the discovery of the North Sea oilfields, Dyce not only became an airliner destination but also a major helicopter operating base for transport to oil rigs and is now hardly recognisable from its wartime origins.

Air Arm (FAA) units. Being close to Edinburgh, there were many visiting transport flights including the USAAF.

When peace was declared, 603 Squadron had already returned in April and was disbanded on 15 August, although it was reformed with Vampires in July 1951 until all auxiliary squadrons were disbanded in March 1957. The station closed in 1961 to allow strengthening of the runways for larger airliners, although commercial flights had started in 1947 when BEA launched services between Edinburgh and London. The airport was transferred from the MOD to the Ministry of Aviation in 1960 and BAA took over control in 1971 following which a new runway was constructed to be more in line with the prevailing winds.

Dyce, the airport for Aberdeen, is located six miles from the city and was first opened for commercial flying by Mr E L Gander-Dower's Aberdeen Airways on 4 July 1934, the initial services linking Dyce with Wick. By 1937, the company had been renamed Allied Airways and services were operated to the Shetlands and Edinburgh, while a five times weekly service started to Norway in July 1937. 612 Squadron was formed at Dyce on 1 June 1937

as an Army co-operation unit used for coastal patrols when war was declared. Dyce became an RAF station on 16 October 1939 and runways were built in the spring of 1940 with a number of hangars erected. Part of 603 Squadron, equipped with Spitfires, was stationed at Dyce on local defence duties from 17 January to 14 April 1940, to be replaced progressively by 602, 145 and 111 Squadrons during the period of the Battle of Britain. From early 1941, the station continued with fighter operations, to which was added Coastal Command patrols, the first being 248 Squadron with Blenheims on shipping strike duties. On 1 March 1943, the airfield ceased to be operational and changed to the training role, initially of photo-reconnaissance pilots flying Spitfires and Mosquitos.

Transport operations by Swedish Airlines were conducted using DC-3s on diplomatic courier flights starting on 16 February 1942 and lasting until May 1944, not without losses. Photo-reconnaissance training was supplemented by photo operations from August 1944 using aircraft from 8 OTU, to which were added unarmed Spitfires of 540 Squadron which completed 26 sorties around the Norwegian coast in November. When the

Spitfire Ia L1004 LO-Q of 602 Squadron with the pilot and ground crew at Dyce in March 1940. *(RAF Museum)*

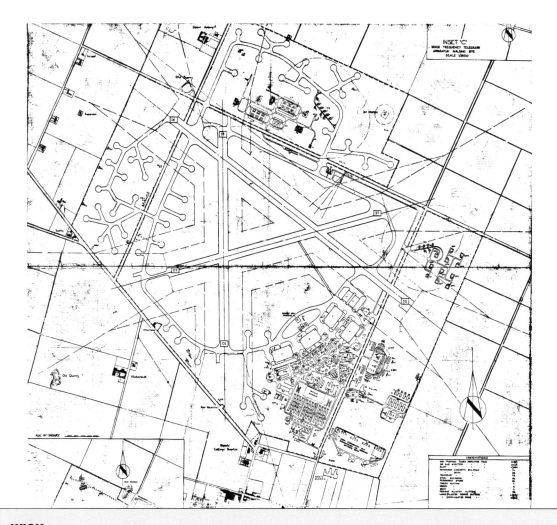

WICK

AP.32; ND360525, one mile north of Wick, Caithness.

RAF Wick was opened on 15 September 1939, and because of the waterlogged landing area, three tarmac runways were laid urgently while flying operations continued alongside the construction work. A perimeter track linked the runways with many bomber type dispersals around the airfield and technical buildings and accommodation were located in the south-east corner. Four large 'C' Type hangars were constructed, which were excellent landmarks for both friend and foe. The first units to arrive were 803 Squadron FAA with Skuas as fighter defence of the naval base at Scapa Flow and coastal patrols by the Ansons of 269 Squadron.

In December 1939, Wick was designated as a 13 Group sector station and more regular fighter squadrons were posted in on rest tours while being tasked with local air defence. The first action was with 43 Squadron Hurricanes from February 1940, and 605 Squadron participated in a battle over Orkney on 10 April when seven enemy aircraft were claimed destroyed by the combined defences. In October 1940, the Fighter Sector HQ moved out to Kirkwall, leaving Wick as a Coastal Command station. With the German occupation of Norway, Wick was on the front line and began to experience enemy bombing raids. On 26 October, the airfield was bombed and three civilians were killed.

More raids took place in 1941, the worst being on 4 June when a hangar and its contents were badly damaged. Coastal operations continued throughout the war with shipping strikes off the Norwegian coast until May 1944 when the squadrons moved south to support the invasion of Europe. Coastal patrols continued until the end of the war with Hudsons, Fortresses and Halifaxes. In March 1946, Wick reverted to civil operations with local services around the Highlands and Islands. However, all that remains are two 'C' Type hangars and most of the buildings are disused.

war ended, Dyce was still used by fighter units, including Norwegian squadrons returning home, after which there was a transition back to commercial operations, although 612 Squadron reformed on 10 May 1946 and converted to Vampires in July 1951 until final disbandment in March 1957. The airport continued to serve Aberdeen in a modest way until the discovery of oil in the North Sea, which not only brought in helicopter oil rig support services, but also increased international air transport operations.

The most northerly Fighter Command Sector Station during the Battle of Britain was the Coastal Command base at Wick, located in the northeast corner of Scotland. The station HQ had been hastily established on 15 September 1939, on an airfield which was having its poor grass surface replaced by runways. Four large C1 hangars were constructed, which unfortunately made excellent landmarks for attacks by enemy aircraft. The first military residents were the Skuas of 803 Squadron FAA, which were allocated to fighter patrols. They were joined by 269 Squadron Ansons on 10 October and reinforcements arrived in the form of a flight of three Hudsons; however, with little activity they returned to Leuchars on 2 December. Wick was made a sector station in December 1939, the task being to provide protection to the major naval base at Scapa Flow and the operations room was located in a local school.

43 Squadron moved into Wick with Hurricanes in February 1940. On 8 April, there were two bombing raids in which three He 111s were shot down, and of the two damaged, one made a forced landing on the airfield with two dead crew members. 605 Squadron arrived with Hurricanes in February and stayed until May, and the first claims were made on 10 April in a major air battle over the Orkneys with seven enemy bombers shot down by the combined forces of 605 Squadron, the FAA and anti-aircraft guns. 504 Squadron took over responsibility for the defence of Scapa in May and moved on 21 June to the satellite at Castletown on the north coast of Scotland. 3 Squadron relieved 43 Squadron at the end of May, 3 Squadron having to re-equip and train new pilots after heavy losses in France. It moved to Castletown on 2 September, and on 17 October, the Fighter Sector was moved to Kirkwall, leaving Wick as a dedicated Coastal Command base.

With the German occupation of Norway, the north of Scotland came within range of the Luftwaffe bombers and Wick was attacked on 26 October 1940. Three He 111s dropped bombs, killing three civilians, destroying one Hudson and slightly damaging a hangar. On 17 March and 26 April, there were further raids by

A pair of 111 Squadron Hurricane Is, including L2001 refuelling and rearming, in early 1940 at at Wick, Britain's most northerly sector station with responsibility for the defence of the naval base at Scapa Flow.

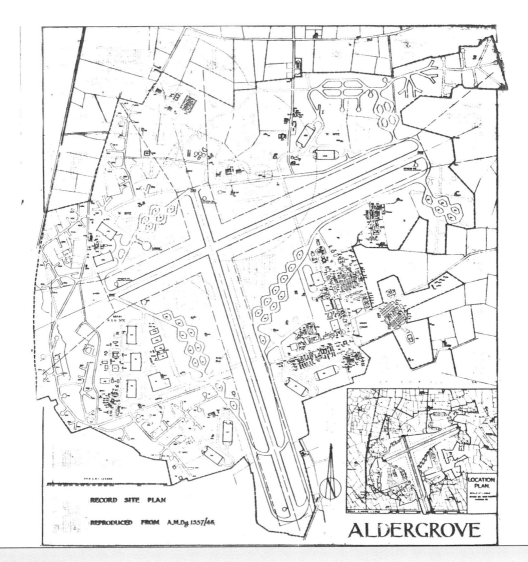

RECORD SITE PLAN

REPRODUCED FROM A.M.Dg 1337/46.

LOCATION PLAN.

ALDERGROVE

ALDERGROVE

AP.33: J150800, by the A57, 13 miles north-west of Belfast, Northern Ireland.

Aldergrove opened early in 1918 as a flight testing airfield for Handley Page bombers built by Harland & Wolff, but only a small number were completed and the airfield closed in December 1919, although it was retained by the RAF for annual exercises. In May 1925, Aldergrove became a night bomber station with 502 Squadron, changing to the day bomber role with 9 Squadron in January 1936. That March, an Armament Training Camp was formed for the benefit of many front line squadrons, the school disbanding in July 1940. In November 1939, 23 MU began the storage and preparation of Wellingtons, Hampdens and Blenheims for operational service.

For the air defence of Belfast, the Hurricanes of 245 Squadron arrived on 20 June 1940 with a Fighter Sector HQ set up. The station was also used by Coastal Command, in particular for anti-submarine patrols, and from November 1941, the station was an arrival point for transatlantic ferry flights from the USA. For both Coastal Command operations and 23 MU two tarmac runways were constructed from September 1941, with the main operational technical site in the south-east corner and the main MU site in the south-west corner. The runways were connected by a perimeter track with many storage dispersals and widely dispersed concrete aircraft storage hangars. The Fighter Sector HQ was moved out in June 1941 and the station reverted to Coastal Command operations on increasing anti-U-boat patrols with a number of successes. A Met flight was also based at Aldergrove to gather vital information on the weather to assist in the planning of bomber operations, and even when operations stopped, Met flying continued, eventually with 202 Squadron Hastings, until it disbanded in July 1964. On 26 September 1963, Aldergrove became Belfast Airport with a new modern passenger terminal and 23 MU continued in operation until it was closed in 1978.

Top: Hurricane I W9200 DX-? of 245 Squadron at Aldergrove for the defence of Northern Ireland. *(RAF Museum)*

Below: Squadron Leader J W C Simpson DFC, commanding officer of 245 Squadron, at Aldergrove in the cockpit of his Hurricane showing 11 victories.

individual bombers which killed a sergeant and airman but without significant material damage. However, on 4 June, a Ju 88 dropped three bombs on No 3 hangar, badly damaging the structure and two aircraft inside. Military flying ceased in March 1945, and the airfield was taken over by BEA for services around Scotland and the islands, which were replaced by Loganair services in 1976. Many of the buildings have been allowed to become derelict and the two remaining hangars are rather dilapidated with two of the three runways in use. The airport is used by helicopters servicing the oil platforms in the North Sea as well as a stopping-off point for short-range light aircraft flying across the North Atlantic via Iceland.

In Northern Ireland, Aldergrove was allocated for the defence of Belfast and convoy patrols, the station being administered by the Air Ministry. 245 Squadron Hurricanes were posted in on 20 July 1940 when a Fighter Sector HQ was set up. There were many scrambles against shipping raiders but no contact was made. On an air-raid in the Belfast area on the night of 7/8 August 1940, 245 Squadron carried out individual patrols and Squadron Leader Simpson shot down a He 111 over Downpatrick. In the final raid on Belfast on 5/6 May 1941, the same pilot claimed another bomber, marking his twelfth victory. After the Battle of Britain, the station became part of Coastal Command as well as housing 23 MU, and on 26 September 1963, Aldergrove became Belfast Airport and the RAF presence ceased with the closure of 23 MU in 1978.

Right: Two flights of well-worn Hurricane Is of 245 Squadron, P3762 DX-F the nearest, airborne from Aldergrove in late 1940.

Right: Defiants of 141 Squadron were based at Aldergrove for the night defence of Belfast following their withdrawal from day fighter duties. The gun turret behind the cockpit was armed with four 0.303-inch machine guns and there was no forward-firing armament. *(RAF Museum)*

ALAN 'AL' DEERE

Alan 'Al' Deere was born in New Zealand and sailed to Britain in September 1937 to join the RAF. Together with two other pilots, Deere was awarded the Distinguished Flying Cross (DFC) on 12 June 1940, which was presented by HM King George VI at Hornchurch on 27 June. Following 'Adler Tag' Deere claimed a Bf 109, two Bf 110s, and on 15 August, shot down a Bf 109 but was outnumbered by enemy fighters who forced him to bail out at low level sustaining minor injuries. He was shot down again on 28 August, but this time by another Spitfire, and parachuted to safety.

In January 1941, while training new operational pilots, Deere collided with one and experienced difficulty bailing out, as a result of which he was ordered to rest and appointed Squadron Leader Operations Room at Catterick. He returned to operational flying as a flight commander of 602 Squadron at Ayr, taking over as Squadron Commander at the end of July for a move to Kenley on 1 August, destroying a Bf 109 on the same day.

As often happened at the end of the war, serving officers dropped rank, in Deere's case to Flight Lieutenant in command of the Polish Mustang Wing at Andrews Field, following which he was commanding officer at Duxford with the return of the base from the USAAF. In August 1945, Deere was awarded a permanent commission in the RAF, and on 26 March 1946, regained the rank of Squadron Leader. On 1 July 1951, he returned to the rank of Wing Commander as Commanding Officer of North Weald. His promotions continued with Group Captain on 1 January 1958 and Air Commodore on 1 July 1964. Following command of No 1 School of Technical Training at Halton, he retired from the RAF on 12 December 1977 and died on 21 September 1995 at the age of 77.

BIBLIOGRAPHY

Ashworth, Chris – *Action Stations – Military Airfields of the South-West v.5* (Patrick Stephens Ltd, 1982)

Barnes, C H – *Bristol Aircraft Since 1910 (Putnam's British Aircraft)* (Brassey's: Putnam Aeronautical, 1988)

Birtles, Philip – *Hurricane* (Patrick Stephens Ltd, 2001)

Bowyer, Michael J F – *Action Stations – Military Airfields of the Cotswolds and the Central Midlands v.6* (Patrick Stephens Ltd, 1983)

Bowyer, Michael J F – *Action Stations Revisited – No.1 Eastern England* (Crecy Publishing, 2000)

Deighton, Len and Hastings, Max – *Battle of Britain* (Wordsworth Editions Ltd, 1999)

Delve, Ken – *The Military Airfields of Britain – East Midlands: (Cambridge, Derbyshire, Leicestershire, Lincolnshire, Nottinghamshire)* (The Crowood Press, 2008)

Dunn, Bill Newton – *Big Wing: Biography of Air Chief Marshal Sir Trafford Leigh-Mallory* (Airlife Publishing Ltd, 1992)

Ellis, Ken – *Wrecks & Relics 21st Edition* (Crecy Publishing, 2009)

Flint, Peter – *R.A.F Kenley* (Terence Dalton, 1990)

Grey, C G and Bridgman (eds) – *Jane's All the World's Aircraft 1940* (Sampson Low, Marston & Co Ltd, 1940)

Halpenny, Bruce Barrymore – *Action Stations – Military Airfields of Yorkshire v.4* (Patrick Stephens Ltd, 1982)

Hunt, Leslie – *Twenty-One Squadrons: The History of the Royal Auxiliary Air Force 1925-1957* (Garnstone Press Ltd, 1972)

Jefford, Wing Commander C G MBE RAF – *RAF Squadrons* (Airlife Publishing Ltd, 1988)

Ogley, Bob – *Biggin on the Bump: The Most Famous Fighter Squadron in the World* (Froglets Publications Ltd, 1990)

Orange, Victor – *Dowding of Fighter Command: Victor of the Battle of Britain* (Grub Street, 2008)

Orange, Vincent – *Park: The Biography of Air Chief Marshal Sir Keith Park, GCB, KBE, MC, DFC, DCL* (Grub Street Publishing, 2000)

Parker, Matthew – *The Battle of Britain, July-October 1940* (Headline, 2001)

Ramsey, Winston G – *Battle of Britain: Then and Now* (After the Battle, 1987)

Smith, David J – *Action Stations – Military Airfields of Scotland, the North-East and Northern Ireland v.7* (Patrick Stephens Ltd, 1983)

Taylor, H A – *Fairey Aircraft Since 1915 (Putnam's British Aircraft)* (Brassey's: Putnam Aeronautical, 1988)

FURTHER READING

Bishop, Patrick – *Battle of Britain: A Day-by-Day Chronicle, 10 July-31 October 1940* (Quercus Publishing Plc, 2009)

Bowyer, Michael J F – *Battle of Britain 50 Years on* (Patrick Stephens Ltd, 1990)

Korda, Michael – *With Wings like Eagles: A History of the Battle of Britain* (Harper, 2009)

Sampson, Wing Commander R W F OBE, DFC & Bar – *Spitfire Offensive: A Fighter Pilot's War Memoir* (Grub Street, 1994)

INDEX